Development on the Periphery

Development on the Periphery

Democratic Transitions in Southern and Eastern Europe

Howard J. Wiarda

With the Assistance of
Dale R. Herspring and
Ester M. Skelley

ROWMAN & LITTLEFIELD PUBLISHERS, INC.
Lanham • Boulder • New York • Toronto • Oxford

ROWMAN & LITTLEFIELD PUBLISHERS, INC.

Published in the United States of America
by Rowman & Littlefield Publishers, Inc.
A wholly owned subsidiary of The Rowman & Littlefield Publishing Group, Inc.
4501 Forbes Boulevard, Suite 200, Lanham, Maryland 20706
www.rowmanlittlefield.com

P.O. Box 317, Oxford OX2 9RU, UK

Copyright © 2006 by Rowman & Littlefield Publishers, Inc.

All rights reserved. No part of this publication may be reproduced, stored in a retrieval system, or transmitted in any form or by any means, electronic, mechanical, photocopying, recording, or otherwise, without the prior permission of the publisher.

British Library Cataloguing in Publication Information Available

Library of Congress Cataloging-in-Publication Data

Wiarda, Howard J., 1939–
  Development on the periphery : democratic transitions in southern and Eastern Europe / Howard J. Wiarda ; with the assistance of Dale R. Herspring and Esther M. Skelley.
    p.   cm.
  Includes bibliographical references and index.
    ISBN 0-7425-3033-7 (cloth : alk. paper) — ISBN 0-7425-3034-5 (pbk. : alk. paper)
    1. Europe, Eastern—Politics and government—1989– —Case studies. 2. Europe, Southern—Politics and government—Case studies. 3. Democratization—Europe, Eastern—Case studies. 4. Democratization—Europe, Southern—Case studies. 5. Europe, Eastern—Economic conditions—1989– —Case studies. 6. Europe, Southern—Economic conditions—Case studies. I. Herspring, Dale R. (Dale Roy) II. Skelley, Esther M. III. Title.
  JN96.A58W53 2005
  320.94—dc22
                                                                           2005021917

Printed in the United States of America

∞™ The paper used in this publication meets the minimum requirements of American National Standard for Information Sciences—Permanence of Paper for Printed Library Materials, ANSI/NISO Z39.48-1992.

Contents

Preface	vii
Acknowledgments	xi
Introduction: Southern Europe and Eastern Europe: Toward a Europe Whole, Free, and Democratic	1

Part I   Background and Context

1	Southern, or Mediterranean, Europe	17
2	Eastern Europe and the Search for a Democratic Political Culture *Dale R. Herspring*	61
3	Transitology and the Need for New Theory	79

Part II   Iberia Transformed: A Closer Look

4	Spain 2010: A Normal Country?	95
5	The New Portugal	120
6	From Foreign-Policy Isolation to Global Presence: Spain in Latin America and Portugal in East Timor	132

Part III East/Central Europe: From Communism to Democracy—Or Something Less Than That?

7	Marxist-Leninist Regimes in Transition	155
8	Defining the Borders of the New Europe	177
9	The Politics of European Enlargement	212

Conclusion: Toward a New Europe	245
Suggested Readings	253
Index	259
About the Author	271

Preface

The transitions to democracy in Southern and Eastern Europe have to be among the most momentous events of the late-twentieth and early twenty-first centuries. Here we have two areas of Europe that had long been poor, underdeveloped, nondemocratic, governed by authoritarian or totalitarian regimes, and isolated from the main currents of European life, often scourged by their wealthier neighbors and sometimes the butt of cruel ethnic jokes. Then, in the mid-1970s, Greece, Portugal, and Spain all began their transitions to democracy, modernization, and integration into European life. Following the fall of the Berlin Wall, the collapse of the Iron Curtain, and the disintegration of the Soviet Union in the period between 1989 and 1991, Eastern Europe also evolved toward democracy, economic reform, and European integration.

It is obviously heartening to see all these countries transitioning to democracy, to a more modern life, and to a higher standard of living. Quite a number of them have now moved on to a second stage, the *consolidation* of democracy. And with the collapse and disappearance of so many authoritarian regimes in the world and the discrediting of Marxism-Leninism in the Soviet Union and elsewhere, it may be that these recent democratic transitions will become permanent. Democracy now seems to be "the only game in town."

While we are encouraged by all these democratic transitions, we still need to study them carefully and ask some hard questions. How solid are these new democracies? Will they be permanent? Have these countries resolved their historic internal conflicts sufficiently for democracy to survive? Is the continuing economic and social underdevelopment of large parts of Eastern Europe a threat to the stability of democracy? How have the processes of integration of these new democracies into Europe (into the European Union and NATO) proceeded, and what are the continuing tensions? What about the areas left behind and not yet integrated into the European mainstreams, such as Belarus, the Ukraine, Moldova, Georgia, Albania, much of the former Yugoslavia and Russia itself? These areas and countries remain poor, underdeveloped, and mainly nondemocratic, and yet they are right on Europe's border. Is there a threat here of future conflict and instability?

The book addresses these important practical and policy concerns but also raises some key theoretical issues for students. Is the Southern European experience of democratization also relevant for Eastern Europe? What are the differences between countries that transition from authoritarianism to democracy and those that go from communist totalitarianism to democracy? Is there one model that fits all democracy-transitioning countries, or are there major differences that need to be taken into account? Are the Southern and Eastern European experiences of transition also relevant to less-developed Third World countries seeking to implement democracy? These are crucial questions, and the book seeks to provide answers to them.

This book takes a different direction and represents an alternative point of view to most of the recent books on democratization. Many of those studies focus almost exclusively on institutions as the agents of change. This book acknowledges, of course, the importance of institutions but takes a much broader perspective that emphasizes the role of history, geography, religion, political culture, political sociology, and political economy in comparing nations and areas. It also has been prepared based on a belief that international influences played a far greater role in these democratic transitions than heretofore acknowledged. The view is thus more encompassing, more broad ranging, and, the author and his colleagues think, more accurate and realistic.

This may be the only book available comparing Southern and Eastern Europe and informed by a deep knowledge of and first-hand experiences in both regions. The book is meant to be provocative and to stimulate discussion. It was designed to serve as a text, as supplemental readings, or as fun, exciting, and stimulating reading in courses on European politics, comparative democratization, Southern Europe, Eastern Europe, post-Communism, or the politics of developing areas. This book is one in a series of books the author has written dealing with Latin America, comparative politics, East/Southern Europe, and American foreign policy.

The author wishes to thank his long-time friend, colleague, and collaborator, Dale R. Herspring, for contributing his well-informed and provocative chapter on East European political culture. Research assistant

Esther M. Skelley contributed so much to the planning, data collection, writing, and editing of the book that she also merits credit on the cover page. Doris Holden, as usual, worked her magic in converting the author's handwriting and editorial squiggles into a readable manuscript. And similarly, Iêda Siqueira Wiarda, herself a political scientist, contributed immeasurably and in all ways to the research life out of which this book emerged. Thanks to all, but the main responsibility for what follows lies with the author.

Howard J. Wiarda
Bonita Hills Road
Athens, Georgia
Summer 2005

Acknowledgments

Although all the materials in this book have been rethought, updated, and rewritten, some of the chapters are derived from earlier journal articles and book chapters. Permission to use these materials is gratefully acknowledged.

Chapter 1. From Howard J. Wiarda, ed., *European Politics in the Age of Globalization* (Fort Worth, Tex.: Harcourt, 2001).

Chapter 2. From Howard J. Wiarda, ed., *Non-Western Theories of Development* (Fort Worth, Tex.: Harcourt Brace, 1999).

Chapter 3. From Howard J. Wiarda, "Southern Europe, Eastern Europe, and Comparative Politics: Transitology and the Need for New Theory," *East European Politics and Society* (Fall 2001).

Chapter 4. From Howard J. Wiarda, "Spain 2007: A Normal Country?" *Mediterranean Quarterly* (Summer 2000).

Chapter 5. From Howard J. Wiarda, ed., *European Politics in the Age of Globalization* (Fort Worth, Tex.: Harcourt, 2001).

Chapter 7. From Howard J. Wiarda, *Introduction to Comparative Politics* (Fort Worth, Tex.: Harcourt Brace, 2000).

Introduction

Southern Europe and Eastern Europe
Toward a Europe Whole, Free, and Democratic

The literature of comparative politics had long suggested that there were three basic routes to national modernization and development: (1) a liberal-democratic route, as exemplified by the United States, most of Western Europe, Australia, New Zealand, and a handful of other countries; (2) a Marxist-Leninist route, as exemplified by the Soviet Union, Eastern Europe, China, North Korea, Cuba, and Vietnam; and (3) an authoritarian or bureaucratic-authoritarian (party or institutional dictatorships as distinct from personal or individual ones) route, as practiced in such countries as Spain under Franco, Indonesia under Suharto, the Philippines under Marcos, and quite a number of developing or transitional African, Latin American, and Middle Eastern countries. Sociologist Irving Louis Horowitz referred to these as the "Three Worlds of Development."[1]

Then, in the period between 1989 and 1991, the Marxist-Leninist model all but disappeared. The Soviet Union basically imploded; the Eastern European countries broke free of Soviet domination, became democratic, and joined Western Europe in the North Atlantic Treaty Organization (NATO) and the European Union (EU); and quite a number of Third World states transitioned away from their Marxist regimes as well. That left only four remaining Marxist-Leninist states in the world: China, North Korea, Cuba, and Vietnam, about which we will have more to say later on.

Meanwhile, the other major alternative to democracy, authoritarianism, was also in decline. Whereas Marxism-Leninism all but disappeared in one fell swoop between 1988 and 1991, authoritarianism declined over a longer period, the last quarter of the twentieth century. What Samuel

Huntington called "the third wave of democratization"[2] began in Portugal and Greece in 1974, included Spain when Franco died in 1975, then spread slowly over Latin America in the 1970s and 1980s (nineteen of the twenty countries are now democratic), encompassed much of East and Southeast Asia (South Korea, Taiwan, the Philippines, Indonesia) in the 1980s and 1990, and penetrated the more difficult areas of sub-Saharan Africa and the Middle East in the most recent decades. The decline of authoritarianism and the rise of democracy constituted one of the most significant transformations of the late twentieth century.

The collapse of both Marxism-Leninism and authoritarianism seemingly left democracy as the only remaining model and alternative, the only surviving route or path to development. As the slogan of the time put it, democracy was "the only game in town." Or, as political philosopher Francis Fukuyama famously said, we had reached "the end of history," and democracy and free markets—that is, the U.S. model—had won![3]

The decline or disappearance of both Marxism-Leninism and authoritarianism and the apparent global triumph of democracy gave rise to a vast new literature, often triumphalist in tone, on "transitions to democracy." The assumption was both that democracy would now become well-nigh universal and that, with so many countries and areas becoming democratic, there were common patterns involved. An almost romantic faith and belief in democracy was involved; the faith in democracy and its inevitability in all countries became almost like a secular religious belief. The "transitions to democracy" literature purported to offer a global model applicable to all countries. It strongly suggested, and often even claimed, that it didn't matter whether the culture of the country was Islamic, Latin-Hispanic, Asian, or African—all countries could and would become democratic. And, more than that, it didn't matter whether they were left-wing Marxist-Leninist or right-wing authoritarian, there was a common guide and road map for them to follow en route to democracy.

But it hasn't quite worked out that way, it turns out, and the following statements form the basis for the discussion in this book:

1. There is no one, single path to, or formula for, democracy; instead, countries can and will pursue many and diverse routes. There is no one model, no single road map to follow.
2. Culture, region, timing, and "neighborhood" all matter; it *absolutely* makes a difference if the country is in Southern Europe, Eastern Europe, Asia, Africa, Latin America, or the Middle East.
3. There is nothing inevitable, automatic, or universal about the process. Some countries make it to full, liberal democracy; others get stalled along the route; still others end up as mixes or hybrids of democracy and something else (traditional beliefs and practices,

patronage and patrimonialism, persistent authoritarianism that coexists with democracy, old Marxist leaders who reinvent themselves [like the performer Madonna] and come back as "democrats").
4. In most countries, the so-called transitions to democracy have produced not full-fledged liberal or participatory democracies but limited democracies, partial democracies, controlled democracies, or other restrictive forms—democracy with adjectives.
5. At the same time, the older corporatism (government-controlled interest groups) and authoritarianism, which were supposed to have disappeared with democratization, have either reasserted themselves and made a comeback or have persisted in various fused and compromised combinations with democracy.
6. Not only is the transition to democracy still incomplete in most countries, but we need a whole new language or nomenclature to account for the various mixed, hybrid, and overlapping types.

FOUNDATIONS OF CONTRAST

The analysis in this book focuses specifically on the contrasts between Southern Europe and Eastern Europe. Southern Europe, for purposes of this analysis, is defined to include Greece, Italy, Portugal, and Spain. Of these four, Italy transitioned to democracy after the defeat and collapse of Fascism in World War II and subsequently was one of the founding members of the European Community (EC). In contrast, Greece, Portugal, and Spain continued as authoritarian regimes even after World War II; their transitions to democracy did not begin until the mid-1970s, at which point they became the leading, initial instigators of the "Third Wave" of democratization.

Eastern Europe is defined here to include all the countries that lie between Russia to the east and the German-speaking countries (Austria, Germany) to the west. These include all the countries that broke away from the Soviet Union when the Cold War ended and the Iron Curtain came tumbling down, as well as those countries that are still part of the Russia-dominated Commonwealth of Independent States. The first group, proceeding from north to south, encompasses the Baltic countries of Estonia, Latvia, and Lithuania; the Central European countries of Poland, the Czech Republic, Slovakia, and Hungary; and the Balkan countries of Albania, Romania, the former Yugoslavia (now further subdivided into Serbia, Croatia, Slovenia, Kosovo, Bosnia-Herzogovina, Macedonia, and Montenegro), and Bulgaria. The second group, also going from north to south, includes Belarus, Ukraine, Moldova, and Georgia.

There are some fascinating comparisons, both parallels and contrasts, that one could draw between Southern and Eastern Europe, and that offer a large reservoir of possibilities for future studies at the levels of term-paper topics or honors, master's, or doctoral theses or books.

First, these are, historically, the two great peripheral areas of Europe. If we can agree that the historical center or core of Europe includes France, England, the Low Countries (Belgium, Luxembourg, and the Netherlands), and Germany, then both Southern and Eastern Europe lie at the far edges of this core, part of Europe but not at its heart, and often isolated from Europe's main intellectual, social, and political currents, such as the Renaissance, the Enlightenment, the Industrial Revolution, the scientific and technical revolution, *and* the movement toward limited, representative, democratic government.

Second, and related to the first point, these two areas have historically been the poorest, least developed areas of Europe. Italy is again an exception here both because of its own internal dynamism and because it was a founding member of the EC and benefited significantly from its economic prosperity. But Greece, Portugal, and Spain remained poor countries right through the 1950s and sometimes beyond; they were closer to the Third World of developing countries than to the First World of already developed ones. Similarly, Eastern Europe remained poor and backward; even today one can find levels of poverty, illiteracy, malnutrition, and disease there that are closer to those in the Third World than in the First.

Third, both Southern Europe and Eastern Europe have long been the most religious areas of Europe. While much of core or heartland Europe has become increasingly secular over the decades and even centuries, Southern and Eastern Europe have been far more intensely religious. For now let us leave it at that, that these countries were intensely religious; later in the analysis we will need to distinguish between predominantly Catholic, Protestant, Orthodox, and Islamic countries. For these societies, religious criteria have been and still often are used to decide who is "in" Europe and who remains outside of it.

A fourth and final point preliminarily has to do with the persistence of tradition and traditional institutions in Southern and Eastern Europe. By this we mean such institutions as the extended family, the clan, the ethnic group, patronage and patrimonialist politics, seemingly old-fashioned notions of honor and trust, special favoritism to the in-group, and other features as well. These institutions are stronger and have persisted longer in the peripheries than in the center or core areas of Europe. They provide an older, alternative model of society and political life that often hinders the development of modern political parties, interest groups, and effective bureaucratic delivery of public programs.

These parallels and similarities between Southern and Eastern Europe provide fascinating possibilities for future research. But at the same time, we must also remember that there are vast differences between these two areas as well. These differences are so great that it becomes difficult to see how the same transitions-to-democracy model can be applied to both areas. Here we outline only a few of the most important of these differences; in the course of the book, other major differences will additionally be set forth:

1. At the time in the mid-1970s that the Southern European countries began their transitions to democracy, they were considerably more developed (more industrialized, more middle class, more affluent—all of which helps if you want to have democracy) than were the Eastern European countries when they began their transitions in the 1990s.
2. The Southern European countries already had a head start: they already had at the time of their transitions more open societies, greater pluralism, freer press, the beginnings of a political party and a competitive interest-group system, and a nascent civil society. All of these conditions were far more advanced in Southern Europe than in Eastern European countries when they began their transitions.
3. At the time the Southern European countries began their transitions, the Cold War was still on and both the United States and the West European allies were fearful that Communist elements in these countries might seize control. Consequently, they were willing to pour in immense amounts of foreign aid to prevent that from happening. In contrast, when the East European countries began their transitions in the 1990s, the Soviet Union had more or less collapsed and the Cold War was already over; therefore, foreign aid was greatly reduced. It became much more difficult for the East Europeans to pry assistance out of the wealthier countries than had been the case for the Southern Europeans at the height of the Cold War.
4. When the Southern European countries began their transitions, they already had banks, financial institutions, stock markets, an entrepreneurial class, many big and small businesses, and government regulatory agencies that speeded their economic—and, hence, political—integration into Europe. By contrast, Eastern Europe had none of these things and had to start almost from scratch to develop them, which also slowed their democratization.
5. It continues to make a *big* difference, therefore, that the Southern European countries were transitioning from generally milder forms of *authoritarianism* to democracy, while the Eastern European countries had to change from *totalitarian Communism* to democracy. The latter is inherently far more difficult than the former and will take a longer time because it also requires a *total* transformation of *all* institutions, whereas the transition from authoritarianism only needs a *partial* changeover of *some* institutions.

Already in these preliminary comments we can see that the East European transition, from Marxism-Leninism or Communism to democracy, is going to be quite different from the Southern European transition from authoritarianism to democracy: East Europe began from a lower developmental base, had a far lower level of civil society, lacked the institutions of a modern mixed economy, was less prepared in terms of both political culture and institutions for democracy, and began its transitions in a post–Cold War context where there would be less foreign assistance from the outside. All this meant that the East European transitions would not only be different from those in the South but also would likely be more difficult, longer, more complicated, and more prone to setbacks and even reversals.

REAL-LIFE CONTRASTS

In the early 1970s Southern Europe was already undergoing profound transformations. Spain was in the last years of the Franco dictatorship; Portugal was in the last years of the Salazar-Caetano regime; and Greece was still governed by the often quite brutal regime of the Colonels. All three of these countries were still under authoritarian rule, and they were often stuck with the "Fascist" labels by their enemies.

The terms *totalitarianism* and *Fascist*, however, were no longer very accurate ways to describe these countries. The use of such labels harks back to the *Fascism* of the 1930s and implies that conditions in these countries had been fixed and static ever since. But that is not the picture that anyone who lived and traveled in these countries during this period would have.[4] Instead, what we had was a kind of old-fashioned authoritarian regime where the controls on political activity, while still present, were seldom enforced anymore. Meanwhile, such vast economic, social, cultural, and even political changes were under way that these countries were all but unrecognizable to those who knew them in past decades. In short, vast societal and other transformations "on the ground" had largely rendered irrelevant the older labels— *totalitarianism, Fascist*—used to try to understand them.

Let us provide a brief picture of what was occurring. Economic growth in Spain in the 1960s and early 1970s was at the "miracle" growth rates of 6, 7, or 8 percent; Greece and Portugal were only slightly behind Spain; and all these vast economic transformations were fast changing Southern Europe from poor to middle income and from Third to First World. As a reflection of these economic gains, vast social changes were under way: rapid urbanization, much greater affluence, a new and dynamic business class, and so on. Third, the political culture was changing: religion had lost its hold; young people were impatient for change; everyone wanted to be "European," which was code for "with-it," modern, and democratic.

Vast changes were also taking place in the political realm. At the domestic level the old censorship had been greatly relaxed; people enjoyed much more freedom to travel and say what they wished; opposition political groups were organizing even while authoritarianism was still in power; and labor-union activity, opposition protests, and collective bargaining were all reasserting themselves. Internationally, Greece, Portugal, and Spain were already far along in ending their isolation and integrating themselves into Europe and the world community.

These are not the images of a totalitarian, let alone Fascist, regime. Instead, Southern Europe had become increasingly dynamic and change oriented, and Greece, Portugal, and Spain, even while their old regimes were still in power, were acting *as if* they were already in a postauthoritarian or democratic transition. Thus, when Portugal rose up in revolt in early 1974, the Greek colonels left power later that summer, and Spain's Franco died in 1975, the transitions in these countries were already well under way. The foundations had already been laid; all that was needed was that final push for the full transition to democracy to quickly take place. When their mid-1970s democratic transitions began, in other words, Greece, Portugal, and Spain were already half, or maybe three-quarters, of the way there. They already had established the fundamental social, economic, cultural, and even political base for democracy; and with that foundation the holding of elections, the writing of new constitutions, and the consolidation of democracy in Southern Europe were relatively easy.

What a contrast, then, in Eastern Europe.[5] In the 1980s, just before the transition, the economies of the area were showing no, stagnant, or negative growth; they lacked the dynamism and the economic cushion of the Southern European countries. I saw poverty, malnutrition, children with bloated bellies, and levels of underdevelopment there that one expects to see in the Third World, not in Europe. Moreover, the changeover from a Socialist to a capitalist economy proved to be far more difficult, traumatic, and disruptive than anyone anticipated at the time.

The East had similarly not experienced the South's vast social changes. It lacked a broad middle class on which democracy could be built. Its people, because of the totalitarian controls, were less well traveled, less sophisticated, less international, and less "globalized" than those in Southern Europe. There was no dynamic business class—except those who ripped off the state-owned properties for their own private advantage—on which a more modern economy could be built.

In terms of values, beliefs, and political culture, Eastern Europe is difficult to describe. Instead of a political culture of dynamism, energy, and change, Eastern Europe, especially old-regime officials, was often surly, sullen, angry, unhelpful, and often downright hostile. The attitude was everyone for him/herself and certainly not one of cooperation, accommodation, and a willingness to be helpful to or to cooperate with others for the greater good. There was little trust or cooperation in the system of the sort that everyone from Alexis d'Tocqueville to Francis Fukuyama has recognized as essential for democracy to survive and thrive.[6]

In the political realm there had been a small measure of a relaxation of the totalitarian controls in the 1970s and 1980s; people were freer (though not completely free) than before to travel and speak their minds. There were the *beginnings* of an opposition civil society in some countries (especially Poland and Czechoslovakia), some new (but limited) interest-group activity, and even some opposition political groups. But this was at nowhere near the level of freedom or of opposition that existed in Southern Europe in the early 1970s. For the most part, Eastern Europe remained a totalitarian, one-party, Communist monolith. Moreover, because of the totalitarian controls, its people as well as its officials had far less chance to travel and/or to gain experience at the broader European, international, or global level than did their Southern European counterparts. In fact, Eastern Europe had been isolated and cut off from the main currents of international life for forty-five years, ever since the Iron Curtain had been lowered. There were gray areas, of course, and some Eastern European countries (Poland, Czechoslovakia, Hungary) were farther along the road to change than others. But the general picture still holds: Eastern Europe started at a lower point in its transition than did Southern Europe.

In the chapters that follow, we provide more systematic and quantitative measures of the differences between Southern and Eastern Europe. Even briefly and impressionistically, however, it should be clear already that there are vast differences between these two regions—so vast, in fact, that it will be difficult if not impossible to develop categories and a model that can be applied to both areas.

THEORETICAL IMPLICATIONS

After the success of the Southern European postauthoritarian transitions to democracy, a spate of books came out based on the authors' experiences, purporting to offer lessons on democracy and democratization to the rest of the world. These books suggested that a model of democratic transitions and consolidation based on the Greek, Portuguese, and Spanish experiences was presumably applicable to other countries and areas as well. These books were directed first at Latin America, many countries of which were also abandoning authoritarianism for democracy, and then at parts of Asia, Africa, and the Middle East, as events unfolded and democracy emerged in those areas. As the Soviet Union collapsed and Eastern Europe was set free, that same model was applied to the post-Communist countries as well.

But is that an appropriate use of the transition-to-democracy model? Quite a large number of problems are involved. Here we offer an introduction to some of them; later in the book, we examine these problems in greater detail.

The first problem involves the use of the term "Southern European model." When we use that term, are we referring to Greece, Portugal, or Spain, each of which had quite different transitions, or to some combination of these three countries' experiences? Portugal went through a revolution in 1974 that could have ended not in democracy but in either Fascism, Communism, civil war, or foreign intervention; Greece's transition was also troubled and produced a form of corrupt patronage politics that was only partly democratic. That leaves Spain as the main Southern European democratic success story, and even Spain's transition looks considerably better and smoother after the fact than it did at the time. So when we talk of the "Southern European model" and its applicability to other countries, that is a very vague, ambiguous term, and we would need to be far more specific than heretofore about which country(ies) we have in mind and what aspects of the transition exactly are included in the model.

Second, the transitions-to-democracy literature fails to take account of the quite different levels of social and economic development between Southern Europe and Eastern Europe at the times that they began their respective transitions. For the facts are that, by any measure used, the Southern European countries in the mid-1970s were considerably more developed than the Eastern European countries were at the end of the 1980s. We know from a vast body of social science literature that, the more socially and economically developed a country is, the better are its chances of establishing and consolidating democracy.[7] Yet in its eagerness to establish a general model applicable to all countries, the transitions-to-democracy literature is strangely silent on these differences.

Third, there are differences in political culture. Political culture, defined as the values, ideas, norms, belief systems (including religious beliefs), behavioral patterns, and standard ways by which people operate, is an essential ingredient in any political system; and the values of trust, tolerance, egalitarianism, dignity of the individual, respect for others, and other basic beliefs are crucial for a successful democracy. We also know that by the mid-1970s the Southern European countries had a political culture far more conducive to democracy than did Eastern Europe in 1989. Yet the transitions-to-democracy literature, again, is woefully quiet about all issues pertaining to political culture—except to assert that political culture doesn't matter. That is both an uninformed comment and bad social science, as we shall see. It seems more of an ideological stance by the authors of the transitions-to-democracy literature than it is solid analysis.

Fourth, the transitions-to-democracy literature also misinterprets the role of institutions. This is particularly odd because the transitions-to-democracy approach focuses on institutions as *the* key ingredient in the transition. But the problem is that it gets it wrong. Where it goes wrong is in having a stagnant model of authoritarian regimes, which means that it completely misses the vast changes that we had previously described occurring in these regimes toward the end and the impressive growth of opposition parties, labor unions, and "study groups," even while the old authoritarian regimes were still in power. Some Eastern European countries had *some* of these type movements toward the end (Poland's Solidarity movement, Czechoslovakia's Charter 77) but the changes were nowhere so extensive as in Southern Europe. In Southern Europe these groups formed the bases of the pluralism, competitive party politics, labor-union competition, and democratic politics that emerged after authoritarianism ended; but in Eastern Europe these groups and the institutionalization of democratic politics lagged far behind.

The fifth problem is the woeful neglect in the transitions-to-democracy approach and literature of the role that international forces played in the transition. We suggest the reason for this is that those who advanced this approach, again, had an ideological preference for giving credit for these successful transitions to the domestic forces while downplaying the international influences. But we know these international forces, including the U.S. government, the Central Intelligence Agency (CIA), the Vatican, several European governments, labor groups, and political parties, were enormously influential in funding and supporting these democratic transitions, both in Southern Europe and, later, in Eastern Europe. In the main books we have, however, the international forces are underplayed or else not mentioned at all.

Sixth, the more we have studied these transitions, the more we become convinced that a crucial difference between Southern and Eastern Europe is the role that banks, financial institutions, markets, business groups, and capitalism played in the transitions. The simple fact is that, as capitalistic countries (although partly state capitalist) with existing banking systems, financial centers, markets, entrepreneurial groups, and so forth, the Southern European countries were well positioned to make a transition to democracy. They already had considerable freedom in the economic sphere, so the transition to freedom in the political sphere was relatively easy. In contrast, the East European countries and Russia were Communist countries; as such, they had no markets, no real banks, no financial institutions, no businessmen, almost nothing for a functioning modern economy. The political transition to democracy in Southern Europe was greatly eased by an existing free-market system, whereas Eastern Europe had to start from the ground up, and *to this day* does not have fully functioning free-market systems. That lack, in turn, has frustrated, sometimes stymied, and slowed their political transitions.

Finally, seventh, we need to keep in mind the fundamental distinction between regimes transitioning to democracy from a rather loose, no longer very brutal authoritarianism (Spain, Greece, Portugal) and those transitioning from the far more strict totalitarianism (that is, total control) found in Russian and Eastern Europe. It really does make a major difference. Now, it is true that in the 1970s and 1980s the East European countries began to open up slightly and become somewhat freer. We can call that totalitarianism modified. But that was nowhere near the degree of liberalization that had already occurred in Southern Europe. Essentially, Eastern Europe remained totalitarian and Southern Europe, authoritarian, and these two fundamentally different starting points profoundly shaped their later transitions. It would prove to be far harder to transition from totalitarianism to democracy than from authoritarianism to democracy. Because after totalitarianism, most countries had no democratic institutions on which to build and had to start from the beginning, whereas the former authoritarian regimes had already permitted a great deal of liberalization and, therefore, had a head start on democratization.

It is plain from the foregoing that we take a broader view of transitions to democracy than do some of the earlier texts.[8] We think the focus in many of these books on institutions and institutions virtually alone in the democratic transitions is much too narrow and confining. To capture the larger picture of democratic transitions we need a wide-ranging lens that encompasses history, religion, geography, political culture, and broad political-sociological and political-economic factors. We are appalled that some of the earlier literature dismisses cultural, historical, and geographic factors as "irrelevant." How can anyone who has ever lived, worked, or even traveled in these areas make such a claim? Good social science and good analysis of transitions to democracy do not start off by ignoring and dismissing some of the most important factors in explaining these changes. All these factors and differences need to be brought into our understanding of the differences between Southern and Eastern European democratization. It should not be too surprising that countries that started at very different points should also experience different transitions and come to different kinds of points. *All* these considerations need to be brought into our understanding of Eastern and Southern European democratic transitions.

THE PLAN OF THE BOOK

Part I of the book provides background and context. Chapter 2 focuses on the common traditions, patterns, and politics of the Southern European or Mediterranean countries. Chapter 3 provides background on East/Central Europe, emphasizing particularly history, geography, religion, political culture, and ethnicity issues—all ignored by the transitions-to-democracy literature.

Part II provides a closer look and becomes more specific. Chapter 4 analyzes Spanish politics, shows how Spain has overcome its historic political and cultural animosities, and argues that Spain has become a "normal" (democratic, European, developed) country. Chapter 5 does much the same thing for Portugal, a smaller and less-developed country than Spain but one that has now also passed the threshold to developed, democratic status. In chapter 6 we show how both countries, now that they are developed, can also afford to pursue a more expansive foreign policy.

In Part III we turn our attention again to Eastern Europe. Chapter 7 discusses the general problem of post–Marxist-Leninist transitions. Chapter 8 wrestles with the question of where Europe ends and where the new border that replaced the old Iron Curtain is in the East, separating those countries being integrated into a developed, democratic Europe from those that still lie outside the democratic fold. Chapter 9 deals with the politics of European enlargement and the degree to which the East European countries are qualified to become members of the European democratic club.

In the conclusion, we return to the themes of this introduction, assessing how useful the transitions-to-democracy literature is, where it needs to be refined or rethought, and where both Southern Europe and Eastern Europe fit within this larger conceptual framework.

DISCUSSION TOPICS

1. Be able to contrast authoritarianism, totalitarianism, and democracy.
2. Why did Eastern and Southern Europe lag behind for so long?
3. Contrast the appearances of Eastern and Southern Europe.

NOTES

1. Irving Louis Horowitz, *Three Worlds of Development* (New York: Oxford University Press, 1972).

2. Samuel P. Huntington, *The Third Wave: Democratization in the Late Twentieth Century* (Norman: University of Oklahoma Press, 1991).

3. Francis Fukuyama, *The End of History and the Last Man* (New York: Free Press, 1992).

4. I first lived in Spain and Portugal for a year in 1972–1973; traveled extensively throughout Southern Europe; returned to Spain and Portugal in 1974, 1976, and virtually every year thereafter; and did extensive research again in Greece, Italy, Portugal, and Spain in 1979–1980 and almost every year subsequently.

5. I first went to Eastern Europe in 1979–1980, returned in 1987–1988 (just before the collapse), returned again in 1991–1992 (just after the collapse), and then again in 1995, 1998, 2001–2002, and 2005, when I lived in Hungary and traveled throughout the entire region.

6. Francis Fukuyama, *Trust: Social Virtues and the Creation of Prosperity* (New York: Free Press, 1995).

7. W. W. Rostow, *The Stages of Economic Growth* (Cambridge: Cambridge University Press, 1960); S. M. Lipset, "Some Social Requisites of Democracy: Economic Development and Political Legitimacy," *American Political Science Review* 53 (March 1959): 69–105.

8. I have in mind here the following books: Richard Gunther et al., eds., *The Politics of Democratic Consolidation: Southern Europe in Comparative Perspective* (Baltimore: Johns Hopkins University Press, 1995); Adam Przeworski, *Democracy and the Market* (Cambridge: Cambridge University Press, 1991) and *The Sustainability of Democracy* (Cambridge: Cambridge University Press, 1995); and Juan J. Linz and Alfred Stepan, *Problems of Democratic Transition and Consolidation: Southern Europe, South America, and Post-Communist Europe* (Baltimore: Johns Hopkins University Press, 1996).

I

BACKGROUND AND CONTEXT

1

Southern, or Mediterranean, Europe

For a long time, Southern, or "Mediterranean," Europe had lagged behind both the core areas of Europe (Britain, France, Germany, and the Benelux countries) and the Northern or Scandinavian countries in terms of economic, social, and political development. But now, Southern Europe has become very much alive, dynamic, and on the go. With dynamic growing economies and democratic political systems, the nations of Southern Europe (Greece, Italy, Portugal, and Spain) have taken their place among the leading countries of Europe.[1] From positions of economic backwardness and political authoritarianism only a few short decades ago, all four of these nations have now joined the ranks of what the World Bank calls "advanced industrial nations"; all four have undertaken successful transitions to democracy.[2]

It is often viewed as a mystery why Southern Europe lagged behind for so long. After all, two thousand years ago Greece and Italy were the cradles of Western civilization, and in the sixteenth century Spain and Portugal were the leading colonial nations and ranked among the strongest powers in Europe. But following their years of glory, all four of these nations went into centuries-long periods of decline. It has taken a long time for them to recover.

Greece, Italy, Portugal, and Spain lacked both the economic resources and industry of the core European countries and their strong political institutions; but why did Southern Europe also come to lag behind Scandinavia, another peripheral European area? After all, in the mid-nineteenth century the Scandinavian countries were at the same underdeveloped level as Southern Europe: poor, rural, unindustrialized, undemocratic.

17

But then Scandinavia forged ahead, industrialized, became democratic, and emerged as among the most, if not *the* most developed, most modern regions in Europe. Meanwhile, for another hundred years, Southern Europe continued to falter. Why?

The answers are complex and are explained in greater detail in the main body of this chapter. Some of the reasons include the facts that Southern European social structure was more rigid and class-ridden than that of Scandinavia, that the inequitable landholding system of Southern Europe held back development, that traditional religious beliefs and ideology postponed and retarded development, that there was no national consensus on the direction these countries should go, that their rural economies were backward and their industrialization late, that political conflict and upheaval prevented stable economic growth, that political institutions and infrastructure were weak, and that neither entrepreneurial spirit and a capitalist growth ethic nor a commitment to democratic ideas were strongly present. All of these deep-seated problems had to be overcome before Southern Europe could enter a period of rapid growth. But now that has occurred, and Southern Europe in recent decades has come alive with energy, spirit, new wealth, and dynamism.

We speak of "Southern Europe" as if it were a single, unified region, and in some characteristics indeed it is. All of the countries border on the Mediterranean—except Portugal, which also faces south but toward the Atlantic. All the countries, despite mountainous areas where snow falls, are baked by the warm Mediterranean sun. None of them have large areas (like the American Midwest or the North European plains) of rich, fertile, level ground suitable to mechanized agriculture; instead, much of their surface areas are stony, rugged plateaus, making it difficult to earn a living from farming, let alone produce a surplus. Hence, the traditional crops of the Southern European countries: grapes, olives, and cork.

It remains controversial as to whether Southern Europe also has a common sociological and political-cultural heritage and, if so, whether that still applies today. For instance, much of Southern Europe long had a two-class social structure whose rigidities impeded development; but now much of the area, as with the rest of Europe, is becoming middle class and thereby changing its politics as well. For a long time it was also said that traditional religious beliefs (Eastern Orthodoxy in Greece, Roman Catholicism in Italy, Portugal, and Spain) not only impeded development but also lent a particular (organic, hierarchical, corporatist) character to Southern European development when it did begin. Now, however, Southern Europe is becoming urban, better educated, and secular just like the rest of Europe, and the social, value, and political systems are changing as well. Similarly, it was long argued that Southern Europe was anti-capitalist, patronage dominated, and without a strong work ethic or sense of trust in one's neighbors; but now Southern Europe has developed a creative entrepreneurial class that is as dynamic and forward looking as any in the world. So the old generalizations, the old stereotypes, don't hold up anymore; and some scholars are now arguing that the advanced Italian economy is really closer to Sweden's than to its Mediterranean neighbors.

As implied in that last comment, the differences among the Southern European countries at this stage may be as great as their historical similarities. Greece is, as noted, Eastern Orthodox in its religion while Italy, Portugal, and Spain are predominantly Roman Catholic; and although there are similarities in these religions and in the political regimes (often authoritarian) they legitimated, there are also great differences—plus the fact that none of these countries is very religious anymore. In economics, all the countries of Southern Europe in the early twentieth century lagged behind their core European and Scandinavian counterparts; but in the period between World Wars I and II Italy took off economically and in the post–World War II period, as a founding member of the European Economic Community (EEC), developed economically and socially, surpassing Great Britain in gross national product and emerging as one of the biggest and most prosperous economies in the world. Similarly sociologically: at one point Italy was, like the rest of Southern Europe, a traditional, two-class, risk-avoiding society in which only family and close friends could be trusted; but now Italy is multiclass and much more socially mobile and cosmopolitan in outlook, like Central or Northern Europe. Meanwhile, Greece, Portugal, and Spain fell behind economically and sociologically until the 1950s, when they initiated new policies and began to catch up, and politically until the 1970s, when these three also experienced democratic breakthroughs. By almost any measure, therefore, Italy is the most developed Southern European country, but Greece, Portugal, and Spain have also made both economic and political breakthroughs and may, therefore, be coming to resemble Italy once again. The question is whether the political cultures and political sociologies of these countries are still similar and whether, as a group, they are still distinguishable from other countries in Europe.

Although Italy as a whole is prosperous and in the top rank of countries economically, the south of Italy, the Mezzogiorno, is still poor and closer to its Mediterranean neighbors. And Greece, Portugal, and Spain are still only at about two-thirds to three-quarters the general Western European standard of living. So Southern Europe, although now forging ahead, still does not measure up to the core countries. But as compared with Eastern Europe, Southern Europe is significantly ahead economically, sociologically, and maybe politically as well. For while Southern Europe is at roughly 70 to 80 percent of the European average economically, Eastern Europe and Russia are way behind at only about 10 to 20 percent of the

European average. Herein lies a good basis for thinking comparatively and placing the countries of Europe in separate categories: wealthy countries in the European core and Scandinavia, countries at 70 to 80 percent of the European average in the South, and still very poor countries (at the level of many developing nations) to the east.

Meanwhile, there are other interesting reasons to study Southern or Mediterranean Europe. First, with the end of the Cold War, the U.S. and NATO's strategic focus has shifted southward. During the early Cold War the main U.S. and NATO preoccupation was a Soviet attack through Central Europe; later, the focus shifted to the Mediterranean: the Middle East conflict and its spillover effects, Cyprus and the Greece-Turkey conflict, instability in the Balkans and especially the former Yugoslavia, and other issues. As a result, U.S. and NATO security planning also shifted toward the Mediterranean area. Some NATO military functions were transferred from Brussels to Naples in Italy; the U.S. Mediterranean fleet was beefed up; and Southern European issues came to have a higher priority in U.S. strategic thinking.

It is also across the Mediterranean that Europe confronted the Third World—North Africa, the Middle East, and the problems of sub-Saharan Africa—and the problems associated with that part of the world specifically and the Third World in general—Islamic fundamentalism, terrorism, drugs, poverty, transmittable disease, pollution, and immigration. For this reason many Europeans began to look on the Mediterranean in the same way that residents of the American Southwest look on the Rio Grande: as a source of both potential possibilities *and* problems. Across the Mediterranean and across the Rio Grande are two of the places in the world where the First World and the Third World come face to face and where the problems in the one tend to become problems in the other. As a result, the nations of Europe, especially Southern Europe, began to reach across the Mediterranean for the first time, to devise cooperative programs on pollution and other hot issues, and to try to find common ground with their neighbors in North Africa. Just as the United States is now reaching across the Rio Grande for the first time, recognizing that unless we do something, Mexican and Central American problems will, through unchecked immigration, start to become our problems, and devising common cooperative, multinational policies, so Europe is starting to reach across the Mediterranean because that is where many of their front-burner issues are kindled.

The nations of Southern Europe and their delayed development are, first of all, interesting in their own right as individual countries. Second, they are interesting because of the comparisons that can be drawn between them, the similarities as well as the differences. Third, Southern Europe is interesting as a bloc, as a group of nations with often common and/or parallel development experiences that are quite different from those of Scandinavia and Eastern Europe, and now facing a common set of problems, across the Mediterranean and elsewhere. And fourth, the nations of Southern Europe are well worth studying because, after decades and even centuries of backwardness and authoritarianism, their economic takeoffs and political transitions to democracy in the 1970s are now being touted as models for Latin America, Russia, and Eastern Europe to follow. Whether Russia and Eastern Europe can or will follow the Southern European model—and what, precisely, that model consists of—is a subject to which we return later.

HISTORY, GEOGRAPHY, BACKGROUND, AND POLITICAL CULTURE

Southern European history goes back a long way, some twenty-five hundred years, to the very founding of Western civilization in Greece and Rome.[3] If one includes the prehistoric cave paintings at Altamira in northern Spain and at Lascaux, Montignac, in France, it is clear that European history stretches back many more thousands of years.

At the time that ancient Greece and then Rome were in their heyday, the Mediterranean Sea was the main center of trade and civilized life, and the countries located on its littoral were leaders in art, philosophy, science, government, and military organization. But with the fall of Rome in 476, the ancient world and much of its culture and society collapsed; society, economics, and politics during much of the subsequent "Dark" Ages reverted to a more primitive form. While society and civilization in the western part of the former Roman empire largely disintegrated and went into a decline during this period, in the east, in Byzantium (including Greece) the Empire, the Orthodox Christian church, and their culture and political structure continued to survive for another thousand years, albeit in attenuated form, with its center in Constantinople (now Istanbul), until it finally fell to the Turks in 1453. Greece's history is thus more commingled with the Near East than with the other Southern European countries.

It took Western Europe a long time—about a thousand years—to recover from the devastation and disintegration brought on by Rome's collapse. And when that recovery did begin, it was now concentrated in the North or central "core" of Europe, and no longer in the South. A key turning point was the crowning of the French king Charlemagne by the Pope in the year 800, which definitively linked the papacy and Christendom to the north of Europe rather than to the eastern church at Byzantium. True, Italy had the Renaissance; Greece flourished off and on as part of the

Eastern empire; and Spain and Portugal roared as colonial powers during the sixteenth century. But the great revolutions of early modern times, the major events that made the beginning of the modern world—the Protestant Reformation, the Industrial Revolution, the movement toward limited, representative government, the Enlightenment, the development of modern, experimental science—all occurred in Northern Europe, not in the South. Hence, the North of Europe—the Low Countries (the Netherlands, Belgium), England, France, Germany, and eventually Scandinavia—was destined to forge ahead into the modern world, while the South lagged behind. Greece's domination by the Turks, and Italy's divided regions controlled in various parts by Austria, France, and Spain, further retarded progress.

Part of the problem of Southern Europe's comparative underdevelopment was geographical. First, all four countries—Greece, Italy, Portugal, and Spain—tend to be stony, harsh, dry, arid, and generally nonfertile, and thus not amenable to the large-scale growing of wheat and grains as in the Northern areas of Europe. Second and related, because of the chopped up, rocky terrain, none of them has navigable river systems capable, as in France or the United States, of knitting these societies together internally. A third factor is that the mountains and distinct geographic regions tended to divide these countries into what Spaniards call *"patrias chicas,"* where loyalty went to the "small country" of the traditional home village rather than to the modernizing nation-state. A fourth geographic factor was natural resources: none of these countries has petroleum, iron ore, aluminum, or other of the essential resources necessary for modernization and industrialization. Hence, while nature has been kind to Southern Europe in terms of sun, moderate temperatures, and gorgeous blue skies, it has been less kind in terms of rainfall, fertile land, and resources.

Not only did the South fall behind, it also remained locked in a quasi-feudal, semi-medieval, and largely traditional sociopolitical mode that continued to hold back its development. In all the Southern European societies, the landholding system remained backward and semifeudal, preventing modernization and perpetuating a two-class social structure that was similarly feudal and medieval. Politics was dominated by ideas and institutions of royal absolutism, authoritarianism, and top-down rule that prevented the flowering of democracy. Science was slow to develop, and intellectual life was closed, formalistic, and based on rote memorization. Traditional religious beliefs (Catholicism in Italy, Portugal, and Spain; Eastern Orthodoxy in Greece) held back progress, discouraged or snuffed out pluralism, maintained unity between church and state, and prevented Southern Europe from modernizing at a pace equal to that of Northern Europe.

The growing backwardness of Southern Europe as compared with the dynamism of Northern, or core, Europe gave rise to one of the main interpretations of European (and other) politics that is still often used today: core-periphery relations. By the seventeenth century, if not earlier, the center of European political and economic life had shifted away from the South, or Mediterranean, Europe and toward the North: Holland, Belgium, England, France, and Germany. This was an important, significant, and curious shift because in the fifteenth century the Italian city-states (Venice, Genoa, Naples, etc.) had led Europe in trade, banking, commerce, and capitalism; and in the sixteenth century, with their vast colonies in Asia and Latin America, Spain and Portugal had been Europe's most dynamic and powerful countries.

But the separate Italian city-states were not able, until much later in the nineteenth century, to consolidate as a single nation-state and thus over time were unable to compete with bigger, unified Spain, France, England, Austria, or Germany. Italy in the nineteenth century was thus dismissed as "only a geographic expression" and not considered a serious country. Meanwhile, Spain and Portugal, though rich in colonies and precious metals, were unable to use their colonial wealth to develop native industries and infrastructure. Instead, the gold, silver, and precious commodities of Asia and Latin America flowed *through* the colonial powers of Spain and Portugal but without benefiting them in any permanent way, and on to England and Holland, where they helped stimulate the Industrial Revolution. Meanwhile, Spain and Portugal remained poor and backward, squandered their power and colonial resources in an unsuccessful, century-long effort to maintain Catholic orthodoxy in Europe in the face of the Protestant Reformation, and by the end of the sixteenth century were already reduced to second-rate power status in Europe.

Spain, Portugal, Greece, and Italy—the Mediterranean countries—were no longer the leaders in Europe. Rather, that distinction in the seventeenth century and thereafter had passed to the North. Southern Europe remained locked in feudalism, backwardness, and the Middle Ages, while the Northern countries assumed the leadership in Western-style modernization. However—and this is at the heart of the core-periphery interpretation—not only did the South lag behind, but it was also exploited and victimized by the North, which, according to the theory, drained the South's resources and used them for its own advancement while keeping the South poor. That other large, peripheral area of Europe, Eastern Europe, was often viewed, or viewed itself, in the same light, as an area of exploitation, conquest, and victimization by the core. In other words, the wealth of the Northern European countries was at least in part based on the poverty and exploitation of the South and East of Europe.

A note of caution is appropriate here for these are controversial themes. For one thing, Northern, or core, Europe's success was also based strongly on its own economic, entrepreneurial, and policy accomplishments, and only in part on its exploitation of other areas of Europe. Second, one needs to distinguish between countries, for while Spain, Portugal, and Greece clearly lagged and were exploited, Italy, at least its northern provinces, continued to do quite well and was better integrated into the core area. Indeed, that is a theme that will emerge several times in this chapter: that Italy is a generally more prosperous and successful country than its Southern European neighbors.

While backwardness and underdevelopment constitute the main picture of Southern Europe during the seventeenth and eighteenth centuries, some further distinctions need to be drawn that make the portrayal more complex. First, already at this early date, we can begin to see the differences not only between Italy and its neighbors but also between a more prosperous Northern Italy and the poor, more traditional South. Similarly, in Spain the provinces of Catalonia and the Basque country (both, like Northern Italy, closer to the more prosperous areas of Europe) forged ahead while the rest of Spain remained poor and illiterate. In Greece, Turkish control for so many centuries (1453–1821) held back Greek development until independence was finally achieved in 1821; and even then Greece remained torn and divided. In all four countries the main cities and the capitals were more prosperous, enlightened, and middle class in the eighteenth century, while the countryside remained poor and traditional.

A similar pattern can be traced in terms of time period: in all four countries a split in the national psyche began to develop in the eighteenth century, carrying over to the nineteenth, between those who were traditional and backward looking and those who were more progressive, rationalist, reformist, and European looking. Often this split had a geographic and sociological basis as well: the cities were modern, and the countryside, traditional; the modern or modernizing sector included the middle class, commercial elements, and educated persons, and the traditional elements included the landholding class, rural elements, and religious institutions. This split divided Southern Europe in terms of its domestic politics but also persisted in modified form through the nineteenth century to produce many conflicts and civil wars that further retarded development, and on into the twentieth century, when it was overlain with class conflict and vast political differences. These political divisions, in turn, further held back Southern Europe's economic development.

The French Revolution of 1789 was a major turning point—and not just in France. In Southern Europe it precipitated an even deeper divide in society than had existed in the earlier centuries and led to a pattern of on-again, off-again civil conflict between liberals and conservatives that tore society apart. In Greece these conflicts were complicated even more by the struggles for independence from the Turks in the early nineteenth century, and in Italy by the *resorgimento*, or movement for national unity. Liberals and revolutionaries, in addition to fighting for independence and unity, sought to change Southern European society in its fundamentals: to abolish special privileges for the elites, to disestablish the official religion, to abolish the guild system and the foundations of traditional corporatism, to introduce individualism and elevate individual rights over group rights and community solidarity, to do away with or limit the monarchy, and to bring in the classic, nineteenth-century freedoms (of press, assembly, religion, etc.). Liberals wanted Southern Europe to be more like their northern neighbors and, idealistically, to immediately catch up to the level of development that it took Northern Europe hundreds of years to accomplish.

Some reactionaries sought to restore the status quo ante, to return to the orderly, traditional, quasi-feudal society that existed before 1789. More thoughtful conservatives recognized the impossibility of turning the clock back but nevertheless feared excessive individualism in countries not prepared for it, the cutting of all the ancient ties of group solidarity and community, the loss of religious or moral values, and a too-fast rush toward modernity and liberalism in societies that at that time lacked the organizational and institutional base to support it. They feared too-rapid change would not produce freedom and moderate democracy but incite chaos and anarchy. The differences between liberals and conservatives in Southern Europe were so great that they brought about repeated conflict and civil wars throughout the nineteenth century.

These fights often focused on the monarchy as *the* symbol of the nation. Liberals wanted to check the monarchy, to have its absolutism limited by a constitution, to fashion a system of government like the British with a constitutional monarchy and an elected parliament. Conservatives, in contrast, sought to preserve the integrity of the monarchy and the strength and centrality of the state, fearing anything less than that in a context of nations with deep divisions and weak, grass-roots associational life would produce national disintegration. Both sides in this debate were at least partially correct, but in the meantime the constant fighting between the two sides produced polarization, conflict, and a lack of progress. Caught up in these repeated crises, Southern Europe continued to fall ever farther behind its northern neighbors.

Following the French Revolution, liberals and republicans in the early nineteenth century made a bid for power. But they were soon turned back by the conservative forces who, in the face of renewed liberal challenges, often turned into full reactionaries. From the 1830s through the 1870s—obviously, varying from country to country—the liberals tried again and again to assert their agenda, only to have it repeatedly frustrated by conservatives. In the core of Europe this period of the early- and mid-nineteenth century was one of industrialization and accelerated economic growth; but in the South of Europe, torn by political and social conflict, industrialization and economic growth were perpetually postponed. Meanwhile, during the 1860s, Italy, which had long been divided into feuding city-states whose rivalries added another retarding element to Italian development, was finally unified under Giuseppe Garibaldi into a single nation-state. Greece also achieved a limited, conditional monarchy in the 1860s.

By the last third of the nineteenth century and including the first decade of the twentieth, *all* the countries of Southern Europe had calmed down somewhat and become more stable. All came to accept one or another form of limited, constitutional government. All accepted some, usually limited, liberties and freedoms. They remained monarchies, but the monarchy was no longer absolute, and checks and balances as well as many basic civil and political rights were introduced. Some of the hottest and most divisive issues—church-state relations, centralism versus local autonomy, monarchy versus republicanism—were smoothed over and compromised, even if not finally resolved. And in this context of greater political stability, investment felt more secure, industrialization could begin, national infrastructure (roads, railroads, port facilities, telephone and telegraph, etc.) was developed, and the economies of the area finally began to take off.

Because industrialization came so late to Southern Europe, the trade unionism that it spawned tended to be considerably more radical than in the north of Europe. The early Greek, Italian, Portuguese, and Spanish trade unions were heavily influenced by anarchist, communist, anarcho-syndicalist, and Socialist ideas. (Anarcho-syndicalists were those who wanted to abolish all government and have power concentrated directly in the hands of the workers' organizations, or "syndicates.") They believed in direct political action—strikes, marches on the centers of power, violence, assassination—over calm, collective bargaining. For example, when the king of Spain married in 1903, the anarchists threw bombs at the wedding party—not an auspicious start for the marriage! Governments of the area often responded to the radicals by refusing to enact any social reforms for the workers and calling out the police and army to beat up striking workers. The so-called labor problem was exacerbated by the immense social and class differences between workers and employers or landowners in Southern Europe that made it almost impossible for the two groups to sit down around a common bargaining table and work things out. So while the general picture is one of increased stability and economic growth in the decades leading up to World War I, beneath the surface there was also increased class conflict, which added one more layer of problems to countries already deeply divided by other issues. There were circulations in power among the elites (*transformismo* in Italy; *rotativismo* in Portugal) but little genuine democratization.

The decades just before World War I constituted what historian Barbara Tuchman called "the proud tower" of traditional European society. Nowhere was that more true than in Southern Europe. There, especially, class lines were still rigidly drawn; the elites monopolized social, economic, and political power; and the masses were expected to accept their lower-class station in life as God given. Southern Europe remained a rigidly hierarchical society, with the class lines sharply defined, and little social mobility. Politics and social life still mainly revolved around the small village, family and clan ties, and patron-client relations. Few of the democratizing or leveling reforms that were already being introduced in the core countries had as yet been introduced in the South.

World War I and its social and political effects had a profound, often devastating, impact on Southern Europe. In the midst of the war, the Russian Revolution occurred, which was then followed by social and economic upheaval in Germany and other countries. These events had major repercussions throughout Southern Europe. The numbers of strikes and bombings increased, and the level of violence went up. There was economic upheaval, recession, and eventually full-scale depression during the 1930s. Class and social conflict increased. Radical groups of both the left and the right became even more radical and also violent; many of them formed their own armed militias. Meanwhile, there were increased popular pressures from below, rumblings of military movements and threatened coups, hardened attitudes on the part of traditional elites, and strong right-wing as well as left-wing movements. Vast political changes were also under way: Portugal abolished the monarchy and declared a republic in 1910; Italy had its last liberal prime minister in 1921; Spain had dictatorship in the 1920s and declared a republic in 1931; while in Greece a new Liberal Party that was elected in 1910 faced repeated attacks from all sides.

Developments on the left almost immediately produced a reaction on the right, and vice versa. In terms of "grand systems," the right-wing reactions at this stage no longer produced a return to absolute monarchy but to corporatism. In 1922 Benito Mussolini staged his march on Rome, seized power, snuffed out nascent republicanism, and turned Italy into a Fascist regime: a combination of personalism, authoritarianism, populism, and corporatism. In Portugal, the First Republic lasted longer, 1910–1926, only to be replaced in that year by a military regime and then the corporatist-authoritarian dictatorship of Antonio Salazar (1928–1974). In Spain, the monarchy sought to perpetuate itself by allying with a military dictatorship (1923–1929), but it gave way to a republic (1931–1936), which triggered full-scale civil war (1936–199) and led to a similarly authoritarian-corporatist regime under General Francisco Franco (1939–1975). In Greece, a reformist monarchy had come to power in the 1860s, accompanied by expansionist economic policies throughout the rest of the nineteenth century, followed by the liberal regime of Eleuthérios Venizelos in the early twentieth century. But Greece was deeply divided politically in the period after World War I, defeated by Turkey in 1921, and devastated by depression in the 1930s. In 1936, the liberal regime was replaced by the corporatist dictatorship of General Ionnis Metaxas.

These corporatist regimes varied from country to country, but they also had many similarities. All were authoritarian. All sought to reestablish "social peace" after the earlier strikes and upheavals. All provided for a strong state that would both maintain order and help promote economic development. All were based at least ostensibly on Catholic or Christian (Orthodox in the Greek case) ideas of organic social unity and national harmony. All sought to organize society along functional or group lines as compared with the earlier system of individual or geographic representation. So within the legislature, advisory councils, and government regulatory and policy-making agencies, for instance, business, labor, fisheries, religious bodies, and other corporate units were all represented *by group* rather than on the basis of one person, one vote. All these regimes also used police-state tactics to keep their peoples in line: repression, jailings, torture, censorship, secret police, and the like. And, over time, particularly as they faced economic and political crises in the 1930s and then war in the 1940s, all of them largely abandoned their earlier religious bases and corporatist representational principles in favor of full-fledged dictatorship that snuffed out all opposition. Of the four countries, Italy was the most successful at stimulating economic growth during this period even though democracy had been extinguished.

During World War II and for the first three decades afterward, the histories of these countries diverged sharply. Italy had allied itself with Nazi Germany in the war, suffered devastating defeat, saw the Mussolini regime collapse and disintegrate, and suffered terrible destruction in the war. Defeat may have been a blessing in disguise, however, for after the war Italy rebuilt, joined NATO and the EEC, became a full-fledged democracy, and saw its economy take off and prosper to become one of the largest and wealthiest economies in the world. In contrast, Spain and Portugal stayed neutral in the war, suffered privation but not wartime destruction or defeat, and emerged from the war without either upheaval or collapse. But that also enabled their longtime dictators to hang onto power, postponed needed economic reforms until the 1950s and 1960s, and prevented democracy, until the Salazar regime was overthrown in 1974 and Franco died in 1975. Greece, like Italy, was the scene of intense fighting during the war, involving not just Allied (U.S., British) versus Axis (Germany, Italy) forces but also a domestic civil war: Socialists and Communists versus conservatives, monarchists, and anti-Communists.

Even after the civil war was settled in 1949, Greece continued to be torn between republican, monarchist, Communist, Socialist, military, and democratic forces.

Only after the mid-1970s did Southern Europe begin to reacquire its unity and cohesion. Recall, Italy had been both prospering and democratic since the end of World War II but the other countries had not. In 1969 the ailing Salazar of Portugal had been replaced by the younger Marcello Caetano, but the old Salazar regime, now more liberal and open than before, lived on. However, in 1974 it was overthrown by a military revolt that went radically to the left for the next year before settling in a moderate democratic direction. That same year the colonels who had been governing Greece for the previous seven years were overthrown, paving the way for democracy. And Spain's Franco died in 1975, which similarly enabled that country to flower into a democracy. The restoration of democracy in the mid-1970s in these three countries not only restored political freedom, it also made them eligible to join the EEC, which Greece did in 1981, and Spain and Portugal did in 1986. Greece and Portugal had long been members of NATO, but when Spain eventually ratified by popular vote in 1986 its earlier (1981) decision to join, the circle of Southern European membership was complete. Thus the two great "clubs" of Europe, NATO and the EC, had become not just exclusive but also democratic.

Greece, Portugal, and Spain are newer democracies than Italy so in the following pages we will want to see if their democratic institutions (civic culture, interest groups, political parties, government institutions, public policy) are still weaker as well. Similarly, in the economic sphere: Italy has the strongest economy in Southern Europe, while Greece, Portugal, and Spain are at only between 70 and 80 percent of the more prosperous European economic average. These economic differences may also help us understand both the relative stability of political institutions and democracy in these countries and the differences between them in their ability to carry out effective public policies for the benefit of their peoples.

Political Culture

Political culture refers to the values, beliefs, ideas, and orientations that citizens have about their political system, and the sociocultural institutions that shape those values. Political cultures can be parochial (backward, traditional, uninvolved, nonparticipatory), subject (aroused but suppressed by authoritarianism or totalitarianism), or civic (participatory, tolerant, democratic).

Historically, political culture in the four Southern European countries has been mainly parochial and subject; only recently has it become civic. It is also deeply divided. The roots of these splits, as we have seen, go back at least to the eighteenth century, perhaps earlier. At that time, a basic division developed in the political culture between those who remained conservative, traditional, deeply religious, and backward-looking and feudal or medieval in outlook, and those (a minority current) who were liberal, progressive, secular, forward-looking, and more modern. These splits, then and in the future, tore Greece, Italy, Portugal, and Spain apart and prevented the growth of unity, democracy, and development. Recall that in Greece these splits were complicated by hatred of the occupying Turks, and in Italy by continued regional divisions and foreign occupations.

Recall that the divisions in the political culture of these countries also had a geographic and a socioeconomic base. The dominant conservative, traditional political culture was strongly entrenched in the nobility, church, army, landholding class, and peasantry, and it was particularly strong in the rural, traditional, often illiterate countryside. The liberal, modern political culture was found among intellectuals, students, and commercial interests and was concentrated in the large cities, especially the capital city. In addition, there were often regional differences: the north of Italy was progressive and modern while the south remained traditional.

The disputes between the traditional Greece, Italy, Portugal, and Spain and the modern; between conservatives and liberals; between religious elements and the more secular, simmered for decades, even centuries. In the seventeenth and eighteenth centuries, these were mainly religious, educational, and intellectual debates confined to handfuls of people. They were sometimes accompanied by important policy debates as well, such as overreform of the school curriculum, the relations of church and state, styles of dress and behavior, and freedom of trade and commerce. Until the French Revolution in 1789, these debates were usually kept within peaceful bounds and did not degenerate into major violence or civil conflict.

After 1789, however, these debates over political culture and, hence, over the future direction of the country, deepened, became more polarized, and sometimes provoked civil war. More people were mobilized and became involved, and the political and economic stakes involved (political power, access to government favors, commercial possibilities) were higher. Greece was torn by religious and political as well as anti-Turkish conflict; Spain was divided by a succession of liberal-conservative civil wars; Portugal was similarly conflictual; and feuding among Italy's still-not-unified city-states was rife.

In the last third of the nineteenth century, we have seen the political situation in Southern Europe began to stabilize somewhat. To end the seemingly perpetual conflicts of the earlier part of the century, a compromise was reached: the monarchy would continue in power, but it would be limited by a constitution, checks and balances, and a parliament and/or constitutionally mandated prime minister.

However, after being long delayed and retarded, this period of the late-nineteenth century was also the period when large-scale industrialization came to Southern Europe. Because of late industrialization and because Southern European workers were often exceedingly poor, the worker movements there that industrialization spawned were often more radical than those in Northern Europe. Their ranks included Socialists, Communists, anarchists, and anarcho-syndicalists. Many of these groups believed in revolutionary violence, assassination, direct action, and the general strike, not collective bargaining, as means of advancing their interests. So in addition to the other conflicts already tearing Greece, Italy, Portugal, and Spain apart, a new, class-based, and ideological conflict was added to the simmering cauldron.

These political and ideological conflicts persisted into the first decades of the twentieth century, through World War I, and beyond. They were accelerated and deepened by the Russian Revolution in 1917 and by the economic and social crises in many countries that followed the war. In Portugal, a democratic republic had replaced the monarchy in 1910; but it was chaotic and riven by violence and conflict, and it was overthrown by a military dictatorship in 1926 that brought longtime authoritarian Antonio Salazar to power. In Italy republicanism and liberalism were discredited in World War I and afterwards and were replaced in 1922 by the Fascist regime of Benito Mussolini. In Spain a similarly wobbly monarchy turned to a military dictatorship for support (1923–1929), but in 1931 a republic was declared; its chaotic existence was followed by a civil war (1936–1939), which resulted in the victory of General Francisco Franco and his authoritarian regime (1939–1975). Greece was also unstable during this period and from 1936 to 1941 turned to the authoritarian-corporatist regime of Ioannis Metaxas.

All these regimes sought to end the conflict that had plagued them for so long over political culture, national values, and the future directions of their countries. They did so, initially, by trying to combine various features of their countries' background into an organic, unified, whole. For example, they sought to eliminate class conflict by combining business and labor in a unified corporatist arrangement; they sought to reconcile religious and antireligious sentiment in a modernized, updated church-state agreement; and they sought to overcome decades and even centuries of backwardness by initiating state-led industrialization. But to achieve these goals and to deal with the opposition trade unions and political parties that objected to the changes being made, they used increasingly authoritarian, even totalitarian, methods of control and dictatorship.

Increasingly, these regimes dealt with an inchoate political culture, the conflict of ideologies, and rising societal pluralism by snuffing out those groups and ideas opposed to themselves. They sought to solve the problem of a deeply divided political culture by imposing the ideas and values (order, discipline, authority, rank, place, religion, top-down rule: no bumper stickers advocating "Question Authority" here!) of one sector of society on the nation as a whole. And to do that required full-scale dictatorship or Fascism.

After World War II, all these regimes were discredited and ostracized, and they eventually fell. Mussolini was assassinated in 1944, Italy was defeated in the war, Fascism collapsed, and in 1946 a new democracy was proclaimed. In Portugal, Salazar suffered a stroke in 1968 and was replaced by his longtime protégé Marcelo Caetano, who was then overthrown in a military coup in 1974 that, after a year or more of instability, led to democracy. The similarly authoritarian Greek colonels who had been in power since 1967 were overthrown only three months after Caetano's ouster, leading to renewed democracy there. And in Spain, Franco died in 1975, ushering in a peaceful transition to democracy that became a model for other countries.

Thus, by the mid-1970s all the countries of Southern Europe had reestablished, or established for the first time, democracy. Moreover, their political cultures had also become more democratic. Nevertheless, in all four countries this transition was still incomplete; not all groups had been reconciled to democracy; and antidemocratic and traditional ideas still dominated in certain quarters. But, of course, these attitudes changed over time and also varied from country to country.

Socioeconomic Background, Class Structure, and Interest Groups

Greece, Italy, Portugal, and Spain have, in the past, been among the poorer countries in Europe.[4] They have often been referred to as marginal, on the periphery, or underdeveloped. Economically, these four countries have lagged behind the more prosperous countries of Northern Europe. In addition, using sociological measures, they have tended to be more illiterate, less urban, plagued by greater health problems, and have lower life expectancy. Prior to World War I and even up to World War II, they were commonly referred to as feudal or semifeudal. Italy was a partial exception, ranking ahead on most measures of its Southern European neighbors but still behind those countries in the Northern core. Similarly, Greece and Spain ranked behind Italy but ahead of Portugal which, along with Albania, was always listed, depressingly, as the poorest country in Europe.

All of these social and economic traits, which characterized Southern Europe as less developed, also carried political implications. There was a two-class social structure, which in politics translated into a nondemocratic system of the elites and the masses. The elites dominated, while the poor, usually illiterate, mass of the population was excluded from political participation. The political system was patronal or patrimonialist, organized on a patron-client basis in which patronage was doled out by those in power in return for loyalty and service on the part of their *clientela*; and in this kind of political environment modern political parties, interest groups, government institutions, and effective public policies had little chance to grow. In addition, in the absence of a strong middle class there was little political stability, frequent conflicts and civil strife, frequent military interventions in politics, and the absence of a strong civil society in the form of groups and associations serving as stable intermediaries between the individual and the state. These conditions of strife and instability, in turn, served to further prevent economic growth and societal modernization.

These conditions of poverty and traditionalism and the economic and political vicious circles that go with them are characteristic of what we would today call developing nations, or the Third World. And, indeed, until the 1950s, Greece, Portugal, and Spain *did* have such low literacy, low per capita income, and low living standards that they were classified with the developing nations rather than the already-developed ones. Italy had made a partial break with its poverty-ridden past somewhat earlier, but even in the 1950s it had, particularly in the South, such extensive poverty that it was still closer to the Third World of developing nations than to the First World of modern, industrial nations. One can understand a great deal about Southern European politics if one understands the low level of social and economic development of these countries, even extending into the post-World War II period.

But now, much of this has changed, even while some of the earlier features remain. Italy has emerged as having one of the most dynamic economies in the world, sixth in gross national product, and with living standards and life expectancy approximating those of the Northern European countries. Spain and Portugal have also moved out of the ranks of developing countries into the category of modern industrial nations, with Spain having a per capita income about 80 percent of the Western European average and Portugal at about 70 percent: still not up to their Northern European neighbors' level but a marked improvement over their underdeveloped past. Because of past political volatility, Greece in 1995 was still listed with the moderate-income countries, although at the highest level in that category; but by 1997 Greece had also made it over the hump into the high-income level.

Since the 1950s, in other words, all or most of Southern Europe has broken the back of underdevelopment and poverty and made it into the ranks of developed modern nations. This is a stupendous achievement in a relatively short time; indeed, much of Southern Europe over the past four decades has experienced miraculous economic and social growth rates second in the world only to those of Japan and East Asia. These are no longer poor, backward, underdeveloped countries but modern, dynamic ones. They still have pockets of poverty, illiteracy, and underdevelopment, as do other modern nations, and some are still poorer than others; but none of them any longer has the society-wide culture of poverty and backwardness that they had in the past.

And, of course, just as poverty and semifeudalism shaped their politics and traditional ways of doing things in the past, so now their rising wealth and modernity call forth a new form of politics in the present. That is what this chapter explores: how rising affluence, accelerated social change, and overall modernization in Southern Europe have fundamentally changed the region's political system as well, toward greater democracy. We begin with some further information on socioeconomic conditions, then discuss changing class and social structure, and finally show how these changes affect the interest-group structure and changing political power relations in Greece, Italy, Portugal, and Spain.

Socioeconomic Background

Up through the mid-1950s, much of Southern Europe remained desperately poor. During the years of World War II, there had been mass privation, impoverishment, and even starvation in Southern Europe, and the depressed conditions continued for a decade or more after the war. But then prosperity kicked in, first in Italy, followed later by growing affluence in Spain, Greece, and Portugal. The rising wealth was fueled by the general peace and prosperity of the times, the European Common Market, which tended to lift all boats, and by increased trade and investment, most prominently from the United States. During this period, Southern Europe went from being part of the poor Third World to being among the affluent of the First World. In the process of these quite remarkable transformations, the social structure of Southern Europe also underwent profound changes, which in turn transformed the political system.

From being generally poor, rural, peripheral, and underdeveloped at the end of World War II, all the countries of Southern Europe have in the past fifty years shot up in the rankings of the world's nations to a position now where *all* are judged by the World Bank to be "high income countries." That is the Bank's highest category. Italy was the first to make that rank, followed by Spain, then Portugal, and, most recently, Greece. The Southern European countries are now up there with the world's richest nations.

With a gross national income (GNI, 2004 figures) of $1.5 trillion per year, Italy is the sixth-largest economy in the world. Spain has a GNI of $875.8 billion per year and is the eighth-largest economy in the world. Greece and Portugal are much smaller countries and, therefore, have considerably smaller GNIs. Greece's GNI is $183.9 billion per year and ranks twenty-eighth in the world. Portugal's GNI is $149.8 billion per year, which makes it thirty-first in the world.

However, on a per person or per capita basis, all the countries rank near the top or in the "high income" bracket. Italy again tops the list with an average yearly income of $26,120 per person. Spain is second at $21,210; Greece is third at $16,610; and Portugal is fourth at $14,350. Thus, while all the Southern European countries are at high-income levels, Italy's per capital income remains almost twice that of Portugal and Greece. Spain is in between.

If we look at social or quality-of-life indicators, we again see high ratings for all four countries, but with considerable disparities between them. Once more, Italy leads the group in virtually all categories. Italy is listed as having virtually no illiteracy, an under-five mortality rate of six per thousand, and life expectancy at birth of seventy-eight, which is among the highest in the world. Italy is 67 percent urban. Spain is listed as having very little illiteracy at 2 percent, an under-five mortality rate of six per thousand, and life expectancy of seventy-eight. Spain is 77 percent urban. Greece also has very little illiteracy at 3 percent, an under-five mortality rate of five per thousand, and life expectancy of seventy-eight. Greece is 61 percent urban. In Portugal there is 7 percent adult illiteracy, an under-five mortality rate of six per thousand, and life expectancy of seventy-six. Portugal is the most rural of the four countries, with a 55 percent urban population.

Two things are striking about these figures. First, how high the rankings are for all four Southern European countries. Second, how improved all the figures are over the situation fifty years ago. Some of the figures are probably exaggerated, but there is no doubt of the remarkable changes for the better. These figures are summarized in Table 1.1.

Classes and Social Structure

For a long time—far longer than in Northern Europe—Southern Europe had what might be called a feudal or semifeudal social structure. That means it was basically two-classes: the elites and the masses, lords and peasants, upper and lower. Of course, in all the countries there were always some people who fell in between, who constituted what is often referred to as the "old" or "traditional" middle class. The traditional middle class consisted of soldiers, artisans, and craftsmen, small

Table 1.1. Basic Indicators of Southern European Social and Economic Life (2002–2004)

Country	2004 GNI**	2004 Economy Rank	2004 GNI** per capita	2002 Literacy (percent of population)	2002 Mortality Rate per Thousand (under age 5)	2002 Life Expectancy	Percent Urban (1997–2003)*	2003 Population (in millions)
Italy	1.5 trillon	6	26,120	99	6	78	67	57.6
Spain	875.8 billion	8	21,210	98	6	78	77	41.1
Greece	183.9 billion	28	16,610	97	5	78	61	10.7
Portugal	149.8 billion	31	14,350	93	6	76	55	10.2

Source: World Bank, *World Development Report*, 2005, available at econ.worldbank.org/wdr, and *World Development Indicators Database*, 2005, available at www.worldbank.org/data/wdi2005/.
*Latest available.
**Cross national income (GNI) in US$ Atlas method: GNI is the sum of value added by all resident producers plus any product taxes (less subsidies) not included in the valuation of output plus net receipts of primary income (compensation of employees and property income) from abroad. Data are in current U.S. dollars, converted from countries' respective national currencies using the Atlas method, which uses a three-year average of exchange rates to smooth effects of transitory exchange rate fluctuations.

merchants and shopkeepers, and some government bureaucrats. But these were small in numbers and did not constitute a coherent, unified middle class as in the North of Europe. Rather, in the South they were weak and divided. So the fundamental two-class system persisted in Southern Europe through World War I and, more so in poorer Greece, Portugal, and Spain than in Italy, even through World War II and beyond. The persistence of this fundamental two-class system into the mid-twentieth century also carried far-reaching political implications. It meant that the mass of the population, the great majority of people, was excluded from participation far longer than in other countries. And it meant that democracy was later in arriving in Southern Europe than in the countries of the North.

The power structure of the Southern European countries similarly reflected this underlying two-class social structure. These were not genuinely pluralist or democratic societies. Instead, they were dominated by a handful of elites, military officers, clerics, landowners, high government officials, and the nobility, or those tied into the royal family. It was often said that politics during this period rested on a triumvirate of power: church, army, and nobility. Usually the same upper-class families dominated all three of these institutions, and the government as well. There were frequent rivalries and conflicts between or among the elites in which the peasants and lower classes were used as "cannon fodder" for the competing elite groups, but no real democracy. This was intra-elite politics without the mass of the population participating except as pawns of the several factions.

In Northern Europe, the "proud tower" of this traditional two-class social structure crumbled in the decades preceding World War I, during the war itself, or even earlier in some countries. But in Southern Europe, with Italy again the main exception, the traditional power structure and its nondemocratic character persisted until at least the mid-twentieth century.

It is not that society and the class structure in Southern Europe were entirely unchanging, only that the elites managed by various means to hang on to their power for a long time despite the changes. For example, in the last third of the nineteenth century, the Southern European countries began to develop a business-entrepreneurial class to go along with its landed classes, but the new business elites were usually absorbed into the older landed and noble class and did not develop as a separate, pluralist group. Concurrently and on into the twentieth century, a new and modern middle class developed. Its demands for greater participation in the political process helped stimulate the founding of the Portuguese Republic in 1910, the Italian Republic in 1921, the Spanish Republic in 1931, and Greek liberalism in the early part of the century. But the middle classes of Southern Europe were also deeply divided politically and ideologically; they could not consolidate their hold on power, and those divisions precipitated conflict, civil war, and the overthrow of republican regimes and the dictatorships of Mussolini, Salazar, Franco, and Metaxas and, later, the Greek colonels. These dictatorships in turn sought to turn back the clock, to hold back and control social change, and to prevent the natural social processes leading to pluralism and democracy from happening.

The trade-union movement and peasant groups followed a similar pattern. By the 1920s and 1930s, all the countries of Southern Europe had significant trade-union movements that could no longer be ignored or dealt with simply by sending out the police or army. The strategy now became to co-opt the compliant unions, create official, corporativist unions that would help control and manage the labor movement, and suppress the radical and intransigent unions. By these means the elites were able, over time, to bend to change and absorb some new social groups while retaining their own power intact. As Southern Europe developed, therefore, it did not necessarily become more pluralist and democratic; instead, the old structure of power continued, modified by change but not destroyed by it.

The process was by no means as peaceful and antiseptic as we have described it. Greece seemed to teeter precipitously on the verge of civil war almost constantly from the 1920s to the 1970s. Italy overthrew the monarchy in 1921 and then had one year of republican government before Mussolini's Fascist dictatorship came to power with its strict state controls over both labor and capital—and virtually everyone else. Portugal experienced a military coup in 1926, a series of labor/left revolts in the 1930s against Salazar's dictatorship and his tight controls on the working class, and, finally, a social explosion in the mid-1970s. Spain is perhaps the paradigm case of the conflict that society produced by the effort to co-opt new interest groups, on the one hand, and their desire to remain independent, on the other: the dictatorship of Primo de Rivera in the 1920s, the fall of the monarchy in 1931, a particularly chaotic and violent republic (1931–1936, full-scale civil war (1936–1939), followed by the long Franco dictatorship (1939–1975).

The rules of the Southern European political "game" during this period, roughly from the 1910s to the 1970s (Italy changed its system of politics earlier than the others) were as follows:

1. A new and rising social group (business, labor, the middle class) had to demonstrate through numbers and political influence a certain level of power capability: the capacity to challenge or threaten the prevailing system. Until it reached that threshold, the group could be, and often was, suppressed.

2. Once a group reached that threshold of power and capability, it could be co-opted into the system, have its right ("juridical personality") to bargain in the political process recognized, and receive certain benefits (jobs, patronage, social programs) from the system.
3. By being co-opted in this way, however, a group was forced to give up its right to challenge the system, to pursue a revolutionary strategy, or to seek to destroy other, already established groups.
4. Those new or aspiring groups, mainly Communists, Socialists, and other radicals, who refused to make this political bargain, who refused co-optation and insisted on maintaining their independence, and who continued to follow a revolutionary strategy, received no recognition from the state, were denied legitimacy, and were frequently brutalized.

The co-optive political strategy thus invited new groups to join the system but usually under state or elite auspices. Those that refused the carrot of co-optation received the stick of repression. Meanwhile, the co-optive strategy itself had as its implication the persistence of an elitist, top-down, basically two-class system instead of genuine pluralism and democracy. The co-optive, statist strategy used to absorb and thus control these rising social groups was called "corporatism," which stood as an alternative to liberal-pluralism, on the one hand, and Marxism or Marxism-Leninism, on the other. Moreover, one can see why the stark, either-or choices posed by this strategy would lead frequently to bloodshed, civil strife, dictatorship, and/or civil war.

The corporatist co-optation strategy and the corporatist-authoritarian regimes (Franco in Spain, Metaxas in Greece, Mussolini in Italy, Salazar in Portugal) that accompanied it in Southern Europe turned back the tide of liberalism, pluralism, and social democracy that had been gradually rising in the North, or core, of Europe. Remember that Southern Europe already lagged behind Northern Europe in terms of industrialization, economic growth, and social modernization. Now with the advent of corporatism, roughly from the 1920s to the 1970s, it came to lag even further behind socially and especially politically. One additional result is that Southern Europe all during this period never developed the networks of civil-society groups, the genuinely competitive and pluralist interest-group structure, that the other European countries had. So here is one more reason for Southern Europe's falling behind the rest of Europe and the absence of democracy in the region, in Italy until after World War II and in Greece, Portugal, and Spain until the mid-1970s.

Southern Europe's social and political development, in terms of the evolution of new groups, genuine social pluralism, and an infrastructure of competitive interest groups, is therefore not a continuous, evolutionary, progressive one. Instead it was (1) late in developing in the first place and then (2) postponed and retarded by approximately fifty years of upheaval, civil strife, top-down or statist corporatism, and often bloody dictatorship. Hence, it is only in the past thirty years (fifty in the case of Italy) that a genuinely pluralist society and competitive interest-group system has begun to develop. And the very newness of the pluralism that exists and the weakness, still, of the interest groups help account for the fact that Southern European democracy is more precarious than we would like it to be.

POLITICAL PARTIES AND ELECTIONS

Most of Southern Europe has not had a very long or happy experience with political parties. The political party system of Italy dates only from the end of World War II and of Greece, Portugal, and Spain, only from the mid-1970s.[5]

Not only has Southern European party history been short, it has also been generally unhappy. For one thing, political parties in Southern Europe have often been viewed in the same way that George Washington saw "factions": as divisive agencies that tear the country apart and are more interested in their own ends (power, spoils, patronage) than in the good of the nation as a whole. For another, the historical political parties in these countries have often been agents of the elites, concerned mainly with maintaining or enhancing the elites' own wealth and power, and devoid of ideology, real programs, or interest in popular participation. Then, under the Greek dictatorships, Mussolini, Salazar, and Franco, the old political parties were destroyed, replaced by one-party states that were agents of control, not democracy. The result of this long and sad political-party history, as well as of the current negative views toward political parties, is that throughout Southern Europe, parties are among the least respected of political institutions, with their public approval ratings generally in the low 15 to 25 percent range.

The origins of political parties in Southern Europe date back to that same eighteenth-century split in the "soul" of these countries that we talked about earlier in the discussion of political culture. The split was between conservative, religious, and traditionalist elements, and more liberal, enlightened, and progressive elements. There were no political parties per se but only factions vying for influence within the *ancien régime*. The nucleus of later political parties was nevertheless formed.

Following the French Revolution and throughout the nineteenth century, these factions and the political parties that followed in Southern Europe became more polarized as well as somewhat better organized. Recall, however, that unlike the United States, the Southern European countries in the nineteenth century were still governed by monarchies. They were not republics or democracies. Nevertheless, the factions that had begun to emerge in the eighteenth century now began to develop into political parties operating within and under the monarchy. In Spain this took the form of Carlists (after one faction of the royal family) versus liberals; in Portugal it was monarchists versus republicans; and in Greece it was liberals versus conservatives and monarchists. Italy also had such factions but it lagged behind in developing national political parties because the country was not unified as a nation until the 1860s.

The parties that existed during this period were almost exclusively elite parties. They had little in the way of programs, ideology, or mass following. Often they consisted simply of rival groups of nobles jockeying for power and influence before the royal court. If they reached out into the country at large, they consisted simply of rival elite families trying to curry favor with the government or seeking to gain jobs, contracts, or special privileges from it. The coin of politics was patronage, still in an almost quasi-feudal relationship: loyalty and support in return for jobs and favors. Because these were still monarchies, there was no democracy or elections; if one elite faction needed to mobilize broader support in one of the innumerable civil wars and constant maneuverings of this period, it would round up its peasants, friends, relatives, and allied clans to do battle with another elite faction. This was not democracy or even political parties as we know them; nevertheless, the seeds were planted.

Toward the end of the nineteenth century and carrying over, depending on the country, into the first two or three decades of the twentieth, more ideological and mass-based political parties began to organize. These included Socialist, Communist, Anarchist, and Anarcho-Syndicalist parties. Often employing violence or violent tactics against the ruling elites and monarchies, nevertheless these more radical parties remained small in numbers. More important were the democratic, republican, and liberal parties that urged the establishment of a republic and the abolition of the monarchy. That step came in Portugal in 1910, in Italy in 1921, and in Spain in 1931. Greece had been moving toward a system of limited constitutional monarchy since the mid-nineteenth century; it had a liberal regime early in the twentieth century; nevertheless, relations between the monarchy and the civilian government were frequently testy, and eventually the monarchy was abolished in 1974.

The establishment of republics early in the twentieth century did not stop the infighting, however; if anything, it intensified it. Now the radical parties came out from the underground and, fueled by the industrialization and urbanization of this period, expanded their mass base among the working class. The emerging middle class also organized for political action. And conservatives and monarchists, in the new republican circumstances, also formed political parties. There was great turmoil and conflict among all these parties; many of them organized their own armed militias; violence spread; and the threat, if not the actuality, of civil war loomed.

Faced with the rise and organization of the lower classes, feeling threatened by the specter of Marxism and Bolshevism, and in the context of the economic and political breakdown of the 1920s and 1930s, the more traditional elements reacted. These included the church, the army, and the elite groups: the same groups that had formed the conservative coalitions of the nineteenth and even eighteenth centuries. They sought to turn the clock back, to restore the status quo ante, to resurrect the monarchy and a more conservative political order. Other, shrewder political leaders (Metaxas in Greece, Mussolini in Italy, Salazar in Portugal, Franco in Spain) sought to capitalize on this conservative backlash while also accommodating somewhat the rising social forces. Thus, they sought in their regimes to repress, illegalize, and snuff out the most radical and revolutionary movements, parties, and labor organizations, even while incorporating the more moderate groups, but under state control and through state-run trade unions and other groups. At the same time, opportunistically, they also moved against the monarchists and other radical-right movements. In the meantime, they used dictatorship and repression against all groups as a way of cementing their own personal controls. Out of this combination of strategies was born the Southern European version of corporatism, or Fascism—less bloody, less warlike, more Catholic, less racial and ethnic persecution, less totalitarian than its Nazi counterpart: authoritarianism rather than totalitarianism.

Once in power, all these corporatist, or Fascistic (Mussolini was the one who coined the term), regimes also had a major effect on the emerging party systems. Arguing that the factionalism and constant infighting among the parties were destroying the country, these leaders abolished *all* political parties: those of the right as well as those of the left. In these respects they were continuing in a long tradition of antiparty, antifaction sentiment in Southern Europe. In their place, they created one-party states: official appendages of the dictatorships serving as patronage instruments to help maintain them in power.

Because there was no democracy and no contested elections under these Fascist, corporatist-authoritarian regimes, the official parties took on other functions. They served as additional instruments of control, alongside the police, the censorship, and other agencies of dictatorship. They functioned to rally the regime's supporters and to exclude all others from participation. And they served as giant patronage agencies, doling out funds, jobs, government contracts, toys for children, sewing machines for widows, and so forth, in return for political support from all these recipients. In addition, anyone who wanted to get a government job, or virtually any other kind of job, had to be a member of the official party. So the official party in these countries was really a giant political machine to serve the goals of the dictatorship and to keep the people under control. They were not instruments of democracy or popular participation.

As these regimes began to wind down in their last years, some of the groups and parties that had previously been suppressed began to resurface. For example, although Communist, Socialist, and other opposition groups had often been brutally suppressed by these regimes, they did not necessarily completely disappear but went into exile or underground. Now, sensing the end of the dictatorship, these groups began to reemerge and prepare the ground for their increased political activity once the authoritarian or Fascist regime was gone. Other groups, which were prohibited from organizing as independent political parties, nevertheless organized "study groups" or "research centers"—ways to get around the prohibition on opposition political activities. These developments occurred when the regimes in power were old, tired, or in collapse and unable or unwilling to continue suppressing them. Thus, many of the political parties that would emerge in the new democratic era already had a nucleus of organization even while the old dictatorships were uttering their last gasps. These parties would now emerge as the party systems that continue to play a strong, democratic role today.

Greece, Portugal, and Spain have fashioned and refashioned their political parties and party systems over the thirty years that they have been democracies; Italy has been a democracy since World War II. All four countries started out with multiple parties (twenty or thirty or more), gradually evolved toward multiparty systems of five or six main parties, and have recently moved increasingly toward two-party, or two-bloc, systems. The parties and party systems in all four countries tend to be fluid and heavily patronage-dominated, but they also, in a democracy, now serve as the main agencies of voter choice and of achieving political power. They stand for real programs, platforms, and ideological differences and no longer just as agencies of elite manipulation and clientelistic politics. But the parties can also be corrupt, inefficient, and unrepresentative; in addition, in all four countries, the corporatist arena of big government bureaucracies and well-connected interest groups (business, banks, labor) continue to function as a parallel and often nondemocratic alternative structure to the party-parliament one.

DECISION MAKING AND THE ROLE OF THE STATE

This section deals with government institutions, decision making, bureaucracy, and the role of the state. By the "state," we mean the vast web of government agencies, ministries, institutions, bureaucracy, kings (in old times, and in Spain still today), parliaments, prime ministers, and the like, that is accorded a legitimate right to rule and makes decisions affecting the polity. In Southern Europe it is not just that the role and function of, let us say, the parliament is different in various particulars from the U.S. Congress; instead, the entire state system and the structure of state-society relations (the relations between government institutions and the various interest and functional groups that make up society) are different as well.[6]

In Southern Europe, the state has long been strong in aspiration but often weak in its reach and ability to implement policy. For example, Southern Europe was the very center of the notion of absolute monarchy, but that did not mean the kings who sought absolute power were always able to implement their policies effectively or enforce their decrees in remote villages. "I obey but do not implement" was often the response of local officials to stupid or poorly informed decrees emanating from royal authority. That way, local officials could be in formal compliance with the authorities even while shielding their people at the grass roots from misbegotten policies.

Similarly, with modern dictators, no one doubts that authoritarian leaders like Franco, Salazar, Mussolini, and the Greek colonels were tough guys who ran strong-arm regimes. But one reason these dictatorships were so tough was that the regular government was so weak, unable to enforce its policies and will on society as a whole. Authoritarianism was often seen as a way to compensate for these other weaknesses, to utilize the instruments of dictatorship to make up—especially following particularly weak regimes or in times of crisis—for the ineffectiveness of the regular government institutions.

At the same time, Southern Europe has never had the same kind of strong societal or interest-group structure as the United States, Great Britain, Germany, or other advanced industrial democracies. It lacks the webs of associability at the grassroots level (local Boy Scouts, Girl Scouts, PTAs, churches, Community groups, etc.) that the perceptive French writer Alexis d'Tocqueville found endemic in American society, and it has never (until recently) had the elaborate system of interest-group pluralism of other advanced democracies. So again, to make up for the absence of strong societal infrastructure, Southern Europe has frequently had to resort to inventing strong, authoritative states as a form of compensation. But even though "strong," the legitimacy and "reach" of these states have often been weak.

The countries of Southern Europe are, therefore, not just different from other modern democracies in the particularities of some of their institutions (presidentialism versus parliamentarism, for example), but also in the entire historical and philosophical bases of the state systems and their relations with the broader society.

Origins of the State Systems and of State-Society Relations

The origins of the Southern European state systems and of state-society relations lie in the feudal past. The Southern European political systems, and those of Europe more generally, are thus fundamentally different from that of the United States, which had no feudal or medieval past. Recall that under feudalism and during much of the Middle Ages, society was decentralized and chaotic, the state system weak, and national political systems virtually nonexistent in most areas of Europe.

This situation began to change by the eleventh and twelfth centuries. More unified monarchies began to come into existence in Greece, Portugal, northern Spain, and the various regions of Italy. These monarchies gradually increased the territory under their control and their power within that territory.

As they did so, they often came in conflict with entrenched societal groups who sought similarly to enhance or protect their own rights and privileges. These included various religious orders and monasteries, a number of military orders (e.g., Hospitalers, Templars, and Malta) left over from the crusades, towns and municipalities that had achieved some level of self-government, and economic groups organized in guilds of sheep herders, goldsmiths, coppersmiths, bankers, and the like. These groups sought to retain their powers, privileges, and right to govern their own affairs against the encroaching power of the central state.

These struggles waxed and waned and went on for hundreds of years, from the twelfth through the fifteenth centuries. Although the outcome was not always clear cut, in most areas the absolutist state and its absolutist monarchs won out. They curtailed the power of the local or corporate societal groups and in some cases snuffed them out altogether. Absolutism emerged as triumphant from the sixteenth through the eighteenth century, and even beyond in some cases. But the triumph of absolutism also meant the end of societal pluralism and of the dynamic tension between a central authority seeking to enhance its power and of societal groups seeking to maintain autonomy and self-government. When these two are in balance, in contrast, Southern Europe has traditionally thought of itself as being governed democratically.

The triumph of royal absolutism also meant that Southern Europe never developed until very recently the institutions of an independent legislature, an independent judiciary, or local government characteristic of democracies. Rather, power remained centralized, absolutist. Not only was societal pluralism snuffed out, governmental pluralism was not allowed to develop either.

As it developed over the centuries, the Southern European state is very different from the U.S. conception of government. For one thing, the state is often viewed as natural and good; but if it is good and natural, there is little reason to check and balance it, limit it, and have separation of powers as in the U.S. system. Another difference is that, historically, citizens tend to look to the state, rather than to their own initiative, for protection, benefits, and social welfare. Even though often ineffective, the Southern European state is nevertheless viewed as a kind of "nanny state," taking care of people and responsible for the general well-being of its citizens.

By the nineteenth century, there were increased pressures for more liberal, republican, even democratic government. But in the face of these pressures, the established monarchies dug in their heels and refused to budge. They were backed by the traditional elite groups—army, church, oligarchy—against the rising social forces of the middle and working classes. Unlike the situation in Northern Europe, where the elites gradually accommodated to change, in Southern Europe they sought to block it altogether. To the earlier conflict over absolutism was thus added new elements: class struggle and social conflict. The result was not pluralism and democracy but polarization, conflict, and civil strife, if not outright civil war.

The dictatorial regimes of Franco, Salazar, Mussolini, and Metaxas represented a continuation of this centuries-long struggle in new form. In the face of rising social and political change and the demands of new groups (labor, peasants, the middle class) for access to power and its benefits, these regimes clamped down and snuffed out the rising social forces or, under corporatism, subordinated them to state control. Absolutism was once again in the saddle but without some of the leavening effects of the monarchy; whatever vestiges remained of pluralism, local government, an independent parliament or court system, or societal-group independence from the central state was eliminated.

Only since World War II in the case of Italy and the mid-1970s in Greece, Portugal, and Spain have democracy and societal and political pluralism returned. But that means (1) that democracy and pluralism are still new and not necessarily fully consolidated and (2) that because of the delays, the political systems of Southern Europe still exhibit some unique features that mark them as different from those of other countries.

State-Society Relations

State-society relations in Southern Europe are still quite different from those of the United States or other Western democracies.

For one thing, the number of groups in the system remains small. It is no longer limited to the nineteenth-century power triumvirate of church, army, and oligarchy but now includes trade unions, farmer groups, middle-class professional associations, business and banking interests, bureaucratic interests, and local and regional forces. However, that still adds up to only ten or twelve major interest groups, compared to the fifty thousand registered national-interest groups in the United States. Southern Europe is clearly more pluralist and democratic than before, but it still practices a form of limited pluralism, not the incredible hurly-burly of the American interest-group struggle.

Second, in a system of limited numbers of interest groups and of limited pluralism, there tend to be fewer moderating, crosscutting loyalties. It is often argued that in the United States, because we have so many interest groups and because each of us tends to belong to several of them at once—religious bodies, labor unions, tenants' associations, student groups, professional associations, parents' groups, political parties, school groups, and the like—our loyalty to any one single group or point of view is therefore moderated, tempered, and compromised and tends to limit intense partisan or ideological commitment to any one single point of view, which is also good for centrist democracy. But this has not been true in the past in Southern Europe. There, people have tended to belong to and go all out for only a single group. Instead of the moderation of crosscutting loyalties, Southern Europe has featured absolute commitment to a single cause. Moreover, people tend to be stock-typed or stereotyped as the military officer, the bourgeoisie, the worker, the landowner, and so forth, which reinforces extremist positions and causes people frequently to actually behave as the stereotypes call on them to do. Limited numbers of interest groups and the absence of crosscutting loyalties tend to reinforce the divisions and polarization that have long existed in Southern European society.

Third, given the long-standing weakness of civil society in Southern Europe, the state still leads. It is usually the state, and not so much private entrepreneurial groups, that guides, directs, and manages the economy. It is the state that doles out funds, projects, and programs so that investment and economic growth can take place. It is the state that largely decides on priorities among pressing social as well as economic issues and directs the national budget in those directions. At the same time, people in Southern Europe tend to look to the state for guidance, direction, and benefits.

The state in Southern Europe is looked on positively as the main source of goods, programs, jobs, patronage, and largesse. Hence, the state does not carry the negative connotations—"big government," "inside the Beltway," "bloated," "irrelevant," "inept"—that it often carries in the United States.

One reason the state has been strong in Southern Europe is that, historically, private groups have been weak. As indicated, Southern Europe has not long had the plethora of interest groups that the United States has. Nor does it have the vast web of neighborhood and community groups— PTAs, Boy Scouts, Girl Scouts, Rotary Clubs, lodges, bowling leagues, and so forth—that the United States has and that is often understood as the essential ingredient in American pluralist democracy. Nor in Southern Europe, until recently, has there been a dynamic, innovative, risk-taking, job-creating, private business sector capable by itself of launching new enterprises, putting people to work, and generating jobs as well as capital for investment. In the absence of this societal and entrepreneurial infrastructure, it is the state or government that has often been required to step into the vacuum and provide the leadership, the guidance, and the investment that the private sector lacks.

A fourth feature of Southern European state-society relations is persistent corporatism or state-sponsored, if not state-created, interest groups. If private interest groups are few and weak, it is up to the state to create them. The issue is similar to that regarding capital and entrepreneurship: if the private sector is weak, then the state must step into the breach. This becomes particularly true in the age of industrialization, when the state must harness all its energies for a coordinated national development strategy. In the absence of much private investment capital, the state must provide the economic stimulus for growth; second, since interest groups are inchoate, unstable, and often disruptive, the state must coordinate, guide, and direct them as well. But as soon as you talk about business, labor, farmers, and other groups being "coordinated" or "guided" under government auspices, you are talking about corporatism, not liberal-pluralism. For that is precisely the definition of corporatism: state guidance, control, and co-optation of interest groups. It is important to remember, therefore, that corporatism in Southern Europe did not just disappear with the end of the Mussolini, Franco, Salazar, and Greek dictatorships. Instead, whenever interest groups are weak and the state has to guide them, assist them, and bring them into governmental decision making, both to get their viewpoint and, in the process, to pacify them, we are talking about corporatism. Corporatism has recently taken on new, more open, more pluralist, more democratic forms—but it did not end with the fall of Fascism.

Now, however, many of these features of Southern European state-society relations are changing. Interest groups are stronger and often more independent of the state, although many interest groups continue to receive subsidies from the state. The climate in which these interest groups operate is now freer and more democratic. And new, better-organized, and more diverse interest groups continue to be formed. Southern Europe is gradually developing the civil society, the vast web of associational life that strengthens the grassroots organization that has long been lacking in the area. New forms of public-private partnerships have also emerged.

The introduction of a common European currency and of a single European monetary unit (the Euro) and central banking system, as distinct from local or national central banks, will also change the system. From now on, it will be harder for governments to subsidize their own interest groups through deficit financing, because the European central bank may not permit that. For the same reason, it will be harder to give favors, vast government jobs, sinecures, and special treatment to favored interest groups. It will be harder to co-opt or buy off dissenting political groups. Although the precise implications of the movement toward a single currency governed by a single European central bank are still unknown, it is clear that these imply not just economic transformations but important political results.

BUREAUCRATIC POLITICS

Most of the Southern European countries have comparatively large state sectors. The state may generate upwards of 30, 40, or 50 percent or more of the national economy. The state may own, subsidize, or have large shares in major industries, utilities, banks, construction, insurance, airlines, tourism, petrochemicals, and other major industries. Again, the state plays such a large and leading role in the economy because the private sector has tended to be weak and small.

The large state sector means the state has also been the largest employer, particularly of educated persons, in the country. Depending on the country, between one-third and one-half of the labor force may work for the state, either directly in the public bureaucracy or indirectly in one of the state's economic enterprises. Hence, in Southern Europe the state sector, rather than the private sector, often offers the best opportunity for employment, for security in one's job, and for a comfortable pension as well as good health, educational, and other benefits.

There are elaborate civil-service laws and rules in Southern Europe, but in the past these have not been followed consistently. In getting and keeping a government job and being promoted in the system, it is patronage, family connections, and political spoils that count at least as much as merit and achievement. Individual persons tend to see their avenue for upward mobility through the state job system; at the same time, governments and political parties tend to reward their friends, supporters, cronies, and even foes by putting them all on the public payroll.

Americans are often used to hearing of individual government jobs being awarded on the basis of political connections, but in Southern Europe entire government programs and whole ministries or agencies are often turned over to well-connected interest groups or political parties for them to dole out, patronage style, to their supporters. In Italy, for example, entire offices within the Labor or Social Welfare ministries would be turned over to the Christian Democratic Party for it to fill with its party loyalists; down the hall, and as a way of buying their loyalty, other offices would be turned over to the other main party, the Communists and their sympathizers. Such practices served important political and patronage functions; whether they served the interests of sound public policy may be another matter.

The state bureaucracy is also the agency through which most interest groups operate. Rather than dealing directly with each other, as, for example, in American-style collective bargaining between labor and employers, most interest groups in Southern Europe try to influence the state bureaucracy. For it is the bureaucracy or government that often determines wages, working conditions, rules, and benefits for the different categories of workers. As an interest group, you always concentrate your energies where power and decision making lie, and in Southern Europe that has long been the state rather than private employers. So you may demonstrate, stage strikes, march on the seat of government, or even try to close down the national economy, all in an effort to get the state to raise wages or decree improved benefits and working conditions. Or you may want to oust the labor or social-welfare minister to bring in a new minister more amenable to your group's interests; alternatively, you may want the state to put pressure on private employers to grant your demands.

Note that this is really a system of political bargaining, through the state system, rather than direct collective bargaining between the affected parties as in the American system. The Southern European labor-relations system is thus more bureaucratic, more indirect, and more politicized than the American system is. And it fits better a group of nations where the state sector is strong, the private sector historically weak, and what we know as up-front, interest-group lobbying is still largely unknown. Southern Europe still largely prefers to handle these matters behind the scenes and bureaucratically, without direct confrontations.

But this system is changing in Southern Europe as well. First, the private sector, especially business, is growing and becoming more independent of the state. Second, and related to the first point, direct collective bargaining between the affected interests—that is, instead of conflicts always being channeled through the state—is becoming more prevalent. Third, pressures for government streamlining and greater efficiency are making it harder for the state to be the employer of first resort and a large reservoir of patronage positions. Fourth, the civil bureaucracy itself is becoming more efficient and professional, less patronage dominated, and more based on merit than personal, family, or political party connections. And fifth, once again, the coming of the Euro and of European-wide monetary policy will make it harder to stuff the bureaucracy with sinecures or to pay for vast new employment programs masquerading as public policies through deficit financing or the printing of more money.

GOVERNMENT INSTITUTIONS

All four of the Southern European political systems are parliamentary systems. Power rests mainly in the parliament and in the government (cabinet and prime minister) that is selected from among its members. In this way the Southern European countries, and Western and Central Europe more generally, are fundamentally different from the presidential system and separation of powers of the United States.

In parliamentary systems the executive and legislative branches are fused. Leaders of the government *must* come from the parliament and simultaneously be elected to represent their districts just like other members of parliament (MPs). Party leaders are chosen by their respective party conventions, and sometimes now in party primaries, to head the ticket and represent the party. If that party gains a majority in the election, then its leaders form a government. And, of course, the government will be able, unless there are extraordinary circumstances, to get its program passed by the parliament because, by definition, it has a majority there. If it had no majority, then it would not be able to form a government in the first place. The opposition, meanwhile, criticizes the government and chips away at its majority, hoping that *it* will win the next election and thus be able to form a government of its own. If there is anything comparable in the American system, it would be like, in the absence of a president and vice president, the speaker of the House of Representatives becoming prime minister and other House leaders of the same party becoming cabinet ministers.

All this presumes a two-party system in which one of the parties is guaranteed a majority, or a multiparty system in which one of the parties is so strong it gets over 50 percent of the votes. But what if, as is the case in Southern Europe presently, there is a multiparty system and no one party gets a majority? Then the leading party, ordinarily, will have to bargain with other, smaller parties to get enough parliamentary seats to form a majority, and thus to form a government. The cost of luring a small party into such a coalition arrangement is usually one or more cabinet seats going to that party, and other favors as well. The term of office in such parliamentary systems is usually five years, but if the balance of political power is close, a few MPs switch sides, or the government loses on a critical vote (a "vote of confidence"), then new elections must be called immediately and the process of organizing a government or of coalition formation begins all over again.

Now, suppose the two leading parties tie in the popular vote or are so close together electorally that there is little difference between them. Or suppose the leading party is unable to complete the coalition arrangements to lure in a second party to form a working coalition. Then there is often trouble in parliamentary systems. New elections may need to be called to resolve the impasse. Or perhaps the king (in Spain) or president (in Greece, Italy, or Portugal—usually a figurehead or ceremonial position but important in these circumstances) may step in to break the logjam. In those situations there may be the possibility of conflict, fragmentation, and breakdown, a remote possibility but not entirely inconceivable.

DOMESTIC PUBLIC POLICY

Historically—that is, up until about the time of World War I—governments in Southern Europe were called on to provide few public-policy programs or initiatives.[7] In those days, prior to the onset of the modern welfare state, governments were generally quite small and had limited responsibilities; most governments had only four or five ministries—treasury, foreign affairs, war or military, interior or public works—and did not feel responsible for a range of domestic social and economic programs. Care of the poor, the indigent, the unfortunate, the lame, the sick, and the insane was seen as the responsibility of the family and, if the family was unable, of the church (Roman Catholic in Italy, Portugal, and Spain, and Orthodox in Greece). In this way, the government's role was kept modest and limited.

Toward the end of the nineteenth century and in the early decades of the twentieth, corresponding with the early stirrings of industrialization in Southern Europe, the "social question" began to be raised for the first time. The social question involved the issue of the rising power of organized labor as well as the debilitating social effects that the early phases of modern industrial capitalism often left in its wake: urban poverty, disease, unemployment, abandoned children, slum housing, and broken families. At first, families and the churches tried to deal with these rising problems in the traditional way, through charity, social programs, and good works. But with massive urbanization as well as frequent impoverishment of large numbers of peoples, the traditional charitable methods proved inadequate. The state or government began to be called on to provide the large-scale resources and programs that private groups were no longer able to provide. In Southern Europe the pressures eventually gave rise in the interwar period (1920s and 1930s) to authoritarian corporatism and corporatist regimes, whereas in Northern Europe during that period the same pressures laid the foundations for the modern welfare state. Hence, the interwar period was a critical juncture, spawning two of the main movements of the twentieth century: corporatism, on the one hand, and welfarism, on the other.

There are a number of useful explanations for Mussolini's Fascism in Italy and the similar authoritarian-corporatism during this same interwar period of Metaxas in Greece, Salazar in Portugal, and Franco in Spain. All of them represented, among other things, an attempt to respond to the "social question": what to do about organized labor as well as the legion of poor and unemployed? Marxism and Bolshevism were unacceptable (remember, the Russian Revolution was also occurring during this period) and the other main alternative, liberalism, seemed to reflect more Anglo-Saxon traditions than the Catholic or Orthodox traditions of Southern Europe. Hence, corporatism was seen as a "third way," alternative to both Marxism and liberalism, and particularly attuned to the histories and sociologies of Southern Europe.

Under corporatism, labor was to be brought into the political process and given certain social benefits, but under state auspices and control. Labor would be obliged to give up its independence as a political movement as well as its revolutionary aspirations (Marxism and anarchism were particularly strong in Southern Europe) in return for being recognized and given legitimacy by the state, and for new social programs being showered on it. To that end, all four countries enacted new labor, social security, and welfare programs in the 1920s and 1930s, meanwhile creating official, government-run unions for the workers.

Organized labor and the workers bore the brunt of government authoritarianism; and they were repressed by the regimes in power, which is why we often label the regimes "Fascist." Meanwhile, the unions that did accept what we may call the corporatist compromise (benefits for workers in return for state regulation) often found that their organizations were rigidly controlled by the state and that the benefits promised in the way of advanced new social programs failed to materialize. In Southern Europe, therefore, the poor and the working class had the worst of all possible worlds: private and religious charity was coming to an end, their previously independent unions had lost their autonomy and were controlled by the government, and the government's promised social welfare, although drawn up on paper, failed to materialize.

This situation could not last indefinitely. In Italy, Mussolini and Fascism were overthrown as World War II was drawing to a close; Italy then embarked on both a more democratic and a more socially progressive course. In Spain and Portugal, the authoritarian-corporatist regimes of Franco and Salazar hung onto power but floundered for the next thirty years, with only modest advances in the area of social policy. Greece experienced civil war in the 1940s, a kind of chaotic and conflict-prone democracy in the 1950s and 1960s, and then a reversion to authoritarianism and corporatism again from 1967 to 1974. It was only after these authoritarian regimes were overthrown or left power in the mid-1970s that Greece, Portugal, and Spain began to adopt the kind of modern social programs that Italy had adopted thirty years earlier and that most of Northern Europe had begun to adopt even earlier still.

Italy now has so many advanced social programs (at least on paper) in so many areas that it can be considered a kind of Mediterranean Sweden. But Greece, Portugal, and Spain still lag behind in many social program areas. In part, their retardation in the field of social welfare can be explained by the fact these countries are still poor compared with Northern Europe, and they cannot afford all of the programs of the modern welfare state; in part, it is because their social-program development was postponed so long by the persistence of old-fashioned social structures and authoritarian regimes. But now there is an explosion of new social programs in all these countries, and a large, pent-up demand at the popular level for all the programs and benefits that their northern neighbors have long enjoyed. Along with aping and imitating all other things "European," Southern Europe is now rushing pell-mell toward Scandinavian-style welfare systems.

REGIONALISM AND GLOBALIZATION

For most of the modern era, 1500–present, Southern Europe was peripheral to, and at the margins of, the European core. After the fall of the Roman Empire, Christendom split into its Eastern and Western blocs; meanwhile, the center of gravity in Europe gradually shifted to the North, while the South or Mediterranean Europe was left behind. Southern Europe was bypassed or came late to all the great "revolutions" that we associate with the making of the modern world: the Protestant Reformation, the Enlightenment, the Industrial Revolution, the scientific revolution, accelerated social change, democratization. Many areas of Southern Europe remained feudal, medieval, and underdeveloped, while the North forged ahead.

The development of the North and the continued underdevelopment of the South bred in both areas a set of attitudes that persist, although now ameliorated, to this day. The North, because of its accomplishments and developed status, tended to feel superior to the South and to look down on it. The South, in turn, felt slighted by these attitudes, resented them, and often harbored a kind of inferiority complex toward the North. Even though the South for many centuries lagged considerably behind the North in economic, social, and political development, it often argued that its culture was superior to that of the North and that it didn't want to be like those "Anglo-Saxon countries" anyway. If Northern Europe insisted on making cruel, ethnic jokes at their expense and didn't really want them in European councils (the EEC or NATO), then Southern Europe had to insist publicly it didn't really want to be in those organizations, even while privately maneuvering to be admitted. The issue of joining or being integrated into Europe was for the Mediterranean countries as much political and psychological as it was geographic or economic.

Italy was the first Southern European country to break out of this syndrome, ironically not because of its success but because of its defeat in World War II. Due to subsequent Cold War considerations, Italy became a charter member of both the EEC and NATO. And then Italy prospered, becoming over time the sixth biggest economy in the world, a reliable ally, and a democracy, with a standard of living on a par with several of the Northern European countries.

The other Southern European countries did not fare so well. Because of Cold War considerations, Greece was allowed to join NATO in 1952, and Portugal, in 1953; but because of the long Franco dictatorship, Spain was kept out until 1981. In the economic sphere, because of their authoritarian regimes, Greece only joined the EEC in 1981 and Spain and Portugal in 1986—considerably later than the earlier European members. Keeping these countries out of the EEC not only prevented them from sharing in the full, post–World War II economic boom that Europe experienced, it also, because of this rejection, increased their anxiety, bitterness, and sense of inferiority vis-à-vis the rest of Europe. Hence, the campaign of these countries to join the EEC was not just economic; it was also tied in with their desires to be considered "normal" *European* countries, with all the political (democracy), social (progressive), and psychological (developed, with-it) characteristics that term implies. Virtually everything the Southern European countries have done over the last several decades has been directed at accomplishing this one, single, overriding goal: joining Europe in *all* its dimensions.

Once they had been admitted to NATO and the EEC—"the Club"—the Southern European countries became among their most enthusiastic members. In part because they had been kept out so long, they participated enthusiastically in EEC councils, were energetic participants in the European parliament, and were among the first to volunteer troops as part of a NATO peacekeeping mission in Bosnia. Three of the countries (Italy, Portugal, Spain) qualified in the first round to be part of the European Monetary Union (EMU); these same three have been among the first to align their foreign policies with an overall European foreign policy. In contrast, Greece during the 1980s was more critical toward the EEC, failed to qualify in the first round for admission to the EMU, and, because of its ongoing conflict with fellow NATO member Turkey, maintains a more independent foreign policy. Nevertheless, Greece too wants strongly to be "in" Europe.

The Southern European countries have been so preoccupied over the last half century with joining Europe and being considered European that they may have neglected global trends occurring simultaneously. In their focus on European *regional* integration, they may have missed what is happening "out there" in the larger world. For the world is becoming a *global* marketplace, not just a regional one. Culture, ideas, trade, and technology are becoming increasingly global, not just local. And the issues of drugs, immigration, terrorism, pollution, the environment, and so forth are increasingly global issues not confined to just one region.

In their rush to Europeanization, it may be that Greece, Italy, Portugal, and Spain have fallen behind somewhat in adapting to these global trends. An integrated Europe is the world's largest and richest market, but that does not mean one can ignore other global markets. It may be good to have a common European foreign policy, but the European countries, as they are finding out in Bosnia, Kosovo, Russia, the Middle East, and other areas, cannot act as if the rest of the universe doesn't matter or doesn't impose on their closed world. And how should Europe or its individual countries react to all those global problems and issues?

We will need more time to see how the New Europe, and specifically the Southern European countries, react to these global trends. The record so far is mixed. Europe's response to the fighting in Bosnia has generally been thought of as a failure. Nor did Europe and its supposedly common foreign policy react coherently to aggression and malfeasance by Saddam Hussein and Iraq. On the other hand, the EU has signed a trade agreement with MERCOSUR in South America, and its relations with other Third World areas have been at least as enlightened as those of the United States. Entering the twenty-first century, it will, in fact, be a major task for *all* nations to adjust their bilateral, regional, and global policies to all these new trends.

Joining the EU will also have a major impact on the domestic politics of the Southern European nations. They now must conform to common European product standards, specifications, quality controls, health and environmental standards, and so on. Their policies on agriculture and in other economic areas are determined as much in Brussels as by their own economics ministries. In addition, because of the common financial policy that membership in the EMU obliges them to follow, the Southern European countries will no longer be able to finance costly social programs through deficit financing, wild borrowing abroad, or the tactic of cranking up the printing presses to produce more paper currency. These restrictions in turn will have a powerful negative effect on traditional Southern European patronage systems and clientelistic politics. No longer will it be so easy to stuff the government with friends and relatives or to dole out whole social programs to groups as a way of buying their loyalty. Instead, the emphasis will be on efficiency, rationality, and a streamlined public service. The European Union and particularly the common currency and monetary policy represent, therefore, not just a new economic program; they will have profound social and political consequences in Southern Europe as well.

CONCLUSION

For a long time the countries of Southern Europe were referred to as "different," and the term was not always meant as a compliment. It was not just the sun, tiled roofs, olive trees, Mediterranean cooking, and deep blue skies that marked them as different, however, but other, deeper forces as well. Socially, economically, culturally, politically, religiously, and even psychologically, Southern Europe seemed both backward and not a part of the European mainstream. The countries of Mediterranean Europe seemed to form a unique culture and society. These differences were summed up in the derogatory comments such as, "Europe stops at the Alps or Pyrenees," "Greece lies beyond the pale," or Italy as a nation was a "figment of the imagination."[8]

From approximately the sixteenth through the nineteenth centuries, Southern European development appeared to diverge from that of the rest of Europe. The Southern European political systems were closed and authoritarian; there was no evolution toward democracy. Socially, they remained rigid and two-class. From the height of wealth in the fifteenth and sixteenth centuries, they fell back into poverty and backwardness. Religious orthodoxy held back learning, science, and intellectual stimulation. Reactionary and backward looking in virtually all spheres, trapped in the Middle Ages, Southern Europe experienced little of the Enlightenment and Industrial Revolution that would lead to modernization. Its social and political systems were long dominated by traditional behavior, patronage, personalism, clientelism, inefficiency, family and clan-based politics, corruption, and authoritarianism. Backwardness in so many areas, in turn, produced national inferiority complexes and a sense that, if Europe did not want or respect them, they did not want Europe either.

When modernization finally began to come to Southern Europe in the nineteenth century, it was terribly disruptive and conflict prone. The old guard and old oligarchies—church, military, elites, monarchy—tried to hang onto their power at all costs, while the often-frustrated newer social forces turned to such revolutionary ideologies as Marxism and anarchism. The result during much of the nineteenth and early twentieth centuries was conflict, fragmentation, instability, and civil war, which held back development even more. Corporatism seemed to offer a third way for these paralyzed, conflict-prone societies and produced such dictators as Mussolini in Italy, Salazar in Portugal, Franco in Spain, and Metaxas and the colonels in Greece.

Hence, it was only in the post–World War II period—Italy first in the late 1940s but Greece, Portugal, and Spain two or three decades later—that Southern Europe began to join the modern world in *all* its dimensions. The economies of the area took off, fueled by the general European and U.S. prosperity of the period; their social systems modernized and became more pluralist; and their political systems embraced parliamentary democracy. In the process, the Southern European countries also embraced Europe as a whole, including the EC, NATO, and the EMU, to say nothing of European mores and behavior, and also broke out of their historical international isolation. The changes in the last several decades in all areas of life have been nothing short of spectacular. This is not your father's or grandfather's poor, backward Greece, Italy, Portugal, or Spain any more. Instead, Southern Europe has become dynamic, alive, often on the frontier of change rather than, as in the past, lagging behind.

Now all the countries of Southern Europe are democratic—for the first time ever. And this condition of democracy seems unlikely to change soon. All the countries of Southern Europe will in all probability continue to develop economically as well as socially, and those conditions are unlikely to change either. All the countries are thoroughly integrated into Europe, not just economically but culturally and psychologically as well. Southern Europe is now an integral part of Europe, no longer apart from it. In all the countries of Southern Europe, however, a major task remains: reconciling the newer forces of democracy, modernization, and Europeanization with the older traditions of patronage, clientelism, and family and class privilege.

Now all the Southern European countries have joined the EMU. No one knows quite how this new financial community will all work out, how the common currency, the common financial policy, and the common foreign and strategic policies will all be harmonized. We do know that there will be economic and, hence, social and political tensions as the European subsidies to Southern Europe decline and as inefficient small firms prove unable to compete in the larger European market. There will also be tensions caused by the European Central Bank's reluctance to allow member states to enact grandiose development strategies or pay for elaborate patronage programs through deficit financing. The precise relations, and degrees of autonomy, between the individual countries and the central European institutions located in Brussels and Strasbourg have yet to be completely worked out, as do the relations between the regional European entities and the larger outside world. The outcome of all these changes on Southern Europe is still uncertain.

While these uncertainties remain, no one doubts that Southern Europe in the last several decades has embarked on a new and very encouraging course that has produced vibrant democracy, accelerated economic development, vast social change, and full integration into Europe. It is clear that Europe no longer stops at the Alps or the Pyrenees. At the same time, Southern Europe has retained its own vibrancy, dynamism, culture, and special ways of doing things. We ought to celebrate both the differences and the progress made toward full integration into Europe.

In this chapter we have emphasized how Southern Europe has often lagged behind the more-developed countries of Northern or core Europe. But in contrast with even more underdeveloped Eastern Europe, Southern Europe has forged considerably ahead. The contrast with Eastern Europe follows in the next chapter.

DISCUSSION TOPICS

1. Describe the political culture of Southern Europe.
2. Describe the socioeconomic background and class structure of Southern Europe.
3. Discuss the main political parties and the party systems of Southern Europe.
4. What is the government like in Southern Europe?
5. What is meant by "bureaucratic politics?"

NOTES

1. For some purposes, France may also be considered a Southern European country, but France is a mixed case in this regard, stretching from south to north, with characteristics of both areas. Similarly with Turkey and the former Yugoslavia: both border the Mediterranean, but they deserve separate and independent treatment and for purposes of this chapter are not considered part of Southern Europe.

2. Some general works on Southern Europe include Giovahni Arrighi, ed., *Semiperipheral Development: The Politics of Southern Europe in the Twentieth Century*

(Beverly Hills: Sage, 1985); Fernand Braudel, *The Mediterranean and the Mediterranean World in the Time of Phillip II* (New York: Harper and Row, 1972); Ernest Gellner and John Waterbury, eds., *Patrons and Clients in Mediterranean Societies* (London: Duckworth, 1977); Beate Kohler, *Political Forces in Spain, Greece, and Portugal* (London: Butterworth, 1982); and Allan Williams, ed., *Southern Europe Transformed: Political and Economic Change in Greece, Italy, Portugal, and Spain* (London: Harper and Row, 1984).

3. For the background, see Gerald Brennan, *The Spanish Labyrinth* (Cambridge: Cambridge University Press, 1971); Raymond Carr, *Spain* (Oxford: Clarendon Press, 1966); John Crow, *Spain: The Root and Flowers* (Berkeley: University of California Press, 1985); James Michener, *Iberia* (New York: Random House, 1968); Stanley Payne, *A History of Spain and Portugal* (Madison: University of Wisconsin Press, 1973), Julián Marias, *Understanding Spain* (Ann Arbor: University of Michigan Press, 1990).

4. See the two books edited by Eric Solsten, *Spain: A Country Study* and *Portugal: A Country Study* (Washington, D.C.: Government Printing Office, 1990, 1994, respectively); also John Hooper, *The New Spaniards* (New York: Penguin, 1995).

5. Thomas Bruneau and Alex MacLeod, *Politics in Contemporary Portugal* (Boulder: Lynne Rienner, 1986); Richard Gunther et. al., *Spain after Franco* (Berkeley: University of California Press, 1986).

6. Ramón Arango, *Spain: Democracy Regained* (Boulder, Colo.: Westview, 1995); Andrea Bonine-Blanc, *Spain's Transition to Democracy* (Boulder, Colo.: Westview, 1987); José Magone, *European Portugal* (New York: St. Martin's, 1997).

7. See Hooper, *New Spaniards*, and Solsten, *Spain* and *Portugal*. Also, note that foreign policy is considered in a later chapter.

8. For a summary and overview, see Howard J. Wiarda and Margaret Macleish Mott, *Catholic Roots and Democratic Flowers: Political Systems in Spain and Portugal* (Westport, Conn.: Greenwood Press, 2001).

2

Eastern Europe and the Search for a Democratic Political Culture

Dale R. Herspring

One misleading assumption held by some outside observers is that the countries of Eastern Europe bear a striking resemblance to one another. These observers often speak of the region as a semihomogeneous entity, primarily because of the Cold War experience. During this high point of Soviet domination, individuality and/or national peculiarities were often repressed in favor of the Soviet, or totalitarian, model. In short, if it was good for Moscow, it was good for Eastern Europe.

This unitary view of Eastern Europe was reinforced first by the heavy-handed approach the Kremlin took in dealing with the desire of some of these countries for greater national independence; for example, the use of Soviet troops against Hungarians in 1956 or the Czechs in 1968. This "unitary" perception was further reinforced by Moscow's creation of the Warsaw Pact and the Council for Mutual Economic Association. These two organizations tied these member countries together (and to Moscow) both militarily and economically, so that many Western observers, especially those concerned about the military threat from the East during the height of the Cold War, tended to view them as a unitary whole dominated by the Kremlin. "The Polish or East German or Hungarian army is a tool in the hands of the Kremlin" was a phrase often heard in governmental meetings set up to discuss the military threat presented by the Warsaw Pact.

There is no question that Moscow exerted considerable control over the countries of Eastern Europe (and especially in the military sphere). However, it would be wrong to assume the existence of a homogeneous social, political, or economic relationship between Moscow and its supposed allies. Deep differences between Moscow and its allies preceded the establishment of Communism, and despite the Kremlin's efforts to enforce political, social, and economic uniformity, significant differences between the USSR and its satellites remained, even during the Soviet period. Similarly, it would be equally fallacious to assume that the Soviets were able to enforce cultural, political, economic, or social homogeneity *among* the countries of Eastern Europe. Just as deep differences persisted between Moscow and its allies, there were important differences between each of the East European states during the Soviet period.

The thesis of this chapter is that the primary defining characteristic of the polities of Eastern Europe is heterogeneity. This characteristic is a result of the very different political cultures that have existed for centuries and continue to exist in these countries. In some, like Poland, there is a highly individualistic orientation; in others, like Serbia, there is an equally strong collectivistic approach to political issues. As a result, some of these countries are closer than others to the Western model—not because of attempts to import the "Western model," but because some political structures are more compatible with some preexisting political cultures than they are with others. Or, to put it another way, the chances of developing democratic political institutions are much higher in some countries than in others. For example, countries like the Czech Republic appear to be well on their way toward adopting a Western democratic political system, while others, such as Serbia and Bulgaria, have a long way to go primarily because their indigenous political culture is less hospitable to democracy than that of the Czech Republic.

The primary impact of the collapse of Communism on Eastern Europe was to permit this heterogeneity in political culture to reemerge as an active political force. Long pent-up pressures for a multifaceted approach to dealing with the problems facing these countries again became part of the political landscape.

The key point is that the approach each polity will take in the future toward the creation of a stable political system will be heavily influenced by its own political culture. And the nature of the political culture in each polity will be a result not only of the Soviet period but of its own historical experience as well.

POLITICAL CULTURE IN EASTERN EUROPE

The concept of political culture plays a key role in our discussion. Political culture, following the definition offered in the introduction of this book, refers to the values, ideas, norms, belief systems, and patterns of behavior of a particular people or country.[1] History plays an important role in transmitting these values and beliefs, but so do other factors, such as religion, language, economic development, political socialization, and attitudes toward authority. What is important about political culture is that each polity develops its own, often unique political culture. For example, for cultural and religious reasons, women are excluded from political life in a country like Saudi Arabia, while they play a vital role in a country such as Sweden. Indeed, one of the underlying assumptions of this chapter is "that autonomous and reasonably enduring cross-cultural differences exist and that they can have important political consequences."[2] Political culture changes, but generally only gradually. From a political standpoint this gradual change means that, despite the major changes that have occurred in Eastern Europe over the past hundred or so years, important differences remain among these countries—differences that continue to influence the way political decisions are made, as well as the prospects for democracy in these countries.

With the foregoing in mind, permit me to note that the extent of Western influence on the countries of Eastern Europe varies country by country. In some cases, such as Serbia and Albania, it is minimal. In others, such as the Czech Republic or Poland, it is considerable. Since this is largely a result of their differing political cultures, let us now turn to a discussion of the major reason for this variation: factors influencing the various differing political cultures of the countries of Eastern Europe.[3]

Language

Languages are important in Eastern Europe not only because they emphasize the diversity of the region, but also because some are more Western oriented than others. Languages in Eastern Europe are split between four different language families: Slavic, Ural-Baltic, Romance, and Albanian. Within the Slavic language group, there are the Western Slavic languages (Polish, Slovak, Czech) and the South Slavic group (Bulgarian, Serbo-Croatian, Macedonian, and Slovenian). The South Slavs (with the exception of the Croats and the Slovenes) use the Cyrillic alphabet, the same one used by the Russians. The only Ural-Baltic language in the area is Hungarian. Romanian is a Romance language much closer to Latin in many ways than it is to the other languages in the region. It also includes a number (about 15 percent) of Slavic words. Finally, there are the Albanians. The Albanian language is part of an Indo-European language group, but it differs markedly from any other Indo-European languages. These language differences have important cultural implications for the countries of the region.

In the north we find the Poles, who, although they are able to understand the Slovaks, find it difficult to communicate with the Czechs, not to mention the Russians. Meanwhile, the Slovaks, Czechs, and Poles are separated from the other Slavic-speaking peoples of Eastern Europe by the Hungarians. The latter language has almost nothing in common with any of the others in the region. The only other languages remotely related to Hungarian are Estonian and Finnish. Indeed, Hungarian is a language with almost no English or Slavic cognates.

East of Hungary is Romania. Romanians can neither understand Hungarians nor easily communicate with any of their other neighbors—with the exception of the Moldovans, who also speak Romanian. South of Romania is Bulgaria, a country speaking a Slavic language that closely resembles Russian. To the west of Bulgaria is Macedonia. Whether or not Macedonian is a separate language is a hotly debated issue. For political reasons (i.e., all have at one time or another claimed this area as their own), Bulgarians, Greeks, and Serbs maintain that it is not a separate language. Needless to say, Macedonians look at the matter differently.

Next we come to the former Yugoslavia. Most observers consider Serbo-Croatian to be a single language, in spite of the battles and wars that have been fought between these two ethnic groups. Slovenian is fairly close to Slovak and includes a number of German words. Albania is believed by some to be a distant cousin of Hindi. There are also some other languages spoken in the region: Romani by Gypsies, Yiddish by Jews, German in parts of Romania, Greek by a minority in Albania, and Turkish by a minority in Bulgaria.

Linguistic factors affect political culture in Eastern Europe in two significant ways. First and most obvious, there are tremendous linguistic differences between the various countries themselves. If language is a key to how one interprets political phenomena, each of these people will tend to view reality somewhat differently.

The second and more important implication is that some of these language groups tend to be Western oriented, while others are more focused on the East. For example, Western Slavs use the Latin alphabet and tend to see themselves as Westerners speaking a Slavic language. As a Polish commentator put it, "Poles consider themselves to be Westerners who should be speaking English or French." The same Western orientation is evident among Czechs, Slovenes, and Croats.

The situation with regard to Hungarians is similar in spite of the unique nature of their language. German is the second most common language in Hungary, and Hungarians resent any suggestion that their Ural-Baltic language does not makes them un-Western. On the other hand, Albanians see little relationship between their language and the West, while the Romanians often romanticize themselves as descendants of the Roman legions.

The situation is very different with regard to the Serbs and the Bulgarians. Relying on the Cyrillic alphabet, they tend to identify linguistically with the

Russians. In fact, the languages are so similar that for many years Bulgarian students were not permitted to claim Russian as a foreign language.

The bottom line is that, when it comes to languages, the Poles, Czechs, Slovaks, Hungarians, Slovenes, Romanians, and Croats tend to see themselves as Western, while the Serbs and Bulgarians find their linguistic identity in the East. The Albanians identify linguistically with neither Eastern nor Western Europe.

Religion

As with languages, there are significant religious differences among the countries of Eastern Europe. Poles, for example, are almost all Roman Catholics. Indeed, many Poles find it hard to accept someone who is not Roman Catholic as a Pole. Protestants were generally presumed to be Germans, while the Eastern Orthodox were believed by many Poles to be Russians. Indeed, for many years when the country was under external domination, the Catholic Church served as the heart of Polish national identify, and the Poles had a saying: "To be Polish is to be Roman Catholic."

In many ways, the Czech lands are the home of the Protestant Reformation—the place where Jan Hus was burned at the stake for his heresies. Slovakia, meanwhile, is almost entirely Roman Catholic. Hungary is split sixty–forty between Roman Catholics and Protestants, while, except for a Hungarian minority, Romania is primarily Orthodox. Bulgaria is also Orthodox, as are Serbia and Macedonia. In addition, Slovenia and Croatia are Roman Catholic, while a large number of Bosnian Serbs are Muslim, as are the majority of Albanians.

What is important about this breakdown is that it parallels the situation in language. Poles, Czechs, Slovaks, Hungarians, Croats, and Slovenes tend to be Western oriented. Poles, for example, look to Rome for religious inspiration, while Czechs are tied closely to the Protestant world. The Bulgarians, Serbs, and Romanians, who have close ties to the Russian Orthodox Church, tend to be Eastern oriented. Macedonia is somewhat distinct, with ties split between the Greek Orthodox Church to the south and the Macedonian Orthodox Church.

Economic Development

While I do not intend to go into the debate over the relationship between a democratic political culture and the level of economic development, I will postulate that there clearly seems to be at least an associational relationship; that is, the higher the level of economic development, the greater the probability of a democratic political system.

Of all the countries of Eastern Europe, the Czech Republic is the most developed. In fact, prior to World War II the Czech lands were among the most developed in all of Europe. Unfortunately, the Communist system did much to undermine the vitality and efficiency of the Czech economy, but it remains ahead of most of its neighbors in the region. The same is not true of Slovakia, however, which continues to lag far behind Prague in economic development. Poland, by contrast, has taken major strides toward the creation of a modern economy and is well on the road toward industrialization. However, it too maintains a large farm economy. Romania is even more underdeveloped than Poland or the Czech and Slovak lands. Indeed, it is one of the most underdeveloped countries in the region. Hungary has made significant progress, especially in mechanizing agriculture, but it too lags far behind its Western neighbors. Bulgaria was the one country of Eastern Europe to benefit from Soviet domination and is far better off today economically than it was in 1945. For its part, Yugoslavia appeared to be making important progress until the country collapsed. The civil war in former Yugoslavia, together with Western sanctions imposed on Serbia, have almost totally destroyed the country's economy. While an end to hostilities would contribute significantly to improving the economic situation, so much has been destroyed and some areas were so underdeveloped even *prior* to the fall of Yugoslavia that rebuilding the economies of Croatia, Serbia, and Bosnia would take a long time. Slovenia is the most developed part of the former Yugoslavia. Finally, when it comes to economic development, Albania is Europe's "basket case." The end of Communism served only to intensify economic chaos in a country that was already far behind the rest of Eastern Europe.

Ethnic Minorities

Another factor affecting the political culture of many Eastern European states is the presence of ethnic minorities in many of them. These minorities not only lead to irredentism (claims on other countries' territories); in some cases their agitation makes the central government more authoritarian in its attempt to check them than might otherwise be the case. The existence of two different cultural entities within the boundaries of the same country can also frustrate the creation of a mutually acceptable, single, broadly accepted political culture. This, in turn, can exacerbate the problems involved in creating a democratic political culture.

When it comes to irredentism, it is important to realize that borders in the region have shifted back and forth over the centuries. In truth, almost everyone in Eastern Europe can make the claim that land somewhere else in the region rightfully belongs to them. Poles, for example, are quick to point out that at one time in history they occupied all of Germany up to the Elbe. In fact, the name Berlin is not German, but an Old Slavic word meaning "place of the nets." Often, the movement of these boundaries leads to intensified feelings of nationalism, or a national sense that one or another country has of having been wronged by history. This is especially true of Hungary. Almost a third of Hungarians found themselves outside of Hungary as a result of what many consider to have been unequal treaties during the early part of this century (e.g., in the Slovak Republic, Romania, and Serbia). Meanwhile, Turks have been upset at their treatment in Bulgaria; Albanians fret under what they consider Serbian and Macedonian repression; and Greeks object to Albanian dominance.

The Poles are among the few populations of Eastern Europe whose ethnic makeup and political boundaries coincide. They inhabit a territory that is almost 100 percent Polish. At the same time, it is important to remember that Poland's borders have been moved back and forth over the past several centuries—indeed, at times Poland ceased to exist as a state. It was only as a result of World War II, when the borders were moved more again, that Poland became almost ethnically pure. The "purification" of Poland did not come without a price, however. Millions of Jews were exterminated, and large numbers of Germans were expelled from what had been traditionally considered German territory. The Russians and the Polish Communist government were able to use this border change as an effective tool in tying Poland to the former USSR. The idea was simple: the Germans had not recognized the annexation of their former territories by Warsaw. West Germany was an American ally; the only guarantor of Polish sovereignty, therefore, was the USSR.

World War II also did much to remove the German minority from the Czech lands. Indeed, with the exception of some Slovaks, the Czech Republic now has almost no non-Czech minorities. The same cannot be said for Slovakia. The latter has a Hungarian population numbering some six hundred thousand individuals. The treatment accorded to this minority was a source of bilateral tension with Budapest under the Communists and has not significantly improved since then. With the exception of the Gypsies and Jews, Hungary itself is relatively homogeneous ethnically. Meanwhile, Romania is home to some two million Hungarians, primarily in Transylvania. Fearful of Hungarian designs on the country, Bucharest has taken a number of actions over the years in an effort to "Romanianize" the Hungarian populace. Hungarian schools have been closed, the use of the Hungarian language prohibited, and efforts made to cut back on ties between Budapest and the local Hungarian population.

Bulgaria has had its own problems with its Turkish minority. Toward the end of the Communist regime, for example, Sofia attempted to forcefully assimilate the Turks into mainstream Bulgarian life. A campaign to end the teaching of Turkish in schools was launched, and all Turkish

Bulgarians were ordered to Bulgarize their names. These policies led to a number of disturbances and the migration of thousands of Bulgarian Turks to Turkey.

Macedonia also has an ethnic-minority problem: about 25 percent of the population is Albanian. So far, the Albanians have not presented a problem for the government, which has been making a strong effort to pacify them. Meanwhile, Albania has a small Greek minority, a situation that has given rise to conflict between Athens and Tirana, the countries' capitals, over the years.

If the former Yugoslavia is nothing else, it is a model of what can happen when the minority problem gets out of hand. Except for Slovenia, all of the remaining republics have until very recently contained significant numbers of minorities. Serbia, for example, includes the Kosovo, the ancestral and emotional Serbian homeland that is now populated almost entirely by Albanians. Croatia used to contain a very large Serbian minority, but one of the results of the recent war has been to drive most of them out of Croatia into either Serbia or Serbian sections of Bosnia. Meanwhile, the various parts of Bosnia are probably more ethnically homogeneous now than at any time in that country's history—a clear result of the policy of ethnic cleansing.

History

For most Americans, history helps integrate their society. But this is definitely not the case in Eastern Europe. Here it contributes to separateness. The primary reason is that divisive events that happened many years ago remain fresh in the minds of the populace through such reminders as poems, legends, or even textbooks. Serbian devotion to the Kosovo, for example, derives from the fact that it contains Serbia's ancestral capital as well as Serbia's most holy church. In addition, Serbian children, regardless of whether they have ever seen the Kosovo, are raised reciting poems that stress its critical importance to Serbian national identity. Given this background, it is no surprise that Belgrade is unwilling to make any concessions over the future of this area, even if it is primarily populated by Albanians. Indeed, one of the justifications used by Serbs for their repressive regime is the need to keep rebellious minorities such as the Albanians in line.

The situation is similar in other parts of Eastern Europe. Serbs continue to feel hostility toward the Croats because of the slaughter of hundreds of thousands of Serbs by the Croatian Ustasha during the World War II. Croats, meanwhile, believe the Serbs have worked overtime in their efforts to dominate every part of Croat life. For their part, Hungarians resent their treatment historically by the Serbs in the Vojvodina, as well as by the Romanians in Transylvania and the Slovaks in Slovakia. Poles harbor deep resentments toward Germans as well as Russians for a number of historical reasons, and the Slovaks have long felt that Czechs discriminated against them.

The important thing to keep in mind when dealing with Eastern Europe is that history to these peoples is not something that is merely studied in school, a subject that one reads about and then forgets. For most of Eastern Europe, history is very much alive. Unfortunately, in most cases it either leads to tensions between countries or it frustrates efforts to integrate various ethnic groups within a country.

THE CLASH OF EAST AND WEST

East European political culture is unique in that it has been a crossroads between the Western tradition of democratic pluralism and the Eastern, or Russian, absolutist approach. In effect, it shows attributes of both traditions.[4]

Western Europe

In the West, the concept of pluralism is very much a part of political life. A ruler's power should never be absolute. This principle emerged directly from the Western Judeo-Christian tradition, which argued in favor of separation of church and state. The idea was that individuals should be provided some private space—space that permitted them to work out their own solutions to moral and political issues. The individual still had a duty to God, but God and the state were not the same thing. A theocratic state was by definition wrong. Theocracy and democracy cannot coexist; Western theorists believed, and still hold, that political leaders have no right to interpret what God wants the rest of the populace to do.

This pluralistically oriented society has permitted the development of many groups independent of the state; for example, in late medieval Europe, cities became independent centers of commerce, and the guilds became important forces within cites. The king often was increasingly dependent on the cities, and the guilds and middle class ran them for money and support, a situation that further limited the king's power. This tradition of many independent power centers gave rise over the centuries to the concept of a social contract: the idea that a deal was struck between the rulers and the ruled. If rulers violate the contract, then the ruled have the right to replace them. Limited sovereignty also led to the rise of the idea of rule by law. The key point was that law was autonomous; it was not the tool of the sovereign.

As with law, the West has also seen education as being autonomous from both church and state. Emphasis was to be placed on speculation, on the development of critical thinking. At base, this idea assumed that knowledge was not just a question of understanding God's will. Rather, it was a matter of asking difficult questions, many of which might not be answerable by looking only to theology.

When it came to developing political systems, Westerners relied mainly on structures invented to routinize the process of changing political leaders via secret ballots. Everyone has—or should have—an equal right to participate in the political system.

The Russian System

The Russian tradition has been almost 180 degrees different from the Western approach. The Russians considered the idea of a balance of power inherently wrong. To be effective, power should not be fragmented. From a moral standpoint, Russians traditionally believed that absolutism was a moral good. All groups in society should be controlled by the center. Besides, an absolutist government could get more done than a democratic one, which many Russians have dismissed as a debating society.

Politically, this belief in unitary absolutist government meant that the main purpose of political institutions was to carry out the sovereign's will. With this concept in mind, why worry about representative institutions? Participation meant the opportunity to carry out the tsar's orders, not the right to have personal input in decision making.

Along the same line, cities were not considered to be—and in fact were not—autonomous. The tsar took what he wanted from the various cities. This, in turn, meant that the idea of a social contract made no sense to the Russians. Leaders were not in power because they were chosen by the people. God put them there. Power went from the top down. Besides, the only contract was between God and the tsar.

From the standpoint of church-state relations, the main idea was that the church should be subordinate to the state. After all, if the tsar was God's personal representative, then doing what the tsar commanded meant doing God's will. Not surprisingly, this meant that belief in the tsar's divinity prevented the development of an autonomous law. The law was nothing more than the expression of the sovereign's will, and its purpose was twofold: first, to make the system run smoothly; and, second, to help the populace understand how to do the sovereign's will.

Education was closely tied to the church. There was little emphasis on critical thinking. Instead, the primary focus was on rote learning. Education was collectivistic: its main purpose was to learn how to behave in a manner that reinforced the group and strengthened the state.

Eastern Europe

Historically, Eastern Europe has represented a transitional stage between Russia and Western Europe. The region shared many of the Western experiences, but these factors were incorporated into Eastern Europe against the backdrop of Russian influence. In this sense, Eastern Europe is halfway between Russia and the West. In some ways, it closely resembles the West, while in others it is closer to Russia and the East.

Take, for example, autonomous groups. While most groups were not nearly as controlled in Eastern Europe as they were in Russia, they were less autonomous than their counterparts in Western Europe. Native institutions tended to be weak because societal bonds were weak. This led to the rise of a bureaucratic state run by a relatively small elite. This elite, in turn, worked to marginalize regime opponents, although bureaucrats recognized that autonomous entities such as independent trade unions had a right to exist—a far cry from the Russian case. Nevertheless, none of these groups was strong enough to deal with the political center in the way similar structures in Western Europe did.

For their part, intellectuals tended to identify with the regime, and much of the opposition to governmental policies tended to take place within the ruling elite itself. This meant that, although there was far more governmental opposition than in the Russian case, the majority of the populace did not actively take part in politics. Participation was limited to a small elite.

Limited popular participation yielded a concept called the discretionary power of the state. Under this idea, the state had the right to act in any area of politics unless expressly prohibited from doing so by law or custom. This formulation very definitely did not mean the same as rule by the will of the majority. Rather, it meant that the government could pretty much do what it wanted, with a few exceptions.

The state's discretionary power led to the creation of a kind of facade of politics. There was outward respect for constitutional principles, and on many occasions the courts delivered objective decisions. In addition, a number of interest groups existed and were active in the political process. The problem, however, was that the efficacy of courts, interest groups, and other actors depended on what concessions the elite was prepared to make.

Education was another area in which Eastern Europe was halfway between the East and the West. Here, as in many other areas, there was a strong difference between the Balkans and the rest of the region. Central Europe (Hungary, the Czech lands, and Poland) had a tradition of critical thought much like that which existed in Western Europe. In the case of the Balkans, the rote learning characteristic of Russia was more the rule.

Finally, unlike Russia, most of Eastern Europe accepted the rule of law. The problem, however, was that the concept was not nearly as developed as in Western Europe. In fact, it was very difficult to enforce laws if the country's ruler did not agree. The one exception was if laws covered either a custom or an area in which the sovereign was specifically prohibited from acting, a situation that provided for more individual rights than was the case in Russia.

As far as church-state relations were concerned, they varied by country. In some places (Poland, Slovakia, Slovenia, and Croatia), the Roman Catholic Church was relatively autonomous. In other cases (Romania, Bulgaria, and Serbia), the obedient role played by the Orthodox Church vis-à-vis the state more closely resembled the Russian model. In countries such as the Czech lands and Hungary, there was a mixture of Protestantism and Catholicism, whereas in Albania, Islam was the primary religion.

THE END OF THE COLD WAR

The major impact of the Communist period from 1945 to 1987 was the creation of a new working class and a massive expansion in urbanization. Peasants did not disappear in Eastern Europe, but their numbers certainly diminished. At the same time, a new elite was created, one that was just as authoritarian as before. Indeed, the postwar Communists had disdained the average citizen. After all, the Communists considered themselves to have a monopoly of knowledge on how society should be organized and engineered to achieve the best social, economic, and political ends.

One of the biggest problems faced by the Communist elite in Eastern Europe was that the people almost always looked upon that elite as an alien institution. To be sure, some believed that Communism was a more just system or that it improved the living conditions of the average citizen. But by and large, most of the region's population saw the Communist period as an opportunity for the Russians to exploit and plunder their countries for Moscow's benefit.

As for the development of a democratic political culture, the major effect of the Communist experience was to further entrench many of the attitudes and values which were least conducive to the development of democracy. For example, the entrenchment of a political elite, who had little interest in public opinion, as well as the introduction of voting procedures that had little impact on political decisions, tended only to deepen the cynicism already prevalent in the countries of the region.

The Communist period also reinforced the belief in statism, the idea that the state could and should resolve all of society's problems. Statism shifted attention away from individual responsibility and convinced average citizens even more that the government owed them a living. This failure of meaningful citizen involvement in politics meant that, almost without exception, few East Europeans were ready for the post-Communist experiment in democracy. The widespread acceptance of statism led many to look to the new regimes to solve most of their problems.

If the new, so-called capitalist economy was not working, then it was clearly the regime's fault. Rather than holding themselves responsible as the body politic for resolving issues, the people of some East European states, frustrated with their countries' failure to move immediately from the darkness of Soviet domination to the dawn of post-Communist affluence, tended to look to demagogic or xenophobic solutions, whether in the form of attacks on scapegoats or reliance on leaders who had simple solutions to complex problems.

ALTERNATIVE SCENARIOS

As should be evident by this point, to suggest that the West has definitively triumphed in Eastern Europe would be inaccurate. Western influence (or the Western model) is stronger in some sections of the region than in others. But to suggest that the East Europeans are consciously following a Western model only recently introduced would be to assign far too much importance to American ability to influence events in these countries. Indeed, one can divide these countries into at least three categories based both on their political culture as well as the current situation in the region: the emerging democrats, The Potential or Transitioning Democrats,[5] and the Imponderables.

The Emerging Democrats

In this category I would place Poland, the Czech Republic, Hungary, and Slovenia.[6] All of these countries have, to varying degrees, embraced what we often call the Western model (i.e., the adoption of a more-or-less democratic political system together with a mixed economy). While a detailed discussion of these countries is beyond the scope of this chapter, what is especially interesting is that all of them have long-standing cultural ties to the West.

When it comes to religion, for example, the Poles, the Czechs, the Slovenes, and the Hungarians are all Western Christians. Similarly, all four of these polities speak a Western-inspired language that draws its inspiration from the West—the Poles, Czechs, and Slovenes with their Latin script, and the Hungarians with their strong denial that their language is

Eastern. These countries also share important economic characteristics: the Czech Republic is the most developed, although the other three are working hard to catch up. None of the four states is faced with significant ethnic minorities. The Hungarians are concerned about the way members of their ethnic group are treated in other parts of Europe, but in all four instances, the lack of an *internal* ethnic problem facilitates the development of a democratic political culture.

Furthermore, in all four cases, there are strong historical ties to the West. Poland is perhaps an exception, having fought for its very existence for the past two hundred years, but even Warsaw sees its history closely bound to the West. Hungary, the Czech Republic, and Slovenia were all closely tied to the Austro-Hungarian Empire, a factor which also helped them identify with the West rather than the East. Finally, Poland, Slovenia, and the Czech Republic are notable for their toleration of autonomous political institutions. The Roman Catholic Church in Poland, in particular, has been a bulwark against external domination; and Prague has shown a willingness to tolerate a variety of dissident groups, including a Communist Party during the interwar period. In this sense, the Communist period was an aberration. Hungary's acceptance of religious tolerance was a sign of how far religious pluralism in that country had come.

The Potential or Transitioning Democrats

In this category I place Slovakia, Albania, Macedonia, Romania, and Bulgaria. All give lip service to the Western model, but all have a long way to go to make it a reality. For example, Romania recently took an important step with the election of a democratic leader, but whether or not that will evolve into a stable, democratic polity remains to be seen.

All of these countries tend to be on the opposite end of a continuum when it comes to the characteristics of a democratic political culture as outlined here. In religion, for example, three of them are Orthodox and one is Muslim. Based on the East European experience, they do not provide the kind of background from which one would expect a democratic political culture to emerge naturally. In this case, Slovakia is an exception. Its apparent Western orientation (Western language, Roman Catholicism) is counterbalanced by other factors. Linguistically, Romania and Slovakia should be on the Western side, with Bulgaria and Macedonia on the Eastern side. In fact, language does not seem to be a sufficient condition to give these countries a Western orientation. As far as Albania is concerned, the most one can say is that its language does not give it a Western orientation.

Economically, all these countries are in the same category: they are faced with serious problems. Most of them are primarily agricultural, and all face the daunting task of trying to put their economies back together. When it comes to history, Slovakia was tied to Hungary, while Romania and Bulgaria have a clear Russian orientation. Albania, as usual, went its own way, and Macedonia has as much of a Greek orientation as it does Serbian and Bulgarian.

The major exception to what conditions one might expect from a country's history to produce is Slovakia. There are three reasons for this situation. First, the Slovaks were treated like vassals by the Hungarians when the latter ruled them. Second, they received little training in political leadership under the Czechoslovak experiment; and, third, they are faced with a serious minority problem. Having said that, with the current authoritarian regime being replaced by a more democratically oriented one, there is a good chance that Slovakia will continue its march toward the West.

The Imponderables

Serbia, Croatia, and Bosnia all fit into this last category. In all three, there has been only limited development of a meaningful democratic polity. This is not surprising when one considers the nature of Serbian political culture: orthodox, Russian-oriented in speech, historically tied to the East, presented with serious minority problems, and underdeveloped economically. Belgrade has a long way to go to become a democratic polity.

Croatia, on the other hand, would seem to have all of the necessities for the creation of a democratic polity. The problem, however, is that a democratic political culture does not flourish well during war, which is a state that Croatia was in for some time. Now that the country's leadership has decided to move toward the Western model, Croatia would seem to have the main prerequisites necessary for the creation of such a system. Meanwhile, there is little one can say about Bosnia. This artificial polity is practically still in a state of war. The fighting may have stopped, but given the continuing bitter ethnic feuds, which were made worse by the recent atrocities, the chances of successfully introducing the Western model into this polity would seem distant at best.

In spite of the uproar that greeted Samuel Huntington's essay on the clash of civilizations cited above, the essay does contain some truth. One can argue that he may have overemphasized the importance of ethnicity, although it remains a serious problem, but the fact is that some countries are more predisposed than others toward democracy. This is not to suggest that countries like Albania have no hope of becoming democratic in the Western sense of the term, only that the road will probably be longer and strewn with more rocks than will be the case for countries like Poland. It is time for Western analysts to dispense with the naive assumption that the entire world is waiting breathlessly for the opportunity to adopt the Western model. The reality is that even those countries that do accept the major outlines of this model will produce a system that places the appropriate institutions within the framework of the prevalent political culture. We can bemoan the continued existence of nondemocratic or less-than-democratic political cultures, but we have no alternative but to learn to live with them.

THE FUTURE

Despite all the problems these countries face, there is a ray of hope, at least for some of them. To begin with, many of the countries of Eastern Europe are now members of NATO. Poland, Hungary, and the Czech Republic joined in 2000; and on March 29, 2004, Bulgaria, Romania, Slovakia, and Slovenia followed suit. While East European membership in this military alliance may not bring about immediate changes, it certainly increases pressure on these countries to become more democratic insofar as civil-military relations are concerned.

On May 1, 2004, Poland, Hungary, the Czech Republic, Slovenia, and Slovakia became members of the EU. As a consequence, these countries will enjoy visa-free travel to the rest of the EU. In addition, most goods will travel throughout the EU without any customs duties, and there will be subsidies from the EU to help them make the transition.

Unfortunately, the transition to full membership in the EU will not be easy. From an economic standpoint, all of these countries lag behind those who have been members for some time. The result will be second-class citizenship—at least, that is how most of the populace sees it. The hope is that, in the long run, wages/salaries between those in the East and those in the West will balance out. In the meantime, there will be serious economic dislocation as small East European shops and factories are faced with the competition and economic power of large supermarkets and factories. Similarly, while some of these countries have serious problems with unemployment, there is no guarantee that EU membership will help. In fact, it could hurt as a better educated and trained Western workforce now has unrestricted access to Eastern Europe.

The East Europeans will also face other problems. For example, most East Europeans see their security (which means countering any Russian action against them) as being tied to the United States, not Western Europe. This is why so many of them answered Washington's call for help during the Iraqi War and went so far as to send troops as part of the American-led coalition in Iraq. Needless to say, this has not endeared them to the French and Germans, who strongly opposed the American attack on

Iraq. Indeed, there have been occasions when some of them—the Poles, in particular—attacked the French for trying to tell them what to do in the realm of foreign policy.

Will this increased integration with Western Europe lead to a common democratic political culture? To begin with, it is worth noting that there will be ongoing problems. Take Poland, for example. Warsaw is far more religious than the secularized West Europeans. There is also a latent suspicion on the part of many in the West concerning the willingness and ability of seventy-five million people who lived under noncompetitive Communist political systems to compete with the more dynamic, individualistic work culture of the West. Likewise, there is a feeling on the part of those in Eastern Europe that the rest of the EU looks upon them as uneducated peasants. Furthermore, if the unification of Germany is any indication, there will also be a problem with many in the East who will expect EU membership to produce immediate prosperity. The road to economic affluence will continue to be a long one.

Despite all the problems involved, there is no doubt that the increasing interaction between the countries of Eastern Europe and the rest of the EU will have a major impact on their political culture, especially as young men and women travel around the EU and see how a free society works and benefits its populace.

As far as those countries that have been left out of either the EU or NATO at this point in time are concerned, the possibility of either of these organizations expanding remains a possibility. Both have made it clear that it is on the agenda. For example, Romania and Bulgaria are scheduled to join the EU in 2007, while countries like Albania, Croatia, Macedonia, Serbia, Bosnia, and Montenegro are still waiting in line, hoping to be asked to join. The one thing that is certain, as far as political culture is concerned, is that those states that have joined NATO or the EU will be under increased pressure to adapt to Western principles of democracy, business, and civil-military relations. Whether the remaining potential democrats or imponderables will make the kinds of changes necessary to make themselves acceptable to the West remains to be seen. Overcoming the kinds of social and economic underdevelopment, institutional deficiencies, and historic political cultures they possess will not be easy.

DISCUSSION TOPICS

1. Define political culture.
2. What are the religions of Eastern Europe?
3. Analyze the languages of Eastern Europe.

NOTES

1. See p. 15. For a full discussion of political culture, see chapter 4 of Howard J. Wiarda, *Introduction to Comparative Politics* (Belmont, Calif.: Wadsworth, 1993).

2. Ronald Inglehart, "The Renaissance of Political Culture," *American Political Science Review* 82, no. 4 (December 1988): 1205.

3. The following draws on my "Eastern Europe: Successful Transitions or Descent into Chaos?" in Howard Wiarda, ed., *U.S. Foreign and Strategic Policy in the Post–Cold War Era* (Westport, Conn.: Greenwood Press, 1996): 85–105.

4. Much of the material in this section is based on George Schoepflin's excellent "Culture and Identity in Post-Communist Europe," in *Developments in East European Politics*, ed. Stephen White, Judy Batt, and Paul G. Lewis (Durham, N.C.: Duke University Press, 1993): 16–34.

5. The line between the "Emerging Democrats" and the "Potential Democrats" follows closely along the lines indicated by Samuel Huntington in his classic essay "The Clash of Civilizations," *Foreign Affairs* (Summer 1993): 30.

6. One could legitimately place the former German Democratic Republic in this category, but it has been left out from this analysis because it is now part of Germany.

3

Transitology and the Need for New Theory

A vigorous polemic has been conducted over the last decade concerning the usefulness of employing in Central and Eastern Europe the model of transitions to and consolidations of democracy fashioned out of the Southern European (Greece, Portugal, Spain) and Latin American experiences.[1] Some scholars of these latter regions have taken to calling themselves "transitologists" and "consolidologists" and have put forth sometimes exaggerated and self-important claims to have invented entirely new areas of the discipline. Actually, the study of the transitions to and consolidation of democracy is a fascinating and important one but, since its theory and empirical material are still weak and underdeveloped, it ought at this stage to be considered merely a new, significant, interesting, but perhaps also topical subject matter, like "liberation theology" or "bureaucratic authoritarianism," rather than a major theoretical breakthrough.

Meanwhile, students of Eastern and Central Europe have often been put on the defensive in this debate. They have been branded as narrow "area specialists," "regionalists," presumably devoid of theoretical interest and insights, and, therefore, out of the mainstreams of comparative politics. Now, it is true that within East/Central European studies there are some narrow area specialists who are not interested in large, comparative studies but, for the most part, this is an unfair, demagogic, and misleading charge.

The question is not whether East/Central European scholars are also theoretically oriented comparativists but rather which body of theory or insights is the most appropriate one to use. Why should we assume a priori, before the evidence is even collected or the East/Central European experience carefully weighed and considered, that Southern Europe and Latin

America have much to teach students of East/Central Europe? Actually, there is much that East/Central European scholars can learn from the Southern European and Latin American experiences, both as to what is relevant in the latter to their own studies and what is not. At the same time we need to recognize that the Eastern/Central Europe experience is so fundamentally different from those of Southern Europe and Latin America that the theory and categories developed out of the latter for studying the former are only of limited usefulness.[2] We need to sort out what insights from studying Southern Europe and Latin America are useful and which are less so; certainly no wholesale, mindless application of the transitology/consolidology literature to East/Central Europe is appropriate.

But I wish to take another tack here. So far, the debate among East/Central European scholars has been over the issue of whether the literature developed by students of Southern Europe and Latin America is relevant for this area. Students of East/Central Europe have largely assumed that the transitologists and consolidologists got the Southern European and Latin American experiences right, without further questioning or investigations of their own. However, I wish to suggest something further and stronger: that the model developed by transitologists and consolidologists is fundamentally flawed, even for interpreting the areas from which it was derived, Southern Europe and Latin America. In other words, I am suggesting that the transitology/consolidology literature got it wrong (or much of it) even for their own area. And, of course, if this literature is wrong or, more accurately, incomplete even on Southern Europe (let us leave Latin America out of the discussion for now; that area is so far removed from East/Central Europe culturally, sociologically, economically, and politically that its utility as a model for East/Central Europe is extremely limited), then it certainly cannot be of great usefulness for East/Central Europe either.

Obviously, this is a big subject area and a controversial one that is certain to generate even more polemic. We cannot in this brief chapter answer all the questions or provide all the data and references to support the case completely. But let us present some of the main themes and arguments as a way of opening the debate. Southern Europeanists and Latin Americanists, East/Central Europeanists, and students of comparative politics are all likely to learn something from the discussion.

THE IMPORTANCE OF POLITICAL CULTURE

Much of the literature on Southern European transitions pays insufficient attention to political culture—the values, beliefs, and orientations that undergird political behavior—and is even, one suspects, on political or even ideological grounds hostile to the concept. Instead, the literature on Southern Europe emphasizes institutional changes (political parties, elections, interest groups, elites, government actors) almost exclusively. These are, of course, important influences but by no means sufficient ones. And yet, one of the leading transitologists claimed that geography as well as political culture no longer matter.[3]

This seems a patently ridiculous statement. Of course geography and political culture count, importantly so, although we may still differ over precisely how much. Those who doubt the importance of geography and political culture in understanding either Southern or East/Central Europe either have not spent any time in the area, did not understand what they saw, or else are so ideologically opposed to political culture–based explanations that ideology has blinded their perception of reality.

I would briefly make three points with regard to political culture in Southern and East/Central Europe. First, there *is* a distinctively Southern European or Mediterranean political culture common to the area (see chapter 1), and one for each of the distinct countries within the region. This political culture has changed enormously over the last forty years and, as a rich literature now suggests, is one of the key explanatory factors in understanding the Greek, Portuguese, and Spanish transitions.[4] Second, as chapter 2, by Dale Herspring, suggests, within East/Central Europe there is an equally, if not more, powerful tradition of political culture, similarly varying by country, region, and/or ethnic group and also changing over time, but with such enormous differences between Christian, Orthodox, and Muslim groups and/or countries that this explanation alone (encompassing aspects of geography, religion, ethnicity, sociology, history, and culturally influenced levels of socioeconomic development) enables us, almost single-handedly (but, of course, in combination with other factors) to differentiate those countries that are "making it" in East/Central Europe (developed, democratic, integrated, or about to be, into NATO and the EU) and those that are not.[5] And third, while there are interesting similarities between aspects of political culture in both areas (a thousand or more years of Christianity, for example), there are essential differences (as between Catholicism and Orthodoxy, for example) that need to be studied seriously as well.

In Eastern Europe, the history, the geographic location between East and West, the repeated foreign invasions, the ethnic makeup, the social and religious base, the cultural attitudes and behavior, and, in short, the political culture are all fundamentally different from those of Southern Europe; we need to take these differences into account as we examine the transitions to democracy in the two areas.

CHANGES WITHIN THE PRIOR REGIMES

Much of the literature on the Southern European transitions ignores or is ignorant of the important and dynamic changes occurring under the previous regimes, especially in their later years. This is not just a plea for an understanding of what is now called path dependency; that is, whether Spain or Czechoslovakia, for example, had a prior democratic experience that facilitated their later transitions to democracy. Rather it is a summons to examine closely the changes under way in the prior authoritarian or Marxist-Leninist regimes to analyze the trends that shaped both the later process of democratization and the kind of democracy that emerged. Here we focus particularly on the Salazar-Caetano regime in Portugal prior to its overthrow in 1974 and on the Franco regime in Spain prior to his death in 1975—especially the latter, since Spain is frequently used as the paradigm in the transitology literature.

The problem is, we (including scholars) are such prisoners of our earlier models, such as "Fascism," "totalitarianism," "Marxism-Leninism," or Juan Linz's famous distinction between "authoritarianism" and totalitarianism,[6] that we tend to reify them and think of them as rigid or static categories, which are useful as simplifying devices but inadequate as full explanations, because they ignore the changes occurring even within these frameworks. In illustration, consider Spain. First, beginning in the late 1950s, Spain began a process of economic reform and subsequent "miracle" economic growth, second in the world only to Japan for almost two decades, that stimulated industrialization, created jobs, reduced poverty and historical underdevelopment, and began to propel Spain into the modern world.

Second, these economic changes helped give rise to mammoth social changes—urbanization, rising literacy, a larger industrial working class, large numbers of women in the workforce, a new middle class, an emerging business/entrepreneurial class distinct from the elite families—that not only helped provide a sociological base for later democracy but was also far more advanced and differentiated than in most of East/Central Europe to that point.[7]

Third, these changes in turn gave rise to vast cultural changes in family structure, the role of women, relations between the sexes, the role of religion (greatly reduced in influence), behavior, and attitudes, even while Franco was still alive. For example, even though Franco's censorship was still in effect, smart journalists and editors learned they could push the boundaries of openness to new degrees provided they refrained from personally attacking Franco or the armed forces. And while "dirty" movies and literature were still prohibited by the official censorship, Spanish tour companies offered regular weekend bus excursions (so large as to constitute bus caravans) to Perpignan across the border in France, where Spaniards could watch or get anything they wanted. Nor should the impact of tourism—more than forty million yearly by the early 1970s, and all those Germans and Scandinavians cavorting topless or bottomless or both on Spanish beaches—be underestimated as a force behind changing Spanish culture and behavioral norms.[8]

Even the political regime was changing quite markedly in ways that defy our usual stereotypes of them as Fascist, for example. First, even though opposition political parties were still illegal in both Spain and Portugal, opposition "study groups" were functioning in both countries that operated much like political parties and served as the nuclei for the open democratic parties that later emerged. Second, within the government there were already known and publicly discussed "liberal" and "conservative" factions that provided some, though still limited, public-policy discussion and debate, and that also served as nuclei for later political groupings and parties. Third, the 1930s-style corporatist system, often linked in the literature with regime authoritarianism, was in the process of being shunted aside, ignored, or transformed and beginning to assume the functions of a more modern, government social-welfare system.[9]

An illustration from my own research experiences in Spain during the Franco regime illustrates a number of these points. One day, residents of Madrid were treated to newspaper headlines proclaiming, "There Are No Strikes in Astúrias" (a traditional coal-mining area known for its violent strikes and radical political action). This was a sure sign, as any adept, between-the-lines reader of Spain's newspapers knew, that there *were* strikes in Astúrias. A few days later a similar banner headline would read, "There Is No Violence in Astúrias," a sure sign that there *was* violence perpetrated by the police, the strikers, or likely both. A few days later, new headlines would blare, "The Government Is Not Negotiating with the Illegal Strikers," a sure sign—you guessed it—that a far more pragmatic government *was* negotiating, even with the "underground" Communist unions (*comisiones obreros*) while ignoring its own official corporatist *sindicatos*, and that it had to negotiate seriously if it wished to avoid disruptive strikes that would undermine the miracle economic growth rate now so necessary for continued prosperity and stability.

None of this is to suggest that the Franco and Salazar/Caetano regimes had transformed suddenly into paragons of democracy, pragmatism, and liberalism. But it is meant to suggest that they were far more open, pragmatic, and changing than the static models (Fascism, authoritarianism, and the like) we use would suggest. Indeed, I would be prepared to argue that by early 1974 (just before the transition) Spain and Portugal were so fundamentally transformed economically, socially, culturally, even politically that, when the actual transition came in the mid-1970s, it was a comparatively easy process. All that was required was a modest push (the death of Franco, a military coup d'état in Portugal) and the entire edifice of the old regime, which our models led us mistakenly to assume was impenetrable, tough, impermeable, and a hardened shell, toppled almost literally overnight. The institutions of democracy were subsequently relatively easy to construct (hence the institutional focus of the transitology literature) because so many other basic *systems* (economic, social, cultural, political) had already been transformed. In contrast, East/Central Europe, which had also been undergoing changes, albeit more limited, in the 1970s and 1980s, had not yet experienced such a deep and thoroughgoing transformation and still had many of its basic systems in place from the old regime, and, therefore, would, unlike Greece, Portugal, and Spain, have to undergo a thoroughgoing economic, social, cultural-behavioral, political-institutional, and international transformation all at once and quickly, rather than taking them more or less gradually and sequentially as had Southern Europe.

THE CRITICAL IMPORTANCE OF MARKETS, FINANCIAL INSTITUTIONS, AND A BUSINESS/ENTREPRENEURIAL SECTOR

Of all the differences between Southern Europe and Russia, Eastern, and Central Europe, perhaps the most important was the presence of preexisting markets, financial institutions, and a business/entrepreneurial sector in the former, and their almost complete absence in the latter. In the focus by transitologists on political institutions, this fundamental economic difference has been all but completely ignored. I first traveled to Russia in 1992, to the city of Nizhny Novgorod, a major industrial center on the Volga River and, with its population of three million, Russia's third largest city. It was one year after the fall of the Communist regime, and there was not a single bank, financial institution, or ATM machine, nor a single hotel, restaurant, or business that accepted Visa or American Express or had faxes or international long-distance telephone service.

Spain and Portugal had largely closed, autarkic, corporatist, and mercantilist, or statist, economic systems until the mid-1950s. But even within a general context of autarky, there were markets that functioned, banks and financial institutions, a nascent business/entrepreneurial class, and an economic and communications system open to international trade and the outside world. By the 1960s and 1970s, although some elements of autarky remained, both Spain and Portugal had opened their markets and allowed supply and demand (rather than the state) to set most prices and wage rates, had well-established banks and financial institutions that had entered into partnerships with big, highly capitalistic international banks, and had a growing, booming business/entrepreneurial sector. All of these continued their rapid expansion begun in the mid-1970s, but the point is how developed, how open, how market and internationally oriented the Iberian economies had become even before the democratic transition.[10]

All this stands in marked contrast to East/Central Europe. We know, of course, that not all of Poland's agriculture had been socialized, that Czechoslovakia (as it was then constituted) had an entrepreneurial element willing to sell almost anything (including, and especially, weaponry) to anyone, and that Hungary's economy also was never completely socialized and had a certain orientation toward capitalist buying and selling. But to say that 5 or 10 or maybe 15 percent of these economies were not socialized and that they had some, still quite limited, markets operating within them is a very long way from being able to compare them with the predominantly market-driven economies of Southern Europe, with their growing prosperity and mushrooming financial institutions, and their already-close, thought not formal integration into the EEC, which helped transform them into the dynamic, prosperous countries that they are. The presence of growing markets, banks, financial institutions, and a business class, even in nascent form, in pre-mid-1970s Greece, Spain, and Portugal may well be the most fundamental difference between these countries and Eastern Europe and may be the most understudied of all the differences.

PACTS AND OTHER MILESTONES OF THE TRANSITION

We need to maintain a broad sense of all the forces involved in the transitions. The transitology literature, we have said, has focused mainly, and at times almost exclusively, on the political institutions emerging during the transitions. But that emphasis may reflect two conditions: (1) unlike in East/Central Europe, Southern Europe's underlying economic, social, cultural, even psychological transitions had already occurred by the mid-1970s and were well under way and even completed in a sense and (2) the political transition, the only transition remaining, was the easiest to accomplish precisely because these other, harder, and longer-term transitions had already occurred and formed an indispensable cultural and socioeconomic base for the political or democratic transition that was about to occur.

A second requirement is that we disaggregate the Southern European model. In most analyses Spain is taken as a paradigm while Greece and Portugal are often conveniently neglected. But Spain may be such a special case (increasingly prosperous, middle class, etc.), and exceptional that its experience is not even faintly replicable in East/Central Europe.

Portugal, after all, experienced in the mid-1970s not a happy, peaceful, evolutionary transition to democracy but a chaotic revolution, near civil war, and such fragmentation and disintegration that it took approximately a decade for the economy to recover (and then only with massive outside economic assistance) and the political system to stabilize. Greece also transitioned to a kind of democracy in 1974, but its political system remained so heavily dominated by patronage, clientelism, and outright corruption that it was seldom presented as an attractive model for East/Central Europe, although for some Central and East European countries it may well be more accurate and realistic. Spain, in other words, is not only a special case, but its peaceful, gradual, reformist (*reforma*, as distinct from *ruptura* in Portugal) route may be entirely unrealistic as applied to the East.

Spain's political-institutional development after the mid-1970s has been portrayed in such orderly and sequential terms that it is antiseptic, almost formulaic: the break by Adolfo Suárez with the old regime, the political reform to allow greater freedom, the reemergence and legalization of political parties, including those of the left, the "social pact" involving business, labor, and the state, the first democratic election in 1977, the new constitution, and the rise of the Spanish Socialist Workers party, culminating in its electoral victory in 1982. All of this seems so neat, organized, and sequential that it appears almost preordained. But I remember it at the time, in Spain as well as Portugal, as considerably more disorganized than that, with great fears involved (of possible revolution, civil war, a right-wing coup, a Communist takeover, national disintegration, a reversion to Fascism: the possibilities, or "systems outcomes," seemed incredibly broad and not at all preordained), and with democracy by no means assured. After the fact, the democracy outcome seems clearer, and even inevitable, in the literature than it did at the time. So to the extent that the transition-to-democracy literature seeks to provide a road map, a formula, a how-to-do-it manual and checklist, it both distorts the actual Spanish experience (remember, the most successful of the Southern European countries and certainly not representative) and presents a false and formulaic model that East/Central Europe, with its quite different experience, history, sociology, and less-developed economic infrastructure at the onset of the transition, could not possibly emulate.

THE AUTHORITARIAN-TOTALITARIAN DISTINCTION

For a long time, the Eastern and Central European countries and the Soviet Union were known as totalitarian regimes, and a quite sharp distinction was drawn in the comparative-politics literature between totalitarianism and its more limited, "softer," less-developed form, authoritarianism.[11] Greece, Portugal, and Spain were considered authoritarian regimes, while the Soviet Union and its satellites were seen as totalitarian.

But then the Soviet Union and some of the Eastern European countries opened up somewhat, allowed somewhat greater freedom, or liberalism, and seemed to be becoming more "pluralist."[12] As these trends continued or occurred, sometimes on an on-and-off basis, the "authoritarian" rather than "totalitarian" label and syndrome of traits began to be used descriptively and analytically in the Soviet Union/East European context as well as in describing Southern Europe. Certainly by the 1970s the Soviet Union and some countries of Eastern Europe were no longer totalitarian in the older Stalinist sense, but how far they had liberalized was open to considerable debate.

I now believe, having traveled extensively in Russia and East/Central Europe, as well as having earlier done research in Southern Europe, that the labels used were misleading. While the Stalinist model of totalitarianism was less applicable to the Soviet Union and Eastern Europe than previously, the leap to the "authoritarian" designation was inaccurate. It put the Soviet Union and Eastern Europe in the same category as Greece, Portugal, and Spain: not an accurate depiction. It likely exaggerated the changes that had occurred in the Soviet Union and Eastern Europe. It probably provided unrealistic expectations for an easy and rapid transition to genuine freedom, pluralism, and democracy. For even though the regimes of Franco and Salazar/Caetano were not exactly freedom loving or democratic for those who lived in them, Spain and Portugal, as it turned out, were considerably freer, more pluralistic, more developed institutionally and in terms of their civil society, and more open than were the Soviet Union and Eastern Europe. And that is another reason why Spain and Portugal were able to make the transition to democracy much more easily and rapidly than could the former Soviet Union or much of Eastern Europe. "Post-Stalinist," or "post-totalitarian," with its accompanying characteristics spelled out, might have been an appropriate label and analytic model to apply to these latter countries; but the use of the authoritarian model, to the extent it equated political conditions in the East with those in the South, was inaccurate and misleading and led to overly optimistic expectations for the ease and speed of democratic transitions in Russia and East/Central Europe.

UNDERESTIMATION OF INTERNATIONAL INFLUENCE

The early literature on transitions to democracy, which has been only partly corrected by more recent analysis, woefully underestimated the role of international influences both on the process and outcome of democratization.[13] In part, this bias likely reflects lack of knowledge about the policy involvement of outside actors; in part also, one suspects, it reflects a preference on nationalistic or political grounds to give the credit for democratization to internal, domestic forces, and to ignore and downplay the crucial importance of international influences. The outside actors, many of whom carried out their efforts through disguised, secretive, and covert operations, would also prefer not to emphasize their earlier interventionist role.

The facts are at odds with this hands-off interpretation. In Portugal, the German Social Democrats, the Swedish Social Democrats, the French Socialists, the British Labor Party, the Socialist International (SI), and the U.S. Embassy, CIA, Defense Department, and even the White House were all involved in the 1970s in a massive, multipronged effort to keep Portugal from "going Communist," to stabilize it and, ultimately, produce a democratic outcome. The amount of foreign aid, after 1986 in the form of EU subsidies, was enormous, helping to transform Portugal from the poorest country in Europe to one of the most successful: stable, middle class, democratic, and a significant voice in the EU. The Portuguese bailout, almost wholly unstudied in the literature, may, along with the Marshall Plan, have been one of the great foreign-aid success stories of the twentieth century.

In Latin America, it was the U.S. presence and effort, and, secondarily, the European one, that were critical. In Central America, the United States engineered elections to provide a democratic middle ground between rightist militarists and leftist guerillas, reformed the armed forces, bought off and/or defeated the guerrillas, and continued to play a quasi-proconsular role in shaping political outcomes. In South America, the U.S. role, in general, was less intrusive and less heavy handed than in the small, weak, underinstitutionalized states of the Caribbean and Central America. But, nonetheless, it was important, offering often critical behind-the-scenes pushing and cajoling, providing inducements as well as advice and pressure even while allowing and encouraging domestic forces to take credit for the successes, and it certainly should not be ignored or minimized in any analysis of democratization processes.

Spain was closer to the South American "model" than to Portuguese or Central American interventionism and proconsularism. The United States and the European allies were hovering and omnipresent at every step of the process, but not often overtly intrusive or as heavy handed.[14] Let us, of course, give credit to the Spanish forces and leadership in the transition, even accord them overwhelmingly the major credit; but once again, we need to acknowledge the roles, both overt and covert, of Austria, Germany, Sweden, Great Britain, France, SI, and the United States in the process. Because Spain's transition, unlike Portugal's, was orderly and peaceful from the beginning (among other factors, Spain learned from Portugal's earlier mistakes), it called forth a less-interventionist policy on the part of the outside actors; but we should have no doubt that, if Spain, like Portugal, had broken down into chaos with the threat of a Communist putsch, the United States and its Western allies were prepared to act more forcefully.

Russia and Eastern Europe are also complicated cases. We know that during the 1980s the United States and others strongly supported the Solidarity movement in Poland, assisted nongovernmental organizations (NGOs) and civil society groups throughout Eastern Europe to find political space for their activities, helped dissidents and opposition voices in the media find outlets for their expression, assisted East European governments in developing greater autonomy from the Soviet Union, and strongly encouraged (and gave a push to) the breakup of the Warsaw Pact. In addition, by this point a host of semiprivate international agencies, including in the United States the National Endowment for Democracy (NED), the national Republican and Democratic international-affairs institutes, and a variety of others, had been created to assist democratization efforts while also serving American foreign-policy goals. It is probably accurate to say that in the Soviet Union the main forces destabilizing the regime were internal: economic backwardness and mismanagement, technological retardation, bureaucratic ossification, political and moral bankruptcy, and maybe even alcoholism. But certainly through its military, technological (including its challenge to the Soviets to compete in the development of a missile-defense system), economic, political, and moral (human-rights) pressures, the United States exacerbated the tensions and cleavages present in Soviet society and hastened the downfall of an already deteriorating regime. And during the actual collapse (1989–1991) of the Soviet Union and afterward in its efforts to build democracy, the U.S. and European influences were, it hardly needs saying, omnipresent.[15]

Understand that in this analysis we are not just talking about "ripple effects," "waves," and "demonstration effects" of democratization from one country to the next. Those we accept as given, and they have been noted in the literature. Here, we are talking about direct, overt, often covert intervention by outside actors in promoting their interests—in this case, stability through democratization—in the internal affairs of other nations. Yet the scholarly literature has been exceedingly reluctant to acknowledge this fact. Why? Only two answers are possible. The first is ignorance—a possible but unlikely explanation given what is known even publicly about these events. The second is a purposeful decision to give all the credit to the domestic forces and thereby deny it to the international actors, perhaps consciously as a political decision not to acknowledge the role of the United States and of a particular administration in power at the time.

CONCLUSION

Beyond the arguments presented here, problems abound with the transitology approach as it derives from the Southern European and Latin American experiences and seeks to find relevance beyond those boundaries. Our list of flaws, problems, biases, and oversights in this approach is illustrative but not exhaustive. The point has been made, however.

The dispute between the transitologists and the East/Central European area specialists has been false and misleading, perhaps purposely so. The so-called transitologists have faulted the area specialists for not using a comparative, more broadly theoretical approach. But what they really seem to have in mind is obliging the East/Central Europeanists to use *their* particular approach and model.

Everyone (well, almost everyone) in the field of comparative politics, including most East/Central European specialists, understands that there is always a dynamic interaction between comparative theory and individual case or empirical studies. Cases and area studies have been the bases of comparative theory (witness dependency theory, corporatism, state-society relations, and others); at the same time, when we use theory to understand new political phenomena or areas (in this case, East and Central Europe), we need also to be prepared to adjust the theory to fit the new research terrain and the new facts discovered. The scientific method in comparative politics means that we do not reify our conceptual frameworks: instead, we adjust, change, or even discard old theories as new facts come in. We emphatically do *not* adjust the facts to fit the theory.

Regarding the question of the utility of transitology and consolidology theory in East/Central Europe, two issues are at dispute. The first, as exemplified by the Bunce-Schmitter/Karl debate, is whether that body of theoretical literature derived principally from Southern Europe (and even more narrowly, from Spain) is relevant to East/Central Europe. The consensus of specialists in the area is that it is not, that at best it has only limited usefulness, that the East/Central European experience is so different from that of Southern Europe, to say nothing of Latin America, that the model developed from the latter two is only of modest assistance in helping us understand the former.[16] And that, of course, is all that such models are useful for: as aides to understanding, but certainly not as holy writ.

In this chapter, however, we have raised an even more fundamental point. We have argued that not only is the transitology/consolidology model of limited use for comprehending East/Central Europe but that much of it is also fundamentally flawed and incomplete even as a tool for understanding Southern Europe.[17] That means we need to return to the sources, to examine the transitology/consolidology model itself, and to reconstruct our basic understanding of democratic transitions in Southern Europe in the light of new facts and interpretations. East/Central Europeanists ought now, on the basis of their research findings, to be at the forefront of reconstructing the new model as much as Southern Europeanists.

I recently interviewed one of former Czech president Vaclav Havel's principal lieutenants. He told me that, as they were plotting their political strategy in those fateful days of 1989, they had open before them the well-known O'Donnell, Schmitter, and Whitehead volume *Transitions from Authoritarianism* (note, no mention of democracy in the title) and were looking there for guidance, a formula, what to do next. "Oh, poor fellows," I commented, "you're lucky you made it to democracy at all." He responded, "Yes, we did not find what we were looking for there; we had to make our own way." Let the model builders take note.

DISCUSSION TOPICS

1. What is "transitology?"
2. What is the critique offered of this literature?
3. Why is political culture so important?
4. Why are markets and financial institutions important here?

NOTES

1. Philippe C. Schmitter and Terry Lynn Karl, "The Conceptual Travels of Transitologists and Consolidologists: How Far to the East Should They Attempt to Go?" *Slavic Review* 53 (Spring 1994): 173–85; Valerie Bunce, "Should Transitologists Be Grounded?" *Slavic Review* 54 (Spring 1995): 111–27; Valerie Bunce, "Comparing East and South," *Journal of Democracy* 6 (July 1995): 87–100; Karl and Schmitter, "From an Iron Curtain to a Paper Curtain: Grounding Transitologists or Students of Postcommunism?" *Slavic Review* 54 (Winter 1995): 965–78; Valerie Bunce, "Paper Curtains and Paper Tigers," *Slavic Review* 54 (Winter 1995): 979–87; Valerie Bunce, "Regional Issues in Democratization: The East versus the South," *Post-Soviet Affairs* 14 (1998): 187–211.

2. My own preliminary contribution to this debate is in Howard J. Wiarda, *Iberia and Latin America* (Lanham, Md.: Rowman and Littlefield, 1996).

3. Adam Przeworski, *Democracy and the Market* (Cambridge: Cambridge University Press, 1991); Adam Przeworski, *The Sustainability of Democracy*, vol. 1 (Cambridge: Cambridge University Press, 1991); and Adam Przeworski, *The Sustainability of Democracy*, vol. 2 (Cambridge: Cambridge University Press, 1995).

4. Samuel P. Barnes, Antonio López Pina, and Peter McDonough, *The Cultural Dynamics of Democratization in Spain* (Ithaca, N.Y.: Cornell University Press, 1998).

5. See especially Lonnie R. Johnson, *Central Europe: Enemies, Neighbors, Friends* (New York: Oxford University Press, 1996).

6. Juan Linz, "Totalitarian and Authoritarian Regimes" in *Handbook of Political Science*, vol. 3, ed. Fred I. Greenstein and Nelson W. Polsky (Reading, Mass.: Addison Wesley, 1975).

7. Eric Baklanoff, *The Economic Transformation of Spain and Portugal* (New York: Praeger, 1978).

8. Howard J. Wiarda and Margaret MacLeish Mott, *Catholic Roots and Democratic Flowers: Political Systems in Spain and Portugal* (Westport, Conn.: Greenwood Press, 2001).

9. See my earlier detailed work on Portugal, *Corporatism and Development: The Portuguese Experience* (Amherst: University of Massachusetts Press, 1977).

10. The best source is Baklanoff, *Economic Transformation*.

11. Carl J. Friedrich and Zbigniew Brzezinski, *Totalitarian Dictatorship and Autocracy* (Cambridge, Mass.: Harvard University Press, 1956).

12. H. Gordon Skillings, *Interest Groups in Soviet Politics* (Princeton, N.J.: Princeton University Press, 1971).

13. Guillermo O'Donnell, Philippe C. Schmitter, and Laurence Whitehead, eds., *Transitions from Authoritarian Rule* (Baltimore: Johns Hopkins University Press, 1986). For a critique and correction, see Gerhard Mangott, Harald Waldrauch, and Stephen Day, eds., *Democratic Consolidation: The International Dimension* (Baden Baden, Germany: Nomos Austrian Institute for International Affairs, 2000).

14. Diplomat Samuel P. Eaton, in *The Forces of Freedom in Spain 1974–1979* (Stanford, Calif.: Hoover Institution Press, Stanford University, 1981), provides a characteristically understated but nonetheless revealing picture of the U.S. role in the Spanish transition.

15. Condoleeza Rice and Philip Zelikow, *Europe Unified and Transformed: A Study in Statecraft* (Cambridge, Mass.: Harvard University Press, 1995); also Robert B. Zoellick, *At the Frontiers: A New Agenda for US-EC Relations* (Washington, D.C.: Carnegie Endowment, 1993).

16. In addition to Bunce's arguments, cited earlier, see among many others M. Steven Fish, *Democracy from Scratch: Opposition and Regime in the New Russian Revolution* (Princeton, N.J.: Princeton University Press, 1994); Piotr Sztompka, "Dilemmas of the Great Transition," *Skisyphus* 2 (1992): 9–27; Sarah M. Terry, "Thinking about Post-Communist Transitions: How Different Are They?" *Slavic Review* 52 (Summer 1993): 333–37; Alejandro Moreno, "The Democratic-Authoritarian Cleavage in New Democracies: Eastern Europe and Latin America in the 1990s" (paper presented at the annual meeting of the American Political Science Association, Atlanta, Ga., 1999); Marc Morje Howard, "Institutional Design, Civilization or Prior Regime Type? Explaining Cross National Variation in Civil Society" (paper presented at the annual meeting of the American Political Science Association, Atlanta, Ga., 1999).

17. Some of the criticisms have been set forth in Anthony P. Spanakos and Howard J. Wiarda, "Comparative Perspectives on Southern European Democratization," *Portuguese Studies Review* 5 (Fall/Winter 1996–1997): 93–6.

II

IBERIA TRANSFORMED
A Closer Look

4

Spain 2010

A Normal Country?

For most of modern history, Spain has lagged behind the rest of Western Europe and has often been referred to as "different," "unique," and "distinctive." Spain not only lagged economically and sociologically, but because it was largely bypassed by all the great revolutions we associate with modern times—the Renaissance, the Enlightenment, the Protestant Reformation, the Industrial Revolution, the revolution in science and learning, and democratization—it was believed to lag its neighbors politically, religiously, intellectually, psychologically, and even morally. Spain was seen as the land of the Inquisition, the Counter-Reformation, royal absolutism, Jesuit theology, closed-mindedness, traditionalism, reaction, and ultimately, the culmination of all these ills, Franco-style Fascism. European attitudes toward Spain were long summed up in the phrase "Europe stops at the Pyrenees, and Africa begins there," words that not only grated on the oft-prideful Spaniards but that were tainted with political, social, religious, and, because of the long Moorish occupation of Spain during the Middle Ages, racial prejudice. In turn, Spain's reactions to these slurs bred resentments, a whole panoply of national inferiority complexes, defensiveness, and, for long periods, a desire to thumb its nose at Europe and go it alone in the world, regardless of what the rest of the West thought.[1]

Now all this has changed. Arguably, no country in the world has changed as much in thirty-five years as Spain has. It is one of the great success stories of modernization; those who knew the country before 1970 would find it unrecognizable today. Spain has been transformed from top to bottom and in all particulars: its political system has been democratized, its political culture has been transformed, and its social system has been modernized. Economically, Spain has moved from being one of the poorest countries in Europe to a position where its per capita income is now approximately 80 percent of the EU average. Spain is no longer the country of quaint customs, fiery flamenco dancers, and long siestas of our fathers' or grandfathers' memories; it is alive, dynamic, urban, sophisticated, and very, very hip.[2]

Spain voted to join NATO in 1986 and was admitted to the EC (now the EU) the same year. Its eager, almost unquestioned adherence to Europe's strict Maastricht budgetary requirements and its inclusion in the Euro Zone demonstrated that it wants to be included in the EU not just on economic grounds but for important national political and psychological reasons as well. Overcoming its past complexes as well as real, tangible measures of underdevelopment, Spain now considers itself and wants to be considered as a normal European country: democratic, economically advanced, and socially and morally progressive. The question we wrestle with here is whether Spain has actually reached that elevated plane, if and how and to what degree it still lags behind, and what the implications are of both the vast changes that have taken place and the continuities with past behavior.

The change processes in Spain have been going on for a long time and are not quite so dramatic as they are sometimes presented as being. Our image of Spain is often that of a country dominated, at least until Franco's death in 1975, by the unholy trinity of army, oligarchy, and reactionary church, and unalterably backward. But, in fact, industrialization in Spain, though retarded as compared with Britain, France, and Germany, began in the last decades of the nineteenth century and the first decades of the twentieth, even while the reactionary monarchy was still in power. Economic quickening led to vast social changes in the early twentieth century and an "explosion" of political participation during the First Republic, 1931–1936.[3] Franco's regime was, of course, based on authoritarianism and a turning back of the clock in the political sphere and, initially, autarky in the economic, but that did not prevent him from initiating an economic opening in 1957 that paved the way for a decades-long rise in prosperity.[4]

Similarly, the political controls were relaxed somewhat in the 1960s and early 1970s, not turning Spain into a paragon of liberal pluralism but making it possible for greater and more diverse political, trade-union, and intellectual stirrings. And although Spain remained in many respects a traditional, conservative, and Catholic society, there were ways to avoid the censorship, to read between the lines of the controlled press, and to take weekend excursions across the French border to watch "dirty" movies. Similarly, the flood of European tourists into Spain, reaching forty million yearly by the late 1960s, and the sight of all these Swedes, Germans, and others cavorting on Spanish beaches had a profound effect on Spanish morals, customs, and interpersonal behavior, especially among young people. In short, by the time Franco died peacefully in his sleep in 1975, Spain was already—culturally, morally, economically, and even to an extent politically—poised to undertake the great transformation that did, in fact, occur. The political culture, society, and economy were already changed or changing; all that was required was a slight shove in the political sphere and the entire edifice of Francoism would topple.

Spain has, for the most part, become a normal, even "boring" country, in the sense that the great systems debate among Socialism, authoritarianism, Fascism, capitalism, and democracy, and even the accompanying potential of breakdown and civil war that many expected to follow Franco's death, never materialized and is now moot. Its transition to modernity and democracy, however, is still incomplete. Most Spaniards as well as the transitologists who have written glowingly of the Spanish transition would prefer that we not pay attention to the persistence of many forms of traditional behavior (elitism, hierarchy, and limited pluralism) that still exist, to the pockets of unreformed institutions (the police, judiciary, and bureaucracy) and to the maintenance of forms of corporatism, organic statism, weak civil society, and authoritarianism that show remarkable continuities with the old regime. Moreover, the transition through which Spain has been and is still going has not been quite as smooth and antiseptic as it is often portrayed; instead, as might be expected given the vast changes in such a short period, there has been considerably more uncertainty and turbulence than at first meets the eye. While we celebrate Spain's quite remarkable accomplishment on the road to democracy and a more developed, modern society, let us keep in mind that such projects are always incomplete, that all countries show lags and discontinuities, that traditionalism and modernity continue to exist side by side and are all part of the same dynamic, and that it is as important to study and stress the continuities as it is to study the changes.

FOUNDATIONS

Geography and History

Spain, or more accurately, Iberia, is a peninsula, a westward-looking promontory of the even larger peninsula that is Europe. It is cut off from the rest of Europe by both distance and the rugged Pyrenees Mountains, in whose passes the French in general, Charlemagne in particular, and even Western Christendom were once famously defeated (see the medieval legends of Roland) by the infamous Saracens (Moors) of Spain.

Spain's historical isolation from Europe is thus geographic, cultural, and psychological and rooted in the seven-centuries-long Moorish occupation of Iberia as well as the five centuries of estrangement and divorce from Europe that followed.[5]

Iberia's topography is rugged and was, before modern communications and transportation, virtually impassable. There is a narrow coastal plain, nowhere near the width or fertility of America's Atlantic Seaboard, that quickly rises to a high elevated plateau. This plateau is rugged, rocky, windswept, cold, and blustery in winter, hot and dry in summer, and generally infertile except for the grasses that are amenable to sheep and cattle grazing. Almost nowhere is the land rich, lush, and agricultural or amenable to large-scale, mechanized agriculture, as in Northern Europe or the American Midwest. The rugged terrain, harsh conditions, and infertile soil mean that Spain never developed the agricultural surpluses that other European countries did on which future industrialization might be built.

Four main mountain ranges and many smaller ones, generally running west to east, cross and crisscross the peninsula, chopping up the terrain even further and making travel between one region or even one village and the next exceedingly difficult. Spain has been called, under the Hapsburgs, the first modern nation-state, but in reality the central state has historically been limited, the regions strong, and loyalty and social life concentrated even more narrowly in small villages. Alongside the *madre-patria* (the motherland) is the *patria chica* (literally, the small country), the small, isolated, local village where life's rhythms, social structure, immobility, and backwardness went on, generation after generation, for centuries. Geographic isolation and separateness reinforced the traditions of regionalism, and tribalism and the role of local caudillos that are so strong a part of the Spanish tradition. One of the great themes of Spanish history, still ongoing and filled with tension (witness the disputes over Basque and Catalan nationalism), is the effort to integrate these diverse villages and regions into a single, unified nation, a process now accelerated by modern highways, high-speed trains, and global-communication technologies.

A parallel great theme of Spanish history consists of the relations and similarly ongoing tensions between Spain's corporate, sectorally organized interest associations and the state. During the late Middle Ages, as the Moors were being driven south out of the peninsula and Christendom reasserted, a centralized monarchy began to emerge. Its centralizing tendencies were often resisted by Spain's strong corporate bodies—military orders, religious fraternities, towns and regions, the sheepherders' guild (the famous Mesta), and others—who sought to maintain their autonomy and self-governance. In this epic, centuries-long struggle, the central state under Ferdinand and Isabella, the Hapsburgs, and ultimately Franco won out, which helps explain the absolute power of the latter-day central state in Spain and the comparative weakness of legislatures, judiciaries, and local representative government. In modern times this debate and conflict between the state and its constituent corporate units was hammered out on the anvil of industrial relations where, again until recently, the central government ruled in an absolute and often dictatorial manner. But even now, in a free and democratic Spain, this historical dispute between the state and the corporate group life that swirls about it is acted out every day in multiple ways in the Spanish system: in the balance and tension between the state and the "autonomous" regions, the state and the church, the state and the military, the state and the university, the state and labor, the state and the business sector, and so forth.[6]

A third axis of conflict is ideological, with a strong base geographically and sociologically. Beginning in the eighteenth century in this hitherto most Catholic, traditionalist, and conservative of nations, a split began to develop in the Spanish soul. On the one side were the absolute defenders of the faith and tradition: the church, the monarchy, the rural aristocracy, the army, and the peasantry. On the other, more liberal side were the secular intellectuals, Free Masons, the urban middle class, and commercial elements who favored rationality, the Enlightenment, and the ability to trade freely (in ideas and goods) with the rest of Europe. This basic split widened after the French Revolution, produced a series of civil wars (the Carlist Wars, named after one of the pretenders to the throne who led the conservative faction) in the nineteenth century, retarded Spain's growth and led to fragmentation in the early twentieth century, produced breakdown and a full-scale civil war in the 1930s that culminated in Franco's authoritarianism of nearly four decades, and eventually led back to democracy in the 1970s. Spain has absorbed the lessons of the past and is not soon about to repeat its earlier, historical conflicts. Nevertheless, the division between what the French often refer to as the "family of order" and the "family of change" is still present, as evidenced in recent elections by the Spanish gravitation toward a two-party system in which the old ideological, geographic, and sociological fault lines are often in evidence.

Demography

Spain's population is slightly less than forty million, half that of Germany and approximately two-thirds that of France, Great Britain, or Italy.[7] Spain is now 77 percent urban and 23 percent rural, figures that represent a dramatic flow of people out of the infertile, inhospitable countryside and into the cities in recent decades. Just as dramatically, Spain's illiteracy rate has been reduced to 2 percent, with the pockets of illiteracy confined to older and rural inhabitants. Life expectancy is at or near levels in the European member countries of the Organization for Economic Cooperation and Development: seventy-five years for males and eighty-one for females. These figures reflect the quite remarkable transformation of Spain since the 1950s from the Third to the First World.

Spain has one of the lowest rates of population growth, or population replacement ratios, of any country in the world. This is due, in part, to natural socioeconomic factors (urbanization, education, and higher per capita income), women's desire to have smaller families, and the declining institutional and political role of the Roman Catholic Church in Spanish society. In 1998, Spain still had slightly more births per thousand population (9.7) than deaths per thousand (9.6), which, when combined with the net number of migrants per thousand population, resulted in a natural population increase of 0.01 percent and a net growth rate of 0.08 percent. However, by the year 2010, births per thousand are expected to drop to 9.3 and deaths to rise to 10.4, a natural *decrease* of negative 0.11 percent. And even accounting for immigration, the population figures remain in negative numbers, at negative 0.06 percent.

These kinds of figures have major implications. The implications are not unusual in the European context, but they may be for Spain, given our still-present image of it as an underdeveloped, backward country. First, they mean that Spain's population is actually shrinking, that its population-replacement ratio has turned negative. Second, they mean that Spain's population, as elsewhere in the industrialized world, is aging. Third, it means that for Spain, again as elsewhere in industrialized countries, there will be fewer and fewer actively employed young persons to help support more and more unemployed older people. And fourth, it means severe strains on those public-policy programs—social welfare, health care, and pensions—aimed at older persons, following directly on the heels of Spain's expensive efforts to elevate all these programs to European standards.

RESOURCES

Spain has considerable mineral resources: coal, iron ore, copper, mercury, tungsten, gold, silver, granite, and marble.[8] Its major shortfall is petroleum. Spain must import virtually 100 percent of its petroleum needs. Almost all of that petroleum comes from the Middle East (including North Africa), although Spain has undertaken efforts to diversify its oil imports by buying from Latin America and sub-Saharan Africa.

This point is critical, because it helps to explain a good deal about Spanish foreign policy. Absolutely dependent on imported oil, far more so than, for example, the United States, Madrid has been much closer than

Washington to the Arab states, including such international "outlaws" as Libya, Iraq, and Iran, and far less close to Israel. Frequently these differences have major policy implications. For example, the United States, after the Pan Am flight 103 sabotage, bombed Qaddafi's Libya but had to fly all the way around the Iberian peninsula from bases in Great Britain because neither France nor Spain was willing, for fear of their oil-dependent Arab alliances, to grant permission for flights over their national territories. These restrictions had nothing to do with Spain's supposed affinity, because of its past history, for the Arab or Moorish world, nor did it have anything to do with any supposed inherent Spanish anti-Semitism reaching back in an unbroken string to the Inquisition. Rather, it had everything to do with Spain's need for petroleum.

The other issue related to petroleum dependence is vulnerability. Spain is absolutely dependent on a continuous flow of imported oil at reasonable prices, and the fact is that most of that oil comes from countries that themselves may have short-lived regimes and volatile politics: the revolutionary regimes of Libya, Iran, or Iraq, or the old-fashioned and potentially doomed kingdoms and emirates of the Persian Gulf. While Spain's economy has shown dramatic, even miraculous growth rates since the 1950s, a new oil crisis could send the economy and, it is often feared, its still fragile political institutions into a nosedive. Hence Spain's current efforts to diversify its dependence by also purchasing from Nigeria, Mexico, and Venezuela.

ENGINES OF HISTORICAL TRANSFORMATION

Of all the European countries, Spain has arguably experienced in recent decades the most profound transformations in all areas of its national life. We are talking here not just of institutional or regime changes or alternations in the governing elites but of paradigm changes, a profound social revolution that fundamentally altered all areas of national life.

The economic breakthrough, building on the slow but real industrialization of earlier decades, came in the late 1950s. At that point Franco shuffled his cabinet ministers and brought in an economic team committed to reducing autarky and opening the economy to trade, competition, and greater market forces.[9] The Spanish economy responded magnificently, triggering the 6, 7, and 8 percent growth rates of the 1960s, referred to as the "Spanish miracle." These growth rates continued for two decades, were interrupted by the 1970s oil crisis instigated by the Organization of Petroleum Exporting Countries (OPEC), and resumed again in the 1980s and 1990s. During this span, the Spanish gross national product (GNP) doubled four times. This sustained period of growth, second among the world's nations only to Japan, stimulated a general economic quickening, attracted immense foreign investment, created vast numbers of new jobs, and succeeded over time in raising the Spanish standard of living to four-fifths of the EU average, a remarkable achievement in a relatively short period of time. Spain had made it to the ranks of what the World Bank calls "high-income" countries.[10]

The second engine of historical transformation, stimulated and accelerated by the first, was social. Here we have in mind not only the vast social changes noted in the previous section—rapid urbanization, rising literacy, expanded educational opportunities, better health care, new employment opportunities, better nutrition, greater life expectancy, and so on. The economic changes of the 1950s and 1960s also stimulated immense class changes: the rise of a new business-entrepreneurial class, a large middle class for the first time, an organized working class, new professional and technical elites, and vast numbers of women in the work force for the first time. It hardly needs saying that these vast social transformations fundamentally changed Spain from an essentially two-class (lord and peasant) society to an increasingly modern and multiclass (but not yet fully pluralist) one.[11]

The third engine of change was cultural. Perhaps in no other country in the world has the culture, specifically for our purposes the political culture, changed as dramatically in so short a time—during the 1960s and 1970s—as in Spain. In that period, Spain went from being a fundamentally conservative, traditional, and exceedingly Catholic society to being liberal, radical, innovative, and secular. Support for authoritarianism and its accoutrements—order, discipline, hierarchy, and rank—was transformed into support for liberty, freedom, even libertinage. Women, children, workers, and maids all became liberated, and some even unionized. Young couples who previously had a grandmother or a spinster aunt along to chaperone on a date now began openly living together, and only recently, as they consider their children's inheritance or their own retirement plans, have they begun, because of the provisions of Spanish law, to formalize their unions in marriage. The pornography available on Barcelona or Madrid streets, once prohibited by Franco-era censorship, is now as bad as anything available in Amsterdam or Copenhagen—not that very many Spaniards buy these degrading magazines; they just want the freedom to buy them. Today's Spain is clearly not the Spain of the past— sleepy, quaint, or different—nor of the classic books of Spanish historical sociology, such as those of Gerald Brennan, José Ortega y Gassett, or Michael Kenny.[12]

Historical memory—or, better, conscious collective amnesia—also played a large part in Spain's cultural transformation. Remembering, or being repeatedly reminded of, the failed republic of the 1930s, the fratricidal civil war that followed, and the long sleep of the Franco period, few Spaniards wished to see that past repeated again in the 1970s and 1980s. In the complex, often difficult transition to democracy that followed Franco's death in 1975, Spaniards were continually reminded by the political parties and government leaders of the horrors of the past, the need to avoid extremism, and the necessity of sticking to the middle ground. There was a conscious campaign to jettison the past, to avoid the tendencies toward a fragmented, conflicted, invertebrated society of which Ortega y Gassett wrote, and to embrace the new and modern in all their dimensions.

It is difficult to say which of these engines of change–economic, social, or cultural–came first or was more important. This is a chicken-and-egg problem, and deciding on an answer may not be all that important. The fact is that these changes were occurring simultaneously; they all fed upon, interacted with, and reinforced each other. Economic modernization and social changes were occurring at precisely the same time that the global revolution in telecommunications was bringing television—and modern life, higher expectations, and alternative lifestyles—into every Spanish household. Nor should we forget all those European tourists—as many per year as there are Spaniards—during precisely the same period gravitating to Spanish beaches and in its towns, exhibiting modes of free behavior that Spaniards emulated as "European" and, therefore, democratic. All these factors occurred together in the 1960s and the 1970s, providing a seamless web of interaction among economic, social, and cultural factors that propelled Spain headlong into the modern world.

The laggard variable was, of course, political: the long-lived and seemingly endless Franco regime. Indeed, the Franco regime, as well as the Salazar regime in next-door Portugal and a host of bureaucratic authoritarians in Latin America, were so long lived and seemingly immutable that scholars during this period were writing books and papers elevating modern authoritarian-corporatism into a third alternative route or framework of development (besides liberalism and Marxism).[13] A steady parade of these Latin American bureaucratic authoritarians and their ministers descended on Spain during this period to discover the key to Franco's success: how the caudillo had achieved such impressive economic and social modernization of this country without implying the hated liberalism, pluralism, and greater democracy to which such trends usually give rise. Hence, the Argentine, Chilean, Brazilian, and other Latin generals traipsed through Madrid and Lisbon during this period searching for the holy grail of socioeconomic development unaccompanied by its usual political concomitants. But in their brief visits they missed some crucial trends: that social, economic, and cultural change in Spain was rapidly undermining the bases of the Franco system even while the aging generalissimo was still alive.

Hence, when Franco finally died, the new regime could move relatively easily and expeditiously to democracy (although there was still considerable tension, frustration, and difficulty) because the economic, social, and political-cultural foundations for such a transition had already been laid. In the mid-to-late 1970s, independent political parties and nongovernmental unions were again allowed; censorship was eliminated; a new and democratic constitution was written; and free elections were held. Spain became a political and electoral democracy. Accompanying these formal institutional changes was a vast sociocultural transformation in which children had more freedom; women were liberated; and art, architecture, and film flourished. With the victory of the Socialist Party in 1982, the belief was strong in Spain that, along with electoral democracy, social democracy had also arrived.[14]

The one engine of change still lagging behind in Spain is that of science and technology. Spain has long prided itself on its humanistic and spiritual tradition, its Renaissance men, and its grand philosophes at home in half a dozen specialties (history, law, religion, philosophy, literature, and politics). It has rarely produced great scientists, engineers, agronomists, inventors, biologists, or Nobel laureates and has even taken nationalistic pride in that fact, arguing that, while the Anglo-Saxon world produces pragmatists, technicians, and scientists, the Hispanic world has devoted itself to high cultural and spiritual matters. In the same vein it condemned the Anglo-Saxon countries for their crass materialism, while Spain and the Hispanic countries presumably devoted themselves to loftier, nonmaterial goals.[15] The latter approach, of course, served to rationalize poverty, disease, malnutrition, and underdevelopment.

But now all this has begun to change. Spain has made a concerted effort to improve its school system and eliminate illiteracy. It has introduced top-to-bottom school reform, built thousands of new schools, and founded scores of new universities. Illiteracy in Spain (less than 5 percent) has been reduced to the level of other advanced industrial democracies and is lower than that of the United States. Moreover, Spain has begun to pay its teachers a decent wage and to emphasize practical and technical training. Along with the growth of universities has come a host of new technical institutes, scientific laboratories, and research centers. In many scientific areas these new facilities are able to compete, for the first time, with U.S. and European universities and research centers in terms of laboratories, salaries, and scientific facilities. Spain is aggressively seeking to lure back its scientists and researchers who earlier felt obliged to go abroad to pursue their careers. So while Spain has not yet redressed its long-standing gaps in science and technology, the steps that have been and are being taken to ameliorate the lopsided dominance of its humanistic legacy are impressive. At the same time, Spain has proved to be just as oriented toward materialism, money grubbing, and conspicuous consumption as the rest of us.[16]

Spain has meanwhile continued to experience vast social transformations. These include the familiar trends associated with modernization: urbanization, bureaucratization, and regimentation. They imply the loss of personalism, family ties, community, local or regional autonomy, intense individualism, organicism, and patrimonialism, for which Spain has long been known. But these traits had been giving way in recent decades; more than that, in its strenuous effort to eliminate all those traits that mark Spaniards as different, Spain has been hurrying these natural processes along, refusing to discuss or even admit that some traditional behavioral traits and institutions still persist, let along that they might be desirable. But now having made it to modernity, to general European levels, more and more Spaniards are rediscovering their history and questioning whether the shucking off of all things that were distinctively traditional and Spanish was such a good idea. While modernity and Europeanness are wonderful, many Spaniards miss the close personal, family, and communal ties of the past and are seeking to rediscover them. It may be too late, and some of the aspects of traditional Spanish behavior may not be worth rediscovering. Nevertheless, it is now once again permissible to (1) study the past, (2) find in it traits that are worth preserving, and (3) fashion a better blend between the many foreign models Spain has imported and the indigenous ones, such as regionalism—the *autonomías*—or the corporate-sectoral organization of society. We return to these themes in a later section.

HUMAN RESOURCES

While the Spanish miracle ushered in one of the greatest economic transformations of the late twentieth century, the continued and ongoing success of which is one of the great EEC foreign-aid success stories, the picture is not entirely rosy. In fact, there are gaps and lags in Spanish development that are not entirely unfamiliar in countries undergoing especially rapid modernization.

For one thing, Spanish unemployment for a long period of time remained extraordinarily high at 22 percent, the highest by far in Western Europe. But with Prime Minister José M. Aznar's economic and structural reforms, unemployment dropped sharply, and now in some areas Spain has a labor shortage that has been filled in part by immigrant labor from North Africa.

A second problem involves the reorganization of the workforce. In the early days of the Spanish miracle, as foreign investment poured in and assembly plants were the main focus of that investment, what was required was a vast supply of cheap and unskilled or semiskilled labor. But today, while it still has abundant assembly operations, Spain's economy is moving to a new, higher, and different stage that requires a better-educated and more technically skilled workforce. Unless and until Spain addresses these problems, it will continue to have difficulty both in reducing unemployment and in adjusting to the new, more efficient, more streamlined economy that the EU and the Maastricht goals now require.

The third problem is the distribution of income. While Spain over the last four decades has had one of the world's most impressive rates of economic growth, the distribution of income remains one of Europe's most uneven. This is due in part to Spain's aristocratic and two-class past, in part to forty years of authoritarianism that closed off possibilities for change even while allowing the uneven distribution of income to worsen, in part to the Spanish government's inability to collect taxes equitably and the Spanish people's unwillingness to pay them, and in part to the fact that Spanish legislation providing for a welfare state and the more equitable distribution of income is still only one generation old.

The issue is not simple, and it is politically charged. On the one hand, the general Spanish economic quickening of recent decades has enabled all, or at least many, boats to rise on the swelling economic tide. On the other hand, it is plain that not all groups have benefited from economic growth, that growth has benefited them differently, or in, in the case of peasants, villagers, and the urban poor, that living standards have actually declined in a period of general economic modernization. On balance, however, the most striking feature of Spain is this: whereas prior to the 1950s Spain was characterized by a generalized culture of poverty that affected upward of 70 to 80 percent of the population, now it has only isolated pockets of poverty (15 to 20 percent) where ill health, illiteracy, malnutrition, and backwardness persist. And in this respect, Spain is not very much different from the United States and other industrialized nations.

Now we are in a new phase of Spanish economic development, that of integration into the EU and the global economy, in which many Spanish small businesses and family firms are not competitive. This is the fourth problem of human resources with which we need to grapple. Sixty to 70 percent of Spanish businesses are small, family based, inefficient, and noncompetitive. They are not competitive with the big German, French, Italian, English, Dutch, Swedish, and other firms that have been operating in these larger environments for many decades. Many of the small businesses in Spain will go under as European integration and globalization proceed. At the same time, pressure to erect tariffs and other barriers to protect these firms and hold foreign competition at bay will surely grow.

If many Spanish firms are not competitive in Europe or in the larger global context, they are competitive in Latin America. The thrust of Spanish firms into Latin America has been one of the most interesting developments in Spanish political economy in recent years. For reasons of language, culture, and history, Spain has long felt especially close to Latin America, but recently the older and often empty concepts of *hispanismo* have been giving way to more concrete manifestations based on real money and investments. It is the Spanish banks—Bilbao, Vizcaya, and Santander—that have led the way with massive investments in Latin America. Spain is now the second largest investor in Latin America after the United States, taking advantage of the benefits that a common language and culture provide. Strikingly, Spanish firms with government support continued to pour investments into Latin America's big emerging markets (Argentina, Brazil, Chile, and Mexico) even after other investors had begun to hedge their bets. Trading in Latin America enables Spanish firms to call themselves multinational corporations, even though on a global basis they are not quite up to that designation.[17]

A fifth problem that Spain must wrestle with is how to replace or substitute for the European subsidies that have poured in during the last two decades. Ever since Spain joined the EC in the 1980s, it has been the recipient of mammoth subsidies provided to help bring its economy up to European standards. Public buses, ambulances, highways, bridges, trucks, trains, and rail lines all bear the imprint of large European transfers to Spain. The program has been enormously successful. A considerable part of Spain's economic growth (and a major reason it could avoid politically costly austerity programs) is due to these European subsidies aimed at bolstering Spain's democracy and preventing its slide toward Fascism or Communism as much as at developing its economy. But now these subsidies are being phased out, and Spain must find new capital. This issue also helps explain Spain's opposition to the eastward expansion of NATO and the EU, since it fears that the subsidies it presently receives will be redirected toward the new and more struggling democracies of Eastern Europe and the former Soviet Union.

It should be said that Spain also paid a price for its membership in the EC. Not only did many Spanish firms go under as protectionist barriers came down, but Spain also began running negative trade balances with a number of its European partners. In addition, Spain surrendered considerable economic sovereignty to those EC agencies in Brussels that determine agricultural policy, production quotas, and now fiscal policy. The old days of solving financial exigencies by cranking up the monetary printing presses or of resolving political patronage needs by expanding public employment may be over.

Finally, we need to mention the issue of corporatism. Under Franco, Spain was an anomaly; along with Portugal it was the only country in Europe that had retained its manifest, statist, and even ideological pre–World War II forms and institutions of corporatism, which in the rest of Europe had been discredited by the war and the Hitler and Mussolini experiences. True, corporatism had been attenuated in Spain: it was no longer the sole institutional basis of the Spanish system, and as an ideology it had all but been abandoned by Franco. Nevertheless, corporatism hung on among some regime ideological stalwarts and as one among several of the institutional bulwarks of the regime. Spain remained both an authoritarian and a corporatist state.

This legacy made it particularly difficult for Spain to transition smoothly from state to societal corporatism, or neocorporatism, after Franco died.[18] In Spain, corporatism was not just an institutional and organizational issue but an intensely ideological and political one. Because corporatism was associated with Franco and he now belonged to the discredited past, corporatism in all its ideological and political forms also had to be eliminated. This did not prevent the post-Franco regime, in the celebrated 1977 Pact of Moncloa that brought together labor, employers, and the state to preserve stability and social peace during the transition, from employing corporatist strategies even if they could no longer be called by that name. Numerous other pacts that are essentially corporatist in nature have subsequently been agreed to between the Spanish state and societal groups. Indeed, it is striking that Spanish newspapers every day report on five or six new public-private, essentially corporatist, agreements that have been reached between the government and societal groups, such as universities, the military, religious bodies, labor groups, farmers, businessmen, and local or regional entities. Yet because of the Franco legacy they cannot be called such. So unlike Germany, Austria, or Scandinavia, where societal or consultative corporatism is a normal, regular, routine feature of the sociopolitical system, in Spain the issue is still controversial, the term *corporatism* is only rarely used outside of academic discourse, and the transition from old-fashioned, authoritarian state corporatism to modern, welfare-oriented, societal corporatism is rocky and irregular. Nevertheless, of the fact that Spain is and remains corporatist, or at least partially so, in both the old (as a control mechanism) and the new (democratic, participatory) sense of that word, there can be no doubt.

REGIONALISM

In perhaps no other country of Western Europe other than the former Yugoslavia is the issue of regionalism and tribalism, historically at least, so intense. France has Brittany, and England has Scotland, Wales, and Northern Ireland, but in Spain, regional, ethnic, and subnational issues may be more important than in any of those countries. They show no sign of disappearing soon, although they are changing and diminishing.[19]

First, the issue of relations between the central state and its various regions has a long history in Spain, nearly a thousand years. Along with the retaking of the peninsula from the Moors and the relations of the central state with its component corporate groups, the regional issue is one of the most important issues in all of Spanish history. Second, for almost five hundred years the dispute was resolved almost entirely in favor of the central state. During Spain's formative years, from roughly the eleventh to the fourteenth centuries, there was often a healthy, nascently democratic competition between an emerging central state and the diverse regions and kingdoms that made up the nation. But the balance slowly tipped in favor of the central state, and with the marriage of Isabella of Castile and Ferdinand of Aragon (after whom Machiavelli's centralizing, amoral prince was modeled), the peninsula's two largest kingdoms were brought together. Under the Hapsburgs in the sixteenth and seventeenth centuries, all claims of local, regional, and corporate autonomy were snuffed out. The Bourbons in the eighteenth and nineteenth centuries were more reformist and Europe-oriented than the Hapsburgs but continued and accelerated absolutist and centralizing policies.

The Franco regime, after the disruptive divisions and conflicts of the nineteenth and early twentieth centuries, was the culmination of this centralizing process: all power was concentrated in Madrid, and at the regional level it was forbidden to teach the local language in the schools, to fly the regional flag, or to advocate regional autonomy. It is said, however, that while Spain was formally united during this half-millennium of history, it was never really unified; regionalist sentiment remained strong, as evidenced most dramatically by the outbreak of armed, terrorist-oriented ethnic violence and separatism in several of the regions even while Franco was still in power. The issue was not just regional or ethnic, however. Spaniards have long believed that the tradition of regional rights and autonomy contains the cradle of their liberties. Hence, regionalism in Spain, especially during periods of authoritarianism, has a strong political agenda that also has national implications associated with it.

Recognizing these tendencies and fearing the possible separatist breakup of Spain, the post-Franco governments and the constituent assembly that drew up the constitution of 1978 tried to reach a compromise on the issue. The constitution says that the nation is indissoluble, but it also guarantees rights of regional autonomy. Castilian Spanish is declared the official language of Spain, but other languages may be recognized as co-official in their respective regions. Unlike in Franco's time, flags and emblems of the region may now be displayed alongside the Spanish flag. The central government in Madrid is responsible for foreign and security affairs but in other policy areas power and/or policy implementation may be devolved upon the regional governments.

The constitution provided for two procedures by which a region may achieve autonomy, one fast, one slow. The fast route was applied to those regions—Galicia, the Basque provinces, and Catalonia—that had sought and achieved autonomy during the 1930s republic before the onset of civil war and the Franco regime; these were also the areas where potentially divisive and even breakaway sentiment was coming to a head in the 1970s. Once approved by the Constitutional Committee of the Congress of Deputies (parliament), all that was required for autonomy was a vote of approval in a regional referendum. On this basis, Galicia, the Basque provinces, and Catalonia quickly opted for autonomy within the Spanish state.

The slow procedure, by contrast, required an initiative on the part of the regional governments as well as approval by the full Cortes (parliament). The degree of autonomy was less for those provinces opting for this route. The stiffer requirements reflected the reality that proautonomy sentiment was less strong and the issue less pressing in these provinces. In 1981 a new organic law was approved by the Cortes governing these procedures in detail, and in 1983 the process was essentially completed when elections were held on the autonomy issue in thirteen other regions. Andalusia received its autonomy under a compromise procedure that represented a mix of the two routes. Hence, by the mid-1980s, all seventeen of Spain's regional governments had opted for some form of autonomy from the central state. Federalism had come to Spain de facto, if not in name.

Each regional entity has its own capital and a unicameral legislative assembly whose members are elected by popular vote. Each regional assembly selects a president from among its members. There is also a council of government in each region, headed by the president and responsible to the regional assembly. Each region may also have its own courts, although they are ultimately subordinate to the Supreme Court sitting in Madrid.

The national government retains exclusive jurisdiction in such areas as defense, foreign affairs, finance, civil aviation, public safety, foreign trade, economic planning, justice, and criminal, commercial, or labor legislation. The regional governments may be responsible for setting municipal boundaries and for setting policy in such areas as town planning, housing, forestry, public works, sports, tourism, and social welfare. In the past, providing one of the prime sources for regional resentments, wealthy provinces like Catalonia and the Basque country paid more into the central government in the form of taxes than they received in the way of programs, a situation that fueled resentment in these regions. Now there is a measure of relief. The regions continue to receive subsidies from the central government, but there are negotiations between the state and the provinces on the particulars, and in these negotiations the wealthier, more populous, and electorally powerful provinces have greater clout than the others. In addition, the provinces may now levy their own taxes, carry out many programs independent of the central government, and conduct their own financial affairs.

When this form of autonomy for Spain's regions was first proposed, many political analysts, knowing Spain's history and the historical power of centrifugal forces, feared that the country might unravel or disintegrate. But that has not happened. Like the American concept of federalism, Spain's system of shared powers between provinces and central government has proved to be both workable and dynamic. Virtually every day the Spanish press carries several stories involving new negotiations between the central state and the regions. Many of the areas of responsibility are ambiguous, such as police power, coast guard activity, and even some areas of defense and foreign-affairs policy. The result is a vigorous form of quasi-federalism in which the balance between the central state and the regions is subject to constant, everyday reinterpretation and renegotiation. Although many problems in the system remain to be worked out, it may be that after five hundred years Spain has finally achieved a workable balance between its centralist and autonomist tendencies. It should also be said that the regional governments provide another layer of bureaucracy by which patronage needs can be met.

Within the regions themselves, other important changes have been occurring. First, since the 1970s there has been a long-term electoral trend away from the more radical regional parties (such as Henri Batasuna or Euskadike Ezkerra in the Basque country), changing the balance within the regions toward more centrist and responsible parties among those with national agendas and those that are regionalist (e.g., the Basque Nationalist Party and the Convergence and Union in Catalonia). Second, as Spain has prospered, as its democracy has flourished, and as regional autonomy has in fact been implemented, the argument of the even more extreme regional terrorist groups, such as the Basque Euskadi Ta Askatasuna (Basque Homeland and Liberty), has been undermined. A good part of its agenda for autonomy has been carried out, and only its most extreme position remains: the demand for a separate country, which in fact has little support within the province. Effective police and security work in arresting, subverting, and even assassinating (with controversial human-rights implications) terrorist leaders has also been effective. It is a classic case of isolating the extremists and co-opting the moderates. In the process, regional autonomy has been increased and the terrorist threat greatly reduced.

Two things need to be said in concluding this section. First, it is striking how much space the autonomy issues take up in Spanish newspapers. These issues may be less dramatic or sensational than the front-page coverage of major-party machinations or the activities of the king or prime minister, but in the long run they may be just as important. Indeed, I would argue that a dual power structure has grown up in Spain, the full ramifications of which would require more space than we have here. On the one hand, there are the Cortes, national elections, the cabinet, the prime minister, party machinations, and government decision making. This is the visible and democratic Spain that has emerged in the past three decades and that has received so much attention and been so lauded in recent years. But on the other hand, alongside this Spain is a parallel pyramid of power, a much more traditional but now updated Spain that goes back centuries. This is the Spain in which the major arenas of politics are the relations between the state and its functional or corporate interests or the state and regional entities. This second pyramid of power has received far less attention from scholars, but it may be just as important as the first one. Not only do we need to understand it better, we also need to know its relations with that other, more visible, formally democratic set of institutions.

The other concluding comment has to do with the question of if, in this dual power structure arrangement, Spain may have actually devised something new and genuinely indigenous. For on the one side, we have the institutions of electoral and parliamentary democracy that have been brought to Spain largely from the outside, from the West, from Europe. On the other, we have a system of quasi-corporatism and of regional autonomies or federalism that is historically very Spanish. And yet Spain, like Japan, seems so far to have been remarkably successful in blending, adapting, and absorbing Western democratic institutions into some uniquely indigenous way of doing things. Not only is there the beginning of a distinctly Spanish model here, but it may have relevance to Latin America and other developing nations that are similarly attempting to reconcile new and imported democratic institutions to local, indigenous habits and practices.[20]

TRANSFORMATION OF AUTHORITY

Of all the European countries, Spain and Portugal, until the mid-1970s, may have been the most conservative. Conservatism, tradition, and a history (from medieval times) of Christianity have deep and powerful roots in the Iberian Peninsula, pervading not just religious life but politics, economics, society, law, government, literature, and intellectual life. Order, discipline, hierarchy, rank, place, position, top-down authority, elitism—all conservative if not reactionary values—were deeply and indelibly imprinted in Spain. It is no accident that Spain had often been described as a nation in the past where the weight of history is especially heavy. Later, a nascently liberal order emerged.

Franco sought initially to roll back the clock and restore what he called the "authentic Spain": again Catholic, conservative, disciplined, anti-Communist, and obedient to God and to him (the two went closely together). In addition, through propaganda, censorship, the school system, a controlled press, indoctrination, low literacy rates, and depoliticization from the frenetic political activities of the 1930s, Franco sought to instill in the population the values he identified with traditional Spain, which, not coincidentally, were the same values that kept him in power: unquestioned authority, the obligation to obedience, a unified and organic state, corporatism, and bureaucratic statism.[21] Meanwhile, other and alternative ideas were snuffed out by the regime's tough controls, repression, censorship, dictatorship, and the conscious fomenting of political apathy.

It should not be entirely surprising, therefore, that the first public-opinion surveys carried out in Spain in the 1960s showed the country to be remarkably conservative. Indeed, what was stunning to the young social scientists—liberals, social democrats, and Socialists—who conducted these surveys was that they showed Spanish public opinion, if anything, to be even more conservative than was the Franco regime itself. No one believed that was possible.

The political events of the Spanish democratic transition are familiar and need not be gone over in detail here. Franco died in 1975. Power then passed to the young monarch, Juan Carlos, whom Franco had groomed, and to Franco's hand-picked prime minister, Carlos Arias. But Arias was colorless, ineffective, and too much in Franco's mold; in 1976 he was replaced by young, charismatic Adolfo Suárez, a friend of the king and a democrat. Under Suárez's and the young monarch's guidance, the democratization of Spain proceeded rapidly. The exiles were allowed back; the Communist Party was legalized; censorship was lifted; free unions were allowed; liberties were restored; the armed forces were reined in; elections were held; and a new constitution was written. Eventually, tiring of the demanding process of governing and disappointed at the bickering within his own party, Suárez resigned in 1981 and was replaced as prime minister. But his successor, Leopoldo Calvo Sotelo, lacked charisma and a solid political following, and in 1982 his center-right political coalition was defeated electorally by Felipe González and the Spanish Socialist Workers Party (PSOE).[22]

González and the PSOE remained in power for the next fourteen years. The economy recovered from the recession of previous years; Spain entered NATO and the Common Market; and the country completed its entry into the mainstream of Western civilization. Spain became a "normal country," albeit a Socialist or social-democratic one; and many progressive Spaniards who supported PSOE thought of the progression from political democracy to social and economic democracy as natural, inevitable, and irreversible. But the González regime over time proved increasingly corrupt and out of touch with the populace, and its electoral support gradually eroded. In 1996 it was defeated by one percentage point by a revived center-right coalition led by José María Aznar and the Popular Party (PP). In 2000, Aznar received a new, stronger electoral mandate and moved the country back toward the center but without tampering with, and often expanding, the social-welfare reforms of his predecessors. The shift from center-right to center-left to center-right again means Spain has accomplished Arend Lijphart's criteria for a consolidated democracy: two successive electoral turnovers where the opposition wins and takes power by democratic means.[23] In 2004, the Socialists returned to power.

To go along with this democratic transition at the formal, electoral level, Spain has also developed a set of democratic institutions that reach farther down into society. It has an active, functioning, mass-based multiparty system that has evolved toward two-partyism. Its trade unions are free and largely independent of the state. Its armed forces have been reduced in size and budget, become more professionalized, and been subordinated to civilian authority. Rather than the historic tripartite power structure of church, army, and nobility, Spain has evolved to a much more pluralist society, although it is still a system of sometimes limited pluralism and not the chaotic hurly-burly of U.S.-style interest-group lobbying. Meanwhile, its political institutions have been modernized and have begun to be more responsive to public as opposed to private demands, and its policy delivery systems have been effective in providing improved education, health care, and social-welfare programs.[24]

Below the level of formal institutions, Spanish society has also changed significantly in recent years. Not only is it more urban and educated—the usual measure of social modernization—but the main institutions of Spanish society have changed as well. In this once most Catholic of societies, divorce, abortion, and family planning are now commonplace. Women work outside the home and increasingly at professional levels; children are more independent of their parents; and young people routinely live together before marriage. The extended family is no longer the all-important institution that it once was; and patronage, spoils, and good family connections are no longer the only route to a high government or business position. Indeed, there was a time in the late 1970s, right after Franco died, when all the societal tapestry and constraints that had long held Spain together seemed to be unraveling: children rebelled against parents; wives, against husbands; employees, against employers; maids, against madams; nurses, against doctors; communicants, against the church, and on and on. All the symbols, to say nothing of the realities, of authority and hierarchy seemed to be under challenge at once. But in the past twenty-five years Spain has settled down, become more socially conservative again, and resurrected such institutions as the nuclear family, even while not abandoning the exhilaration and "liberation" of the early, heady, post-Franco years.

With all these economic, institutional, and societal changes, it would be surprising if Spain's underlying political culture had not changed as well. This is the acid test of the transition, for while it is relatively easy and comparatively painless to change institutions, if the underlying values, beliefs, and political culture are not concomitantly transformed, then the system has only superficially changed and may well revert to earlier practices. Spanish political culture, however, has indeed been transformed. For example, while Spain remains culturally and nominally a Catholic country, only about 8 percent of Spaniards are active, practicing Catholics. Moreover, the traditional Catholic virtues of acceptance of unquestioned authority, obedience, discipline, and hierarchy are no longer widely accepted.

By 80 percent or more, Spaniards believe in democracy, tolerance, freedom, political participation (voter turnout in parliamentary elections is still in the 70–80 percent range), and pluralism, even while—and this should be a disturbing feature to democrats—having little faith in what we think of as democracy's necessary supporting institutions, such as parliament, political parties, and labor unions. Support for these institutions has declined over the years to the 15–20 percent level.[25]

While most indicators point toward a solid and robust Spanish democracy, there are enough disturbing features to raise concerns. First, although Spanish democratic institutions are firmly established, they are sufficiently dominated by old and bad habits—corruption, patrimonialism, family or clan favoritism, and ascriptive criteria, in general—that one needs to worry about them. Second, there are many institutions—the police, judiciary, bureaucracy, armed forces, local and regional governments, and security services—that have been only weakly or incompletely affected by the modernizing, democratizing trends. Third, corruption and special favoritism in awarding contracts, access, and jobs, while in decline for a time, are again on the rise. Fourth, the underlying political culture, even with the changes mentioned above, has still only incompletely been transformed; many high governmental as well as day-to-day transactions are still dominated by a pervasive sense of hierarchy, place, position, elitism, disdain for those lower in the social scale, and authoritarianism.

Fifth, civil society remains weak, with only limited growth of political parties, trade unions, or associational life since the 1970s.

Finally, while Spaniards overwhelmingly support democracy in the abstract, what many of them mean by that term—organicism, a strong state, corporatism, top-down authority, a Rousseauian as distinct from a Lockean conception, and patrimonialism[26]—has to be of concern to true democrats. This subject deserves far more attention than it has so far received.

ANXIETY, ALIENATION, AND ANOMIE?

Spain at present remains an optimistic, positive, hopeful nation and people. One finds little Euro-pessimism there; indeed, because Spain still identifies all things good (prosperity, democracy, a modern culture and society) with a somewhat mythologized Europe, Spain was, surprisingly to some, one of the first European countries to qualify fully for the New Europe under the Maastricht Treaty requirements. Although Spain in 2005 has a soberer and more realistic assessment of Europe than it had when it joined the EC in 1986, one finds in Spain almost none of the anomie, alienation, and pessimism that one finds in other European countries.

The main reason for this positive and optimistic faith, one suspects, is that Spain is still new to both Europe and democracy. It had such faith in both Europe as an abstract ideal and in democracy—and for many years its robust economy provided ample reasons to be optimistic—that it has not yet had time to become disillusioned and pessimistic. Prosperity also helps.

But in recent years the signs have become abundant that those early, heady, transformative, positive, and optimistic years may be coming to an end. Spain may be entering a second, less optimistic post-Franco period. In other words, Spain has so far avoided the widespread Euro-pessimism, alienation, and disillusionment that characterize other Western nations not because it is ahead of these others but because it lags behind. Alienation, pessimism, doubt, disillusionment, anomie, and a negative human psychology are not things of the past in Spain. Rather, they are likely the vision of the future.

The signs of this change are everywhere, and they are both economic and political. First, the economy has slowed considerably from its earlier miracle growth rates. Second, the European aid and subsidies that have been so critical in the past three decades will be drying up. Third, Spain's economy is not yet fully competitive with the rest of Europe or the larger developed world. Fourth, with a slowed economy, there are fewer pieces of the economic pie available to hand out to aspiring groups or to cover up and gloss over the fault lines and problem areas (corruption, inefficiency, and noncompetitiveness) that are increasingly showing up. Fifth, voter turnout is gradually declining; apathy is increasing; and there is widespread disillusionment and distrust with the main institutions (parliament, parties, and unions) of democratic life. Sixth, while Spain is still proudly pluralist, the balance (as in other countries) within that pluralism has clearly shifted away from the popular institutions, where it was increasingly lodged in the late 1970s and early 1980s, toward more elite, less popular, and less trusted institutions—government, business, and bureaucracy—which are in the process of forming a new iron triangle in Spanish political life.

All this is not to say that Spain's democratic transition is threatened or about to collapse. But it is to say that one era is slowly coming to an end and another, less certain one beginning. It is also to say that, as Spain still lags by almost every index behind the rest of Europe, its harder tests still lie ahead.

CONCLUSION

By all accounts, Spain has made a remarkable series of transitions in recent decades: from Third to First World economically, from traditional to modern sociologically, and from authoritarian to democratic politically. The political culture is now participatory, and Spain's international frame of reference is now European rather than isolationist. We should not denigrate Spain's accomplishments in any of these regards, nor can we ignore the numerous hopeful and optimistic indicators.

By virtually every index of social and economic life, Spain is at approximately 70–80 percent of the EU average. While that is a remarkable improvement by almost any standard over the situation forty years ago, we also need to worry a bit about the other side of this coin: the 20–30 percent of Spain that is not "European." This is the part of the glass that is not two-thirds or three-quarters full but is one-quarter to one-third empty. We know what the full part looks like: democratic, prosperous, and European. The question is what the part that is still empty looks like. And here we have to emphasize those remaining, perhaps now residual areas of Spanish life that are still nonmodern, Third World, or "Latin American," implying persistent underdevelopment in some areas, major social gaps and inequalities, a political culture that is both democratic and statist, and weak and uneven political groups and institutions.

For Spain, therefore, the prognosis is one of cautious, tempered optimism. And optimism, even with adjectives, has not in the past been what we were used to hearing regarding Spain. Democracy is secure; economic growth is going forward; and Spain's place in a modern Europe is institutionalized. So now such cautious optimism is justified; Spain is a Southern European country that works. Spain has made it to the ranks of being a "normal country."

DISCUSSION TOPICS

1. What have been the main disputed issues in Spanish history?
2. Describe the Franco regime.
3. What is corporatism and why is it important?
4. Analyze regionalism in Spain.

NOTES

1. For an overview, see Howard J. Wiarda and Margaret M. Mott, *Catholic Roots and Democratic Flowers: Political Systems in Spain and Portugal* (Westport, Conn.: Greenwood-Praeger, 2001).
2. A good readable account is John Hooper, *The Spaniards: A Portrait of the New Spain* (London: Penguin, 1987).
3. See Samuel P. Huntington, *Political Order in Changing Societies* (New Haven, Conn.: Yale University Press, 1968), which explores such explosions of participation and their political consequences.
4. The best study is that of Eric Baklanoff, *The Economic Transformation of Spain and Portugal* (New York: Praeger, 1978).
5. Useful factual summaries may be found in Eric Solsten and Sandra W. Meditz, eds., *Spain: A Country Study* (Washington, D.C.: Government Printing Office, 1990).
6. See the author's study, *Corporatism and Development: The Portuguese Experience* (Amherst: University of Massachusetts Press, 1977), and *Corporatism and Comparative Politics: The Other Great "Ism"* (New York: M. E. Sharpe, 1997).
7. The data in this section are from the World Bank, *World Development Indicators (1998)* Washington, D.C.: World Bank, 1999); United Nations, Population Division and Statistics Division, Social Indicators home page, available through www.un.org; and the U.S. Census Bureau, *International Data Base*, at www.census.gov/ipc/www/idbnew.
8. Solsten Meditz, *Spain*.
9. The best study is Charles W. Anderson, *The Political Economy of Modern Spain* (Madison: University of Wisconsin Press, 1970).
10. World Bank.
11. Hooper, *New Spaniards*.
12. Gerald Brennan, *The Spanish Labyrinth* (New York: Macmillan, 19343); José Ortega y Gassett, *Invertebrate Spain* (New York: Norton, 1937); Michael Kenny, *A Spanish Tapestry* (Bloomington: Indiana University Press, 1962).

13. Phillipe C. Schmitter, "Still the Century of Corporatism?" *Review of Politics* 36 (1974): 85–131; Howard J. Wiarda, "Toward a Framework for the Study of Political Change in the Iberian-Latin World: The Corporative Model," *World Politics* 25 (1973): 205–35.

14. Richard Gunther, Giacomo Sani, and Goldie Shabad, eds., *Spain after Franco* (Berkeley: University of California Press, 1986).

15. The classic statement, written by a Latin American, is José Enrique Rodó, *Ariel* (Austin: University of Texas Press, 1988).

16. Hooper, *New Spaniards*.

17. Eric N. Baklanoff, ed., *Economic and Business Perspectives on the Centennial of the Spanish-American War* (Tuscaloosa: University of Alabama, Bureau of Business and Economic Research, 1999).

18. Howard J. Wiarda, *Iberia and Latin America: New Democracies, New Policies, New Models* (Washington, D.C.: Rowman and Littlefield, 1996).

19. Robert P. Clark, *The Basques* (Reno: University of Nevada Press, 1979).

20. For further speculation on this theme, see Howard J. Wiarda, *Politics in Iberia*, and, by the same author, *American Foreign Policy toward Latin America in the '80s and '90s* (New York: New York University Press, 1992), especially the chapter, "State Society Relations in Latin America: Toward a Theory of the Contract State."

21. Richard N. Nuccio, "The Political Content of Public Education in Spain under Franco" (Ph.D. dissertation, Department of Political Science, University of Massachusetts, 1975).

22. E. Ramon Arango, *Spain: Democracy Regained*, 2nd ed. (Boulder, Colo.: Westview, 1995).

23. Arend Lijphart, *Electoral Systems and Party Systems* (New York: Oxford University Press, 1994).

24. Richard Gunther, ed., *Politics, Society, and Democracy: The Case of Spain* (Boulder, Colo.: Westview, 1993).

25. Wiarda, *Iberia and Latin America*.

26. See Howard J. Wiarda, *The Soul of Latin America: The Cultural and Political Tradition* (New Haven, Conn.: Yale University Press, 2001).

5

The New Portugal

Portugal likes to claim that it is the oldest nation-state in Europe. Its history goes back to the twelfth century, when Portugal succeeded both in driving the Islamic Moors out of its territory and in holding off the incursions of its larger and more powerful neighbor, Spain. Portugal early on became an independent country, but for most of the succeeding nine centuries it remained isolated and underdeveloped as compared with the rest of Europe. Its poverty was such that it vied with Albania to wear the label of "the poorest country in Europe."

From the twelfth through the fifteenth centuries, Portugal struggled to consolidate a central administration, to reduce the power of the local and regional nobility, to develop farming and agriculture, and to build national infrastructure, including roads, ports, a fishing fleet, and cities. The chief methods for achieving these goals were authoritarianism in the political sphere, Catholicism, a rigid social class structure, isolation from the rest of Europe, and a corporatist system of nascent interest groups that kept everyone in their place and subordinated to the state.[1]

Portugal roared in the late fifteenth and sixteenth centuries on the basis of its explorations, discoveries, and colonization of vast areas in Africa, Asia, and the Americas. The wealth of the colonies flowed into the mother country, enabling it to build vast palaces and gold-lined churches and to take its place, though only temporarily, among the great colonial empires. Sadly, Portugal attributed its newfound wealth and international stature to the authoritarianism, rigidity, and closed nature of its social and political institutions. But Portugal was still a small, poor country and could not sustain its global role. After its initial spurt, it sank into a four-centuries-long period of decline, isolation, and lack of development. It was bypassed by the great revolutions in science, industry, ideas, religion, politics, economics that we associate with the modern age.

Liberalism and republicanism came to Portugal in the nineteenth century in the aftermath of the French Revolution. But Portugal lacked the social, economic, cultural, and political base on which strong representative government could be based. It remained unstable, uninstitutionalized, unmodern, and very poor. When a republican form of government was finally established in Portugal (1910–1926), it experienced, over this sixteen-year period, more bombs per capita than any country in Europe. Beset by economic crisis, social conflict, and weak political institutions, the republic quickly fell.

THE SALAZAR REGIME

What to do next? Socialism and Marxism were unacceptable in conservative, Catholic Portugal, and liberalism and republicanism had seemingly failed. Economist and dictator Antonio Salazar claimed to have the answer.

Salazar's response was corporatism. In those days corporatism seemed to provide a "third way," between capitalism and Socialism and to democracy or totalitarianism. It called for a strong central state that would regulate and direct the economy. Harking back to the middle ages and Portugal's "glorious" earlier centuries, it wanted class harmony between labor and capital, as distinct from the Marxian class conflict. It was strongly Catholic in its beliefs and ideology. It also called for an authoritative, if not authoritarian, political system that guaranteed order and stability. At one level Salazar's corporatist system represented an effort to recapture Portugal's historic, if perhaps mythical, past; at another, it sought to deal with the modern world by repudiating both liberalism and Marxism and opting for a quasi-Fascist system. Unfortunately for Portugal, the Salazar regime proved no more able to solve Portugal's manifold problems of underdevelopment, social retardedness, and institutional weakness than had other "magic formulas" in the past.[2]

When Salazar died in 1969, he was succeeded for the next five years by his student and protégé Marcelo Caetano. Caetano was more liberal and open than Salazar and tried to modernize the regime, carry out limited reforms, and open Portugal up to European influences. As in Spain in the early 1970s, the result was a flowering of new political groups (so-called study groups as distinct from political parties, but providing the basis for the latter), a relaxation of the censorship and greater openness in the press and media, economic growth, and accelerated social change. All these changes went far beyond anything Eastern Europe experienced in the 1970s and 1980s and prepared the way for the even greater economic expansion and democratization in Portugal that followed.

TRANSITION TO DEMOCRACY

Caetano's reforms had caused consternation among the reactionary elements. In addition, Portugal had been fighting a costly and draining series of guerrilla wars in Africa in attempting to hold onto its colonies (Angola, Mozambique, and Guinea-Bissau) there. These pressures came to a head in 1974 when a group of younger military officers conspired to overthrow Caetano.

Over the next five years, Portugal went through a tremendously chaotic revolution. Almost all work stopped as seemingly everyone poured out into the streets, all the old social hierarchies were upended, what government there was fell into chaos, and the Communists made a bid for power. It was hardly a peaceful, orderly transition to democracy. Eventually, out of the chaos, the Socialist Party emerged victorious in the first election held after the revolution, and the political system began to settle down a little.

It took over ten years. Gradually, a functioning political party system began to emerge. A new constitution was written, but it was so anticapitalist that no new investment came into the country. The economy remained a disaster area until it gradually began to recover in the 1980s and when Portugal was admitted to the European Community (EC). The country continued in a state of near-chaos: almost no employment, dirty streets in what before had been a clean, whitewashed country, much social upheaval (not just workers against employers but also students against teachers, children against parents, nurses against doctors, etc.), and great political uncertainty and upheaval.

Only in the mid-1980s did Portugal recover to prerevolution levels. The economy recovered; investment came in; and Portugal began to receive massive subsidies from the EC to rebuild its infrastructure. On the political front, the centrist Social Democratic Party (PSD), under Aníbal Cavaco e Silva, an austere engineer who reminded voters of the aloof and technocratic Salazar, achieved for the first time ever in Portuguese history a working majority in the parliament in the 1985 election, thereby setting Portugal on a stable, middle-of-the-road course that has continued to this day. Portugal began to boom economically, and its democracy is now thriving.[3]

But is this the kind of model that Eastern Europe, or anyone else for that matter, would want to follow: economic backwardness for centuries, stagnation, a throwback to medievalism under Salazar, then revolution, chaos, ten years of economic decline, political instability for over a decade, and social unraveling? Clearly, the Portuguese revolution does not provide a model for anyone. Eventually, the country settled down again, but not before great damage had been done to its social, political, and economic infrastructure. The costs were simply too high for anyone to consider Portugal an example for Eastern Europe to emulate.

In the next sections of the chapter, we examine the main components of the Portuguese political system: the political culture, class structure and interest groups, political parties, government machinery and the state, and public policy both domestic and foreign. In the conclusion we return to the theme of the modernizing changes taking place in the country and the appropriateness of the Portuguese "model" for Eastern Europe.[4]

Political Culture

Portuguese political culture has long been conservative, traditional, and devoutly Catholic. For a long time, Portugal was known as the most conservative and Catholic country in Europe. But since the eighteenth century, there has been also a liberal, rationalist, progressive, and European-oriented current in Portuguese political culture, derived from the Enlightenment. Long a minority view, in the nineteenth century this liberal current burned brighter in the form of growing republican sentiment, checks on royal authority, growing (but still limited) liberal reforms, and, eventually, the establishment of a republic in 1910. But the republic was unstable, chaotic, and opposed by conservative forces who conspired to overthrow it in 1926.

When Salazar came to power in 1928, he sought to turn the clock back, to restore the traditional, Catholic, conservative society of the past. To do so, he used dictatorial methods—not the full-fledged Fascism of Mussolini but nevertheless authoritarian—to suppress and snuff out the liberal, radical, and Socialist elements. To tourists, Portugal looked like a quaint, whitewashed throwback to medievalism, but beneath the surface the other, liberal Portugal continued to exist. In 1974, this "other Portugal" exploded in revolution.

Portugal went through a period of instability in the mid-to-late 1970s. At one point, it appeared that the more radical elements would seize power and do to conservative Portugal what the conservatives under Salazar had done to them: snuff them out. But over time the moderate and conservative elements recovered.

Today, Portugal is a functioning democracy. Public-opinion surveys show overwhelming support—80–85 percent—for democracy. Moreover, sentiment in favor of extreme solutions, from either the right or the left, is declining. It is inconceivable that either of the options that still seemed possible only thirty years ago—Fascism or Communism—would garner wide support.

Nevertheless, there are still disturbing elements in Portuguese political culture. Some groups have not yet or fully reconciled themselves to democracy, and the traditions of elitism and top-down rule by a small elite are still strong. In addition, when the Portuguese are asked what is the best government they have had in the past forty years, a stunningly large percentage still say, "Salazar." That does not mean that Portuguese democracy is in danger, only that many Portuguese still favor the authority, discipline, and law-and-order of the old regime.

Socioeconomic Background, Class Structure, and Interest Groups

Portugal was an elite-dominated (church, aristocracy, army) society through the nineteenth century and beyond—some would say through the revolution and upheavals of the mid-1970s. But for much of the twentieth century, corresponding to the periods of military rule and the Salazar dictatorship, that elite dominance was maintained by suppressing the working class and keeping the emerging middle class apathetic.

Only since the mid-1970s has Portugal begun to emerge as a genuinely pluralist, and hence democratic, society. Although Portugal's population is still one of the most Catholic in Europe, the church as an institution has considerably less political power than it once had. The aristocracy has also declined in power, having lost much of its wealth and political influence in the 1970s upheavals. The third leg of this traditional triumvirate of power, the army, has returned to the barracks, been reduced in size and budget, and is generally subordinate to civilian authority.

Meanwhile, other, newer interest groups have risen in influence. The trade-union movement threw off the shackles of authoritarian control in the 1974 revolution and has emerged as a major political force, but its power has often been diluted by internal rivalries between Socialist and Communist unions. The main labor organizations are the General Union of Workers (UGT) associated with the Socialist Party, and the General Confederation of Portuguese Workers–National Intersindical (CGTP-IN) closely tied to the Communists. Peasant groups also rose up in the mid-1970s, but they have since become less activist. Student and street groups were also active as protesters in the 1970s.

As Portugal has settled down politically since the 1974 revolution, joined Europe, and become more prosperous; a new interest-group power balance has emerged in the country. The middle class and its myriad groups and associations—the state bureaucracy, doctors' associations, lawyers' associations, university groups, and so on—is emerging as the dominant class in the country. At the same time, the business class, which is seen as essential if the country is to remain prosperous, has emerged as the most influential group and is able to influence government policy on a variety of issues. Its argument, that without the jobs and prosperity that business creates, the entire national economy and, with it, the political system, will falter, is powerful; even recent Socialist governments in Portugal have recognized the influence of such essential groups as the banks, commercial establishments, industrialists, and importer-exporters.

Portugal is more socially pluralist now than ever before in its history, which has provided a more solid base for democracy. But Portugal does not have the incredible interest-group hurly-burly of American interest-group lobbying; its system is still one of more limited pluralism than is seen in the dominance of interest-group lobbying in the United States.

Political Parties and Elections

The present-day Portuguese political-party system emerged only after the 1974 overthrow of the long-lasting Salazar-Caetano regime.[5] Some of these parties emerged from the clandestine underground; some came back from exile; others developed out of the study groups that emerged, disguised as political parties, in the last few years of the old regime. Within a year, by 1975, a new but full-fledged party system was already in place.

The main Portuguese political parties, proceeding from left to right, are as follows:

Portuguese Communist Party (PCP). The Portuguese Communist Party (PCP) is an old-time Communist party formed in the Stalinist mold. It was long headed by Moscow-oriented Alvaro Cunhal and is now run by younger leaders who are trying to guide it in more moderate directions. The PCP is strong among trade unions around Lisbon and among peasants in Portugal's impoverished south. In 1975, the party made a bid to take power through a Communist putsch but failed. Its electoral strength has declined from 18 to 19 percent in the mid-1970s to less than 5 percent today.

Portuguese Socialist Party (PSP). The Portuguese Socialist Party (PSP) has emerged as the largest party on the moderate left. Long headed by exiled politician Mario Soares, who upon his return to Portugal became prime minister and later president, the PSP has moderated its view away from Marxism to a social-democratic position. The Socialists won the first parliamentary election in 1975, formed the first post-Salazar democratic government, headed a coalition government in the late 1970s and early 1980s, and came back to power in 1995 under a new leader, Antonio Guterres. The party's voting support fluctuates between 40 and 45 percent when it is victorious and 25 and 30 percent when it is down. It returned to power in 2005 after a three-year absence.

Social Democratic Party (PSD). The Social Democratic Party (PSD) began in the mid-1970s as a liberal-democratic party and has since become the country's main center-right party. Like the Socialists (and as its mirror image), the PSD gets about 40–45 percent in good times and 30–35 percent in bad. It stood in opposition to the Socialists in the mid-1970s, in coalition in the late 1970s, and as the single governing party under Prime Minister Cavaco Silva from the mid-1980s to the mid-1990s. It returned to power in 2002 but lost again in 2005.

Social Democratic Center (CDS)/Popular Party (PP). The Social Democratic Center (CDS) is a more conservative Christian-Democratic Party. It is not a radical-right party, however, and is frequently looked on by the other main parties as a potential coalition partner. Because the Portuguese electorate has again become more conservative since the upheavals of the mid-1970s, the CDS was expected to be the chief beneficiary of the rightward trend; but, in fact, the PSD has profited most from this trend. With its electoral support declining, the CDS morphed into the neoliberal Popular Party (PP).

In addition, Portugal has other, smaller leftist groups as well as a monarchist party that have some support but not enough to meet the requirement (5 percent of the vote) for being recognized as a political party.

Although Portugal is a multiparty system, two of the parties, the PSP and the PSD, have become larger; and there may be a tendency toward a stable, centrist, multiparty system. At the same time, the extreme elements on both the left and the right have been isolated and have become smaller. With the PSP and PSD now having alternated in power through a series of regular democratic elections, Portugal may have achieved the democratic political system that was impeded for so long.

Government Institutions

Portugal has a parliamentary system and a president. The government is headed by a prime minister, who is the leader of the majority or top-ranking party and, as in all parliamentary systems, a member of the parliament. The presidency is usually a ceremonial, ribbon-cutting, and baby-kissing office; but if no party has a majority and cannot reach an agreement on a coalition or if the government is paralyzed, then the president has the power to twist arms, dismiss the government, or call for new elections. In addition, the presidency in Portugal had been filled since the establishment of democracy in 1975 by unusually strong and capable individuals: Ramalho Eanes, Mario Soares, and Jorge Sampaio.

The winner of the first democratic elections in 1975 was the same Mario Soares who was then head of the Socialist Party. Soares and the Socialists dominated the first democratic governments in Portugal and were instrumental in consolidating the fledgling democracy. In the late 1970s and early 1980s, however, Portugal was governed by a series of weak coalition governments in which no party had a majority and the leadership was generally ineffective. But by the mid-1980s, Portugal was reversing course and returned to a center-right government under PSD leader Anibal Cavaco Silva. For the first time ever, in the elections of 1987 and 1991, Portugal had a government that was able to command an absolute majority; after ten years in power that saw a remarkable growth of the Portuguese economy, however, the center-right government lost support and gave way in the election of 1995 to a renewed PSP headed by Antonio Guterres. But Guterres also followed a pragmatic, centrist policy course that kept Portugal close to the middle of the road, and he was reelected in 1999. In 2002, the PSD returned to power.

Portugal is a small country, and it has been a unified and unitary one ever since the Middle Ages. Almost all political and governmental power, as well as economic, social, and cultural leadership is concentrated in the capital city of Lisbon. There is, unlike Spain or Italy, little regional or separatist sentiment, except perhaps in the Azores Islands or the north of Portugal, both of which are more Catholic and conservative. That did not stop the government of Portugal, however, based on the Italian example, from launching a campaign to decentralize power and establish a new system of government at the regional level. But that effort was seen by most Portuguese as a ploy to create a new layer of regional patronage or an opportunity for the political parties (primarily the Communists, who were strong at the local level) to compensate for their weakness nationally by qualifying for European subsidies given directly to local and regional governments, without those going through the government-party-controlled central ministries in Lisbon. The initiative was killed in a popular referendum. Even though Portugal's democracy is only thirty years old, it has become a stable, pragmatic, and centrist democracy, with alternation in government between the main parties, a widespread consensus on democracy, economic development though a modern, mixed economy, and close adherence to stringent European financial (balanced budget, low inflation) requirements.

Domestic Public Policy

Throughout its history, Portugal was one of the poorest countries in Europe. The poverty stemmed from a lack of resources, from deep social and class cleavages, from political divisions, and from reactionary authoritarianism. Portugal's social problems were equally severe: malnutrition, high illiteracy, debilitating disease, and inadequate housing. The dictatorship of Antonio

Salazar put in place the first advanced social programs in the 1950s and 1960s, but implementation was slow.

With its revolution in 1974, Portugal destroyed the old-fashioned political regime, but its economic underdevelopment persisted and was exacerbated for several years by chaotic political conditions. Not until a decade later, in the mid-1980s, corresponding with the coming to power of a stable, business-oriented government, as well as Portugal's joining the European Common Market and receiving massive European subsidies, did the economy take off. By now Portugal has reached a level of 70 percent of the EEC average, still poor by European standards but far better off than it was in the past. New highways and housing construction, as well as a new middle class make traditionally poor Portugal look like a boom area. Surprisingly, Portugal was one of the first countries to qualify under the Maastricht Agreement (which required balanced budget, low inflation) for the European Monetary Union. It is interesting that even the coming to power of a Socialist government in Portugal in 1995 did not alter the fiscal restraint and tight monetary policy of its probusiness predecessor, a departure from the divisive debates of the past.

Socially, Portugal has made equally impressive strides. Illiteracy has been all but eliminated, except among some in the older, passing generation. Urban as well as rural slums still exist, but overall the housing situation has greatly improved. Medical and health care have improved; the incidence of disease and malnutrition has declined greatly; and life expectancy is now close to European (rather than Third World) levels. At the same time, the government social programs that lagged for so long—pensions, welfare, unemployment, health insurance, and the like—are now finally being implemented. But it must also be remembered that Portugal is still not as wealthy as Scandinavia (or, closer to home, Italy or Spain) and, therefore, cannot afford the elaborate social programs that the advanced social-welfare countries have. Nevertheless, major changes have occurred in the last twenty-five years so that Portugal now only has pockets of poverty rather than a society-wide culture of poverty.

Economically, Portugal has also taken off. Its major problems remain a lack of resources, a small internal market, the eventual reduction of its EU subsidies, and stiff competition in the larger EU and global economies.

Foreign Policy

Portugal was once a global power with extensive colonies in Africa, Asia, and Latin America. But Portugal had gone into a centuries-long decline, and by the 1970s had left only small enclaves in Asia (Macao, East Timor) and sizable territories in Southern Africa (Angola, Mozambique), which it was desperately trying to hang onto. However, national liberation armies in these African territories had fought the Portuguese to a draw, and, in 1974–1975, convulsed in a domestic revolution that the protracted colonial wars had helped bring on, Portugal granted independence to these last remnants of its once-great colonial empire.

For several years thereafter, Portugal was so preoccupied with its debilitated economy and unstable domestic politics that it had virtually no foreign policy at all. The United States and Western Europe helped Portugal with economic assistance and political advice during this difficult period, but Portugal was mainly passive internationally. As its political system stabilized in the 1980s and its economy began to expand, Portugal once again turned serious attention to international affairs.

Portugal's number-one priority was and is Europe. Portugal received massive aid and subsidies from Europe in the1970s and 1980s, and in 1986 it joined the Common Market. Socially, economically, and politically, Portugal wanted desperately to be considered a European country (that is, democratic, progressive, modern); and it bent all its resources in that direction. In 1999 it became a charter member of the European Monetary Union.

Meanwhile, Portugal reached out in other foreign-policy directions too. Its location at the entrance to the Mediterranean and its oil needs meant it kept close track of North African and Middle Eastern politics. It sought to form a Luso-phonic (Portuguese-speaking) confederation much like the British Commonwealth (Australia, New Zealand, etc.) but found that its former colony bigger, stronger Brazil also had ambitions along those lines. In Africa, Portugal served as a useful go-between to help solve the long civil wars in Angola and Mozambique. In Asia, it turned its former colony Macao over to China in 1999 and tried to pressure Indonesia into better human-rights behavior in Portugal's former colony of East Timor while helping to securing East Timor's successful transition to independence.

In its relations with the United States, several issues are salient. Because of the Cold War, the United States has long had an interest in Portuguese stability and prosperity, specifically, in the strategic benefits of its location overlooking the Atlantic and the Mediterranean and of the Atlantic islands (Azores, Madeira) it possesses. Considerable U.S. trade and investment and tourism occurs in Portugal, and the Portuguese community in the United States is sizable and of growing political importance. The relations are good, solid, albeit sometimes distant, but the tensions associated with the Portuguese revolution of the mid-1970s have waned.

CONCLUSION

Portugal is a very different country now from what it was thirty or forty years ago. In the early 1970s, it was still conservative, Catholic, traditional, and backward. The political system was authoritarian; the economy was still quasi-autarkic; and the society was rigid. Prerevolutionary Portugal was quaint, whitewashed, quasi-medieval, and a mecca for tourists, but it was a very inefficient, poor, unmodern, and difficult place to live.

Since the mid-1980s, Portugal has made a spectacular recovery. Its social structure is more open; its economy has boomed; and its political system is democratic. Those who knew the country before would not recognize it today. New superhighways run the length and breadth of the country; Lisbon has been cleaned up and transformed; and construction cranes are everywhere. The Portuguese are taller (from better nutrition); life expectancy is twenty years longer; literacy is all but universal. Social services (health, education, housing, etc.) are also much better; the quality of life is higher; and living standards are now close to Northern European standards. The old two-class system has given way to a vast middle class; huge new housing developments and shopping malls attest to the prosperity of the country. The country is now so wealthy that, like Spain, it must import workers to do the manual labor, a sharp contrast from its long history of exporting surplus laborers because of high unemployment.

While we must obviously be pleased with Portugal's recent successes, for the purposes of the argument of this book we must be concerned with the intervening years, the decade from 1974 to 1985, before stability and relative prosperity came to Portugal. That was a period of chaos, revolution, social disintegration, political instability, economic reversion to a poorer lifestyle, and of foreign intervention. It is a period that has little to commend it, either to Portugal or to anyone who would want to elevate Portugal into a model for others to emulate. Right now, Portugal looks good and successful; but if this earlier period is also to be considered a part of the Southern European model and an example of a successful transition to democracy, it is not an attractive example for other countries to follow, either in Southern or Eastern Europe or anywhere else.[6]

DISCUSSION TOPICS

1. Describe the Salazar regime and the role of corporatism in it.
2. Describe Portuguese political culture.
3. Is Portugal now solidly democratic?

NOTES

1. For the background, see Walter Opello, *Portugal's Political Development* (Boulder, Colo.: Westview, 1985).

2. Howard J. Wiarda, *Corporatism and Development: The Portuguese Experience* (Amherst: University of Massachusetts Press, 1977).

3. Kenneth Maxwell, *The Making of Portuguese Democracy* (New York: Cambridge University Press, 1995).

4. Good summaries of all these aspects may be found in Eric Solsten, ed., *Portugal: A Country Study* (Washington, D.C.: Government Printing Office, 1994).

5. For more information on political parties and elections in Portugal, see Thomas Bruneau, ed., *Political Parties and Democracy in Portugal* (Boulder, Colo.: Westview, 1997).

6. For a summary, see Howard J. Wiarda and Margaret MacLeish Mott, *Catholic Roots and Democratic Flowers: Political Systems in Spain and Portugal* (Westport, Conn.: Greenwood Press, 2001).

6

From Foreign-Policy Isolation to Global Presence

Spain in Latin America and Portugal in East Timor

For a long time, Spain and Portugal were too isolated, too poor, and, during the long Franco and Salazar regimes, too much viewed as pariah states to have a vigorous and far-reaching foreign policy. It was only after they transitioned from authoritarianism to democracy, joined the modern, developed world, and became more affluent that they were able to invigorate their foreign policies and resume their role, which had been lost for some three-and-a-half centuries, as countries with significant and innovative foreign policies. It should be borne in mind in this respect that Spain is four times larger than Portugal, four times more populous, quite a bit richer and stronger, and, therefore, more able to sustain a far-flung foreign policy than is Portugal. Nevertheless, from these opening remarks, it seems clear that there is a close correlation between levels of development and the possibilities of countries being able to carry out a vigorous foreign policy.

In the preceding chapters we provided some brief overviews of Spanish and Portuguese foreign policy; in this chapter we zero in on two fascinating cases: Spain in Latin America and Portugal in East Timor. In both cases we are dealing not just with countries that, because of greater affluence, are now able to carry out more expansive and effective foreign policies but with countries that have discovered particular foreign-policy niches for themselves. We may call this niche foreign policy. Niche foreign policy may be defined as policy toward a certain region, country, or issue in which one particular state has, because of history, culture, language, proximity, or foreign-policy specialization, advantages over other states. In the two cases explored here, Spain has the advantage in Latin America of a common history, language, culture, affinity, and way of understanding; similarly, Portugal has the advantage in East Timor of common history, language, cultural background, modes of understanding, and even common educational backgrounds among the elites. Countering these positive factors, however, is the negative one that in both these cases Spain and Portugal are the former colonial powers; hence, there have been bad vibes in the areas where they have reestablished their presence, as well as good ones. The two cases are interesting in their own right but can also perhaps shed light on other, similar cases of niche foreign policy, for example, France in Francophone Africa or the Netherlands in the Dutch Caribbean.

SPAIN IN LATIN AMERICA

Spain in the 1950s was one of the poorest countries in Europe. Its per capita income placed it in the Third World category; its culture and society were still traditional and rural; its political system under the aging Generalissimo Francisco Franco was authoritarian and, some would say, Fascistic; and in the international realm, Spain was isolated, a pariah state. But by the time of Franco's death in 1975, an economic "miracle" had taken place: Spain had risen to the level of what the World Bank calls an "industrialized country," and its society and culture were rapidly modernizing. Subsequently, Spain embarked on a process of democratization that was both successful and served as a model for other nations. Spain joined the European Community (now the EU) in 1986 and continued its rapid economic climb, reaching the standards of the advanced industrial nations, with a per capita income now about 77 percent of the EU average and an economy that is the eighth or ninth largest in the world. Consequently, Spain's presence abroad both politically and economically has also grown.

From the low point of its defeat by that "upstart" United States in 1898 in the Spanish-American War, Spain has reemerged as a major cultural, political, and now economic actor in Latin America. Spain has also helped redirect Europe into a larger role in Latin America, serving as a bridge between Latin America and the EU, and has emerged as a political and economic competitor to the United States in the region. As a result of Spain's resurgence, the United States and its investors are now facing levels of competition from Spain and the EU more generally that they have not felt since at least World War II. Hence, it behooves us to understand the background and current realities of this new trilateral relationship between Spain, the United States, and Latin America.

European interest in Latin America, seldom large since the early twentieth century, began to increase again in the 1960s. The new ties between

Europe and Latin America were the product of both increasing European prosperity and desire to play a greater global role, and of Latin America's desire to diversify its international trade and relations away from too great a dependence on the United States. In 1985 the EC opened a sizable office in Madrid devoted to advancing European–Latin American relations.

But one needs to distinguish further between the European countries and their goals. France has concentrated its efforts in Francophone Africa and not paid much attention to Latin America. Great Britain under Margaret Thatcher and her successors focused on commercial ties in the Southern Cone (Argentina, Chile, Uruguay). The often sanctimonious Scandinavians believed Latin America was full of noble savages just waiting to be liberated from their "evil" oligarchies who would then become good social-democrats just like the Scandinavians themselves; but their commercial interests in the region have been limited. West Germany developed the most sophisticated policy, encompassing political, economic, and cultural ties; but with Germany's costly reunification and concentration on the new democracies to its east, some of that interest has flagged.

That leaves Spain as the major European actor in Latin America. Spain is important both in its own right and as an interlocutor for other European countries and the EU. Spain, after all, has over three hundred years of history as the colonial power in Spanish America, and even longer in Cuba and Puerto Rico. Spain's cultural, political, social, religious, legal, and language imprint is stamped indelibly on Latin America, which has now been overlain since 1898 with one hundred years of U.S. influence. Because of this long history and the heavy baggage it carries, Spain's relations with Latin America have been on a love-hate basis with the pendulum now swinging back to the former. Following independence in the early nineteenth century, Spain, as the former colonial master, and all things Spanish were greatly reviled in Latin America. Spain was blamed for all of Latin America's shortcomings, including economic backwardness and lack of preparation for republicanism and democracy. Except for Cuba and Puerto Rico, which Spain retained as colonial possessions, and Hispaniola, which it tried to reconquer, Spain largely withdrew from Latin America throughout the nineteenth century.

After the embarrassing debacle of 1898, which capped a two- to three-hundred year decline from great power status, Spain went through an agonizing self-appraisal. Who are we as a nation? Why are we lagging behind other nations? What is our future and destiny? Out of the reappraisal came the notion of *hispanismo*, or *hispanidad*, the concept that Spain and Latin America shared not only a common history, language, religion, culture, and colonial past but a common future as well. Ironically, it was

Spain's defeat by the United States that prompted Latin America to look on the former mother country more sympathetically.

For many decades *hispanismo* floundered both because Spain lacked the resources to implement the concept effectively and because Spaniards themselves disagreed over the concept's meaning. In the early years of the twentieth century, there were some exchanges of artists, orchestras, and cultural events between Spain and Latin America, but at the concrete diplomatic, strategic, and economic levels only limited activity occurred.

During the long rule of Francisco Franco (1939–1975), an effort was made through greater cultural exchanges, diplomatic activity, and some limited Spanish investment in Latin America to give *hispanismo* a firmer base. Franco created a special government institute to deal with Latin American affairs; he also politicized the concept of *hispanismo* by urging Latin America to follow the example of his own regime. Under Franco, therefore, *hispanismo* came to mean discipline, authority, religion, order, hierarchy, social peace—all very conservative and Catholic values—and a political system based on corporatism. To be Spanish or Hispanic in this conception, one was obliged to subscribe to the values Franco cherished; if one did not subscribe to these values, one could be denounced as non-Spanish, non-Hispanic. From the 1930s through the 1970s, this concept of *hispanismo* helped give rise to or cement dictatorship, not only in Spain but in much of Latin America (Somoza, Trujillo, Perón, Batista, etc.) as well. It also implied a closed, autarkic, quasi-mercantilist economic policy.

But, by the 1960s, the Franco-authoritarian vision of *hispanismo* was being increasingly challenged in Latin America as well as in Spain itself. In 1958, Franco had broken with the autarkic economic policies of the past, ushering in an explosion of economic growth and development that lasted for two decades and more. The economic growth gave rise in turn to vast social and cultural changes that served to modernize Spain and also to undermine the base of the Franco system. Meanwhile, Spain began to be inundated every year with millions of European tourists whose free lifestyles helped force major cultural change in Spain itself. In Latin America, too, the hold of dictatorship began to loosen during this period.

Hispanismo now resonated differently depending on one's political point of view. Some more traditional Latin Americans as well as the military dictatorships of the 1960s and 1970s continued to admire Franco-style authoritarianism, but liberals and democrats of various stripes—including more liberal Catholics—sought to break from that mold. In Spain this issue was no less complicated. To emphasize order, discipline, social peace, and Spain's "unique" national character identified one as a Franco supporter. But by the early 1970s, more and more Spaniards in the younger generations repudiated the older version of *hispanismo*. They wanted to disown the tourist posters that proclaimed Spain as "different" and instead they wanted to join Europe—not just in an economic sense (the EEC) but psychologically, culturally, and politically as well. To speak of joining Europe in the context of the early 1970s was thus a code for freedom and democracy. Hence, the debate over *hispanismo* and its meaning was, in microcosm, a debate over the future of Spain.

After Franco died peacefully in his sleep in 1975, Spain began a remarkable transition to democracy. This political transition accompanied the economic, social, and cultural transitions already well under way. In other words, Spain had significantly moved away from Francoism even while the aging caudillo was still alive. All that was necessary after 1975—which was nevertheless still a tense period—was for the post-Franco politicians and political parties to erect democratic institutions and put into practice the ideas and habits toward which the Spanish population was already gravitating. This massive shift in the economy, society, and culture prior to Franco's passing is what made the later transition away from authoritarianism and to democracy relatively smooth. Note here the contrast with Russia and Eastern Europe, whose transition was far more abrupt, with everything occurring at once and, hence, not so rapid, complete, or successful.

The transition was first in the hands of moderate Francoists such as Carlos Arias, then as King Juan Carlos, became more assertive, it shifted to the center under Adolfo Suárez and Leopoldo Soreto, and then, in 1982 and for the next fourteen years, the PSOE under Felipe González won power. The shifts signaled a major change in the Spanish notion of *hispanismo* and foreign policy; they also led to initial tensions with the United States and, to a lesser extent, Latin America.

Rather than the authoritarian-corporatism of the Franco period, *hispanismo* now came to mean democracy and human rights. Moreover, as the Spanish transition to democracy was consolidated, Spaniards began to talk openly of exporting their model to the many still-existing dictatorships of Latin America. The Spanish experience with building democracy after Franco, along with that of Greece and Portugal at the same time, was now being touted as the beginning of the "third wave," the worldwide phenomenon of democratization and freedom that next encompassed Latin America and soon came to include much of Asia, Eastern Europe, Russia, and parts of Africa and the Middle East as well.[1]

The first post-Franco concept of hispanism was quite moderate and restrained, but once González and the PSOE took power it became more radical and anti-American. Several factors were operating: first, González and the PSOE were Socialists, and many of their supporters shared the European Left's hostility to things American, and to the Reagan administration in particular. Second, this was the period of the great Spanish debate over joining NATO; criticism of U.S. policy in Cuba and Central

America was used to offset González's support of the more important NATO initiative. Third and related, the PSOE itself was split between its radical and more moderate wings; an anti-American stand in Latin America where the stakes were low enabled González to satisfy his domestic left even while taking the party in a moderate direction. Fourth, within the Spanish foreign ministry was a group of radical, anti-American officials who were given the Latin American bureau. Finally, it must be said that both González and many within his government were genuinely opposed to the U.S. Latin American policy at that time.

Spain's efforts in these early post-Franco years were not always appreciated in Latin America either. Some Spanish officials tended to treat Latin Americans as primitives or "noble savages" (Jean-Jacques Rousseau's phrase). These officials demonstrated attitudes tinged with racial, patronizing, and condescending biases. Spain began also to present its transition to democracy and human rights as a "model" for Latin America to follow, but many Latin Americans felt that they were quite capable of achieving democracy themselves and had no need for someone else's model. Similarly, corresponding with its entry into the EU, Spain offered to serve as a bridge for Latin America into Europe, but most Latin American countries thought of themselves as being capable of managing their own European relations without Spanish intermediation, thank you. Finally, because of history, culture, and language, Spain thought that it intuitively knew Latin America, but in fact, without the university research centers and think tanks devoted to Latin America, many Spanish officials were woefully ill informed and out of date.

With time and maturity, Spanish policy in Latin America began to settle down, to become more realistic, more normal, and less confrontational. González sacked his radical and often offensive foreign minister Fernando Moran and put a more moderate team in charge of Latin American policy. The government became surer of itself and less inclined to rhetorical posturing. At the same time, the move by the Reagan administration away from confrontation in Central America and toward a negotiated peace process removed a particularly contentious issue in the U.S.-Spain relations. Repeated visits by the king, the prime minister, and other Spanish officials to Latin America also helped increase Spain's knowledge level about the area and its great diversity. Similarly, the Iberian nation's entry into the EU, the continued prosperity of its economy, and the clear success of its democracy served to reduce Spain's historic inferiority complexes and its sometimes testy defensiveness in its relations with other countries. Rather than being different, Spain was now seen as a normal country, and its foreign policy reflected greater normalcy and pragmatism.

Whether the right-wing variety as exported by Franco or the left-wing type of the early González administration, Spanish policy in Latin

America has been long on rhetoric and short on substance. But now that has changed, often quite dramatically. Spain has at last begun to put real money into its old colonies. Indeed—and it is a critical turning point for any country—Spain is investing so much money in Latin America that, for the first time in its history, it has turned into a net exporter rather than a net recipient of direct investment. In the popular press the new Spanish entrepreneurs in Latin America are referred to as "the new *conquistadores*."

In the mid-1980s, the most thorough study of Spain–Latin America relations had concluded that there was more rhetoric than substance to the relationship.[2] But that conclusion, correct at the time, did not forecast the large influx of Spanish capital into the area during the 1990s. Indeed, on all fronts—economic, political, cultural, diplomatic—Spain has proved to be a considerably stronger presence in Latin America than previously anticipated.

On the political and diplomatic front, Spain has taken the lead in championing Latin American issues in Europe and in reaching out to build better relations with Latin America. It was Spain that organized the Iberoamerican summit, a regular meeting of Iberian and Latin American heads of state that pointedly excluded the United States and has emerged as a major sounding board to rival the Organization of American States and other inter-American bodies. Spain has significantly increased its political and diplomatic presence in Latin America, and its knowledge and sophistication in dealing with the area have grown apace.

But it is in the economic sphere that the most concrete and impressive gains have been made. Spain has gone full force into Latin America. It has replaced Germany and Great Britain as the biggest European investor in the area and is now second only to the United States itself. Latin American countries absorb 43 percent of Spanish direct foreign investment. Spain's banks and companies want to be big players in the region. Spain views Latin America as a growth frontier; its businessmen see their investments there as a financial rediscovery of America. With all this new Spanish capital pouring into its former colonies, there is fresh talk of a Castilian-speaking commonwealth—analogous to the old British commonwealth—which Spain would, naturally, like to lead and turn into a zone of economic cooperation and influence with itself at the head.

Several features of this new Spanish "discovery" of Latin America deserve special mention. First, although U.S. attention has largely been focused on Spanish relations with Cuba and the efforts of some firms to bypass Helms-Burton restrictions on trade with the island, that is really quite a small part of the broader Spanish "invasion" of the hemisphere. Second, although the Spanish thrust into Latin America has been led by its banks—Banco Santander, Banco Central Hispano, and Banco Bilbao Vizcaya—big Spanish companies such as Endesa (utilities), Mapfre (insurance), Repsol SA (oil), and Telefónica (telephones) have also established a large presence in the region.

Most Spanish companies in the past were small and mainly national; their Latin American ventures have enabled them for the first time to become genuine multinationals. In addition, by taking advantage of the United States's reluctance to extend NAFTA beyond Mexico and general indifference to the area's importance, Spanish companies have themselves moved into what everyone agrees is a big, booming area now offering expanding markets because of stability, democracy, open economies, and a growing, consumption-oriented middle class. It was Spain and its companies, for example, that introduced the EU to MERCOSUR, the Southern Cone common market and that began cooperative negotiations with MERCOSUR because the short-sighted Americans were largely ignoring it. Significantly, too, Spain has moved sharply into Brazil, a Portuguese-speaking country. Spain has not allowed the language differences to hold back its investments into the largest and most dynamic economy in Latin America that is also the ninth largest in the world.

This is the most serious Spanish incursion into Latin America since the sixteenth century. It is no longer based on the rhetorical posturing of *hispanismo* in its various incarnations but involves real, serious *money*. And because it is serious, Spain has been very careful not to engage in gratuitous partisan or ideological differences with the Americans, on the one hand, or any longer to be condescending and patronizing toward Latin America, on the other. The new Spain–Latin America relationship is a partnership; and under the center-right government of José Maria Aznar, Spain's presence, and especially its economic policies, it expanded even more.

At the same time, because of indifference, neglect, and the negative political fallout from the free-trade debate, the United States runs the risk of losing ground in the area. For the first time in sixty years, the United States is now facing stiff competition from Europe, the EU, and, above all, Spain. While the United States is standing still or ignoring the area, the EU, led by Spain, is busily negotiating agreements with MERCOSUR, the Andean Pact, and CARICOM, as well as with Cuba, Mexico, and Brazil. U.S. firms have also been frightened by the seeming volatility of Latin American markets and by the threat of the so-called Asian virus to the area. Thus, the United States is losing ground, opportunities, and markets in the region.

English economist John Maynard Keynes was wrong: it is not that we are all dead in the long run. Rather, in Latin America it is only the short run that looks unstable; the long term looks awfully good indeed. With its stable, democratic governments, booming open markets, expanding middle class, and prospering consumerist economies, Latin America looks like an excellent long-run investment. In its policies, the United States has been threat oriented so long that it has nearly forgotten how to be opportunity oriented. And, clearly, the opportunities in Latin America are vast.

There is plenty of room—and opportunity—in Latin America for Spain, the EU, and the United States. Not only is there room for all these countries and ruling bodies, but there are marvelous opportunities for cooperative and joint ventures as well. It would be a shame as well as a terrible loss if either the U.S. government or private business or both were to ignore and continue to neglect Latin America. Spain has recognized these opportunities and is moving vigorously toward taking advantage of them.

PORTUGAL IN ASIA: EAST TIMOR

Portugal from the fifteenth to the seventeenth century was one of the great seafaring nations of all times, perhaps *the* greatest seafaring nation.[3] It discovered, colonized, and held vast territories in Africa, Asia, and Latin America. But as Portugal itself declined from the seventeenth century on, it lost most of these colonies either to independence (Brazil, Angola, Mozambique) or to other larger, more powerful (Dutch, English) colonial empires. Only recently, rather like Spain, has Portugal recovered sufficiently to be a more significant international player. And part of its new foreign policy is to use comparative advantage, what we have here called niche foreign policy, to recover at least some of its influence in its former colonial possessions. Here our focus is on East Timor.

East Timor is one of the most unfortunate countries in the world. A Portuguese colony for hundreds of years, it was nonetheless largely ignored by Portugal because it had few resources or advantages and little to offer to a colonial power. After Portugal was convulsed in domestic revolution in 1974–1975 and precipitously abandoned the island, East Timor's independence was cut short after only a few months by rampaging Indonesian military forces, which absorbed East Timor into Indonesia. As Indonesia's rule proved, by the 1990s, brutal and rapacious, East Timor's popular forces rallied again for independence; but after the country was allowed in 1999 to formally cast a vote for independence, rampaging thugs and militias, mainly from Indonesian West Timor but aided and abetted by the Indonesian armed forces as well as anti-independence forces in East Timor, rose up again and sought to thwart independence by burning, looting, killing, and destroying everything in sight. East Timor subsequently was occupied and became a ward of the United Nations, with UN peacekeeping forces and civilian administrators effectively running the country until sovereignty was restored and full independence was achieved in 2002.

Not only has East Timor had a sad history, but it is also one of the least-developed countries in the world. Per capita income is under $300 per year; unemployment or underemployment affects 90–95 percent of the population; and East Timor has few and limited resources. Agriculture is plagued by poor soils and the absence of rain, and the country's main export crop, coffee, is currently at rock-bottom prices in global markets. There is very little commerce even at the capital city, almost no industry or tourism, and practically no investment. The only new jobs are those provided by the UN and the myriad international agencies operating in East Timor, but these will soon be drying up as the aid agencies reduce their staffs.

In addition to suffering from social and economic underdevelopment, East Timor is a very traditional society with poor roads, underdeveloped educational and communication facilities, and a precapitalistic work ethic. It may be that oil and natural gas fields in the Timor Sea will help alleviate underdevelopment and serve as a substitute for salaries paid by the UN, but that is ten to twelve years from realization and may not be the bonanza that East Timor hopes. Given East Timor's underdevelopment and, worse, the sense of hopelessness that often pervades the territory, we must ask why Portugal remains interested in it and willing to commit resources. Portugal has by now made a major commitment to East Timor, sending in military forces, technicians, businessmen, and a sizable diplomatic presence. But given the absence or low level of resources, trade, and commerce, there must be other reasons for Portugal's renewed interest in its former colonies. Among the possibilities are Portuguese guilt for past actions or inaction on the island and a desire to make up for earlier colonial mistreatment; close ties between Portugal and the new East Timorese political elite, many of whom were educated in Lisbon; an emotional attachment to its former colonies; a continuing long-term policy of advancing the concept of a Lusophonic commonwealth led by Portugal; and a desire to reassert Portuguese foreign policy in areas where the Portuguese language, culture, and background make that feasible. Or could it be an interest in all that potential oil and natural gas from the Timor straits? Whatever our answers to these questions, we must also weigh the question of *whether* it is worth it for Portugal to pour so many resources into such a hapless country.

History

East Timor has long been the neglected, bedraggled, tail end of the once-vast Portuguese empire in Asia.[4] It is not now a wealthy or resource-rich country, nor was it wealthy in colonial times, the result being that East Timor was long characterized by colonial neglect. No one wanted it. From

Portugal's point of view, its most valuable Asian colonies in the sixteenth-century (and thereafter) were Goa, Malacca, and Macao; in what is now the Indonesian archipelago, it was the Moluccas and the entrepôt at Jakarta that made the enterprise worthwhile, not East Timor. East Timor had little or no rich agricultural land, little or nothing in the way of valuable spices, and no precious minerals worth exploiting. Hence, the Portuguese paid little attention to the island. An especially telling statistic is that there are more Portuguese in the country now, about 1,500, than there ever were during the centuries when East Timor was under Portuguese colonial rule.

During the early 1500s, the Portuguese had captured much of the trade in cloves and other spices grown on the Spice Islands not far from Timor, and, as early as 1512, the Portuguese had apparently scouted the island of Timor. In 1520, the Portuguese established a landing point at Lifau on the northern coast of Timor, but it was mainly a rest stop for occasional merchant ships and not a permanent settlement. The area's first sizable European settlement was on the nearby island of Solor in 1516; the settlement at Lifau meanwhile waxed and waned depending on Portuguese interest. Over time, Portugal all but abandoned the colony, which then sank into poverty and torpor. Its lack of value to Portugal is illustrated by the fact that the closest Portuguese administrative center was located in Macao, about two thousand miles away. Because of the lack of resources, East Timor was of little worth to the Portuguese Crown, or to the Portuguese republic that followed in 1910. It was isolated at the far eastern end of the Indonesian archipelago, with little strategic, political, commercial, or diplomatic worth.

Over time, Portuguese merchants, sailors, and soldiers had mingled with the native peoples of the islands, producing a sizable mestizo population known as Topasses. They spoke Portuguese as well as native languages, converted to Catholicism, and accompanied Portuguese merchant parties to Timor to trade in sandalwood. Relations between the Portuguese and their rivals, the Dutch, were not always harmonious, however, and included armed conflicts and the establishment of rival trading posts at Lifau. Under siege by their Dutch neighbors, in 1769 the Portuguese moved their garrison eastward to Dili and established a new European settlement. But that also removed the Portuguese farther from the sandalwood trade and led to further neglect. In the early nineteenth century, a visitor described the colony as "squalid, demoralized, and in a state of half siege." Ironically, it was the very absence of value and resources in East Timor that enabled the Portuguese to hang on to it for so long. Neither the Spanish, the Dutch, the British, nor the French were interested in the colony. It simply wasn't worth the effort. As Indonesia became a Dutch colony, the Dutch similarly showed little interest in impoverished East Timor. And, even as Indonesia became independent after World War II, it expressed little interest, at least at first, in conquering this part of the archipelago. As a result, Portugal was able to retain the territory. But recognizing its limited value, Portugal for long periods neglected the island and failed to put its resources to work there—far less, for example, than Portugal put into its main African colonies of Angola and Mozambique. As a result, East Timor languished in underdevelopment and much of its traditional, quite primitive ethnic/tribal culture and society remained intact. That is why Portugal is still blamed today by many Timorese for the island's lack of progress and modernization.

Meanwhile, the Dutch had gone beyond the entrepôt stage in Indonesia and were moving to colonize and effectively settle the islands. The Dutch claimed West Timor but left the Portuguese in charge of what was viewed as a worthless colony in East Timor. Over time, the Dutch possessions far outstripped the Portuguese in wealth and value. In addition, as the Dutch influence spread, Portuguese settlers from the Spice Islands and other island settlements gravitated toward East Timor. The colony remained bedraggled, but it did receive something of an economic stimulus from the Dutch presence and expanding production of coffee. However, Portuguese influence and personnel in the colony remained minimal, and that was the way the colony remained well into the twentieth century. Portugal did little to develop its colony economically or socially.

The vestiges of this neglected Portuguese colonial outpost are still present in the capital of East Timor, Dili, today. Facing the harbor and newly renamed Human Rights Avenue is the seat and former administrative offices of Portuguese colonial administration in East Timor, a building that reminds one architecturally of the Praça do Comércio in Lisbon and was the headquarters of the vast UN administration on the island. In front of this building is a park that looks like the parks in front of the Jerónimos in Belém on the Tejo river in Portugal, the central point of which is a damaged statue of Prince Henry, the navigator. Behind is a school, the Camões Institute, where the small Portuguese community once brought their children but which is now used to teach Portuguese to the Timorese, few of whom below the infinitesimally small educated class speak the language. On one side is the *fortaleza*, the most recent incarnation of which dates to the early nineteenth century but which now lies in ruins, a burned-out hulk, the victim of rampaging Indonesian militias. On the other side of the main square is a shamble of buildings that once housed the municipal government; that will be the location of the new, or renewed, Portuguese embassy in Dili. The cathedral still stands, bypassed by the rampaging militia mobs of 1999, as do several Portuguese-style churches.

When Indonesia achieved independence after World War II, political tensions in the area increased. On the other hand, although Portugal retained control of East Timor, it was clear that Indonesia had designs on the territory and would someday move to incorporate it into the Indonesian state. At the same time, the Portuguese dictatorship of António Salazar was determined at all costs to hang onto its far-flung colonies, including not just East Timor but Goa, Diu, Damão, Macao, Angola, Mozambique, and Guinea-Bissau. A third new element in this volatile mix was the national independence movements growing after 1974 in East Timor itself. These included the conservative, Catholic, middle-class-dominated Timorese Democratic Union (UDT) which favored a go-slow approach; and the Timorese Social Democratic Association (ASDT) which advocated immediate independence and, taking a cue from its more Marxist, anti-colonialist orientation, changed its name to the Revolutionary Front for the Independence of East Timor (FRETILIN). Another group on the island, Apodeti, favored integration with Indonesia as the only way for East Timor to grow economically.

These conflicts came to a head in the early 1970s. The more radical FRETILIN launched an anticolonial campaign against Portugal that received considerable international sympathy as a "national liberation" struggle. Then, in 1974–1975, continental Portugal itself was convulsed in revolution, which for a time swung radically to the left. At the height of this leftward stage, Portugal unilaterally granted independence to East Timor, turned power over to FRETILIN, and precipitously abandoned the island. With no or few resources, no training in self-government, and Indonesia already plotting to annex the territory, East Timor faced a bleak future.

For a brief time, FRETILIN and the UDT were able to work together. But then the coalition broke up, the situation degenerated into civil war between the contending factions, and Indonesia stepped up its meddling in East Timor's affairs. FRETILIN sought to move the newly independent country radically to the left, which only gave the conservative, military-dominated Indonesian government of General Suharto another pretext for intervening and also antagonized the United States at a time of heightened Cold War tensions. Hence, in December 1975, after East Timor had been independent for only a few days, the Indonesian army, with the quiet approval of both the United States and neighboring Australia, invaded the island and annexed it to Indonesia. East Timor disappeared as an independent entity.

Initially, Indonesian rule was cruel, brutal, and repressive. But by the 1980s, the worst of the repression ended and East Timor actually experienced a measure of prosperity, integrated as it was into the growing Indonesian economy. But then in the 1990s, Indonesia went into an economic downspin that, along with Thailand, Russia, and Argentina, was one of the world's worst. Meanwhile, the Indonesian military again increased the repression; FRETILIN launched a renewed guerrilla struggle, this time aimed at achieving independence from Indonesia; the Timorese Catholic Church and other groups rallied to the independence cause (the church vastly increased its flock as a result of its support for independence); and an international campaign was launched to champion East Timor's independence struggle, culminating in the awarding of the Nobel Peace Prize in 1996 to the two main independence leaders, Bishop Carlos Felipe Ximenes Belo and independence advocate José Ramos-Horta.

By this time, a number of religious and human-rights groups had taken up East Timor's cause and were strongly critical of Indonesia's human-rights violations; the Pope visited the island in a move that not only strengthened the church's position but also provided enormous publicity for the cause of independence; the Cold War had ended, making FRETILIN's leftist positions appear less worrisome; and dictator Suharto was in his last days. When he was forced from power, a more democratic Indonesia permitted East Timor in 1999 to vote on independence.

The vote for independence was overwhelmingly favorable. But in the aftermath of the vote, anti-independence forces in East Timor, armed militia gangs from Indonesia-controlled West Timor, and irregular forces aided by or part of the Indonesian armed forces went on a rampage in East Timor, seeking to prevent independence from being implemented. It is almost impossible for anyone who has not been to East Timor to appreciate the extent of the damage. These forces killed, looted, raped, terrorized, vandalized, and burned their way through the country and destroyed almost every building in Dili and elsewhere. Almost nothing was left. Poor East Timor, which had almost no economy, no institutions, no infrastructure, no civil society to begin with, was now left with a totally destroyed, anarchic, burned-out territory.

Faced with a massive humanitarian disaster, the United States, Portugal, Australia, and the UN determined to intervene. They sent military forces to keep the peace and civilian forces to rebuild, or build from scratch in most areas, the country. East Timor became a ward or protectorate of the UN. The UN and other military forces reestablished peace; some rebuilding was done; a new constitution was written; and East Timor became a fully independent republic on May 20, 2002, even though UN and other forces are likely to remain in the country for many years to come. Meanwhile, East Timor faces so many problems as to almost seem insurmountable: stifling poverty, lack of resources, pervasive violence, absence of investment or jobs, weak or nonexistent infrastructure, absence of institutions, absence of civil society, lack of experience with self-government and democracy, little experience of the outside world, unemployment that may reach 90–95 percent of the population, and a traditional political culture that is not supportive of a free-market economy or of pluralist, democratic participation.

When East Timor became independent in 2002, Xanana Gusmão was elected as its first president. These events were widely celebrated both on the island and globally. But if one looks at the low per capita income of East Timor, its high unemployment, the absence of investment and dismal state of the economy, the traditional character of much of the culture and society, and the potential for renewed conflict, violence, and ethnic strife, then one cannot be so optimistic. Much of the island still lies in ruins, desolate and destroyed, a vestige of the Indonesian rampages and destruction. One, of course, feels terribly sorry for poor East Timor and hopes that it does well, but a hard and objective examination of the facts and figures leads one to be quite pessimistic.

East Timor is a very difficult terrain in which to operate. Roads and communications are woefully underdeveloped; violence, crime, and gang activities are still widespread; there are few functioning institutions; there are few restaurants, hotels, and commercial establishments; living conditions are often difficult; and East Timor is now independent but the UN and other missions will need to stay there for many years to come. Its future is uncertain, unsettled.

The above points require some elaboration since they affect the likely future success of the Portuguese mission in East Timor. There are very few commercial establishments in Dili, and they have few goods to sell. Violence is widespread and is only kept in check by the UN peacekeepers. The UN has created few jobs for the Timorese, has not stimulated the economy, and has not attracted essential new investment. The UN mission is big, bureaucratic, and inefficient; the real peace keeping occurs between the UN missions and agencies, not between the UN and the local forces. Little nation building, in the sense of institutional development, has been accomplished. Privately, UN, U.S., and Portuguese mission officials said that they regarded the situation as "hopeless," a "disaster area," and "unsalvageable," although their official positions preclude them from saying this openly. But if this is the actual situation, what is the purpose of having such a large Portuguese mission and private Portuguese Foundations office in such a woebegone place?

In terms of the legacy of Portuguese political ideas and institutions in East Timor, here are some of the results of interviews the author conducted in 2001:

1. The Portuguese language is spoken by a dwindling number of persons. It is mainly the older, educated, upper-class Timorese who speak Portuguese, and they are decreasing in numbers. If there is a second language in East Timor, it tends to be Indonesian; if there is a second *European* language, it now tends to be (because of the UN and

U.S. presence) English. This is particularly true among the younger generation.
2. The educational system (what there is of one) is now mainly Timorese and Indonesian. Again, the older, elite generation was often educated in Portuguese schools and universities, but the younger, nonelite generation has mainly been educated in Indonesian schools and universities. At present, there are some 170 Portuguese-language teachers in the educational system.
3. During the colonial period until 1975, East Timor was 20–30 percent Catholic; now, because of the church's identification with the independence movement, the conversion recently of many practiced animist religions, and the driving out of many Muslims, the country is 80 to 90 percent Catholic. One might assume that this recent surge in Catholicism would also be beneficial in terms of preserving and enhancing Portuguese cultural influence, but that is not necessarily the case. In fact, the church in East Timor (and increasingly the church in Goa) is mainly advancing its own interests, identifying with East Timorese nationalism, which may or may not be in accord with Portuguese state interests. In both areas there is considerable antagonism over this issue.
4. Portuguese law is still in effect in East Timor in some limited areas. But during its twenty-five-year occupation, Indonesia imposed a great deal of its law system on the territory; there has also been, because of the upheavals of recent decades, a reversion to indigenous and consuetudinary law; and at present what law and order there is largely mandated by the UN. The new constitution, drafted with the assistance of legal technicians from the Portuguese National Assembly, contains numerous Portuguese and some Mozambican influences. This is one of the areas where the Portuguese have had a considerable impact.
5. Local government in East Timor is likewise a mix of indigenous, Indonesian, Portuguese, and UN organization. The UN has been running just about everything in East Timor, including what there is of local and district administration. Indonesian control for twenty-five years also left its imprint. But in many areas, local government authority has devolved to traditional elders and tribal authorities. In the cities, however, traditional Timorese authority (the *chefe de suco*) corresponds to the longtime Portuguese system of *aldeias* and *freguesias*. Additionally, what is referred to as the *liurai* (a kind of administrative decree) in East Timor is the same as a *régulo* in Portugese. Regional administration still corresponds to the Portuguese system of parishes.
6. Civil administration (birth, marriage, death, property records) in East Timor is presently in almost complete chaos, because the Indonesian

invaders and militias burned all the archives. None of these records is left. The (UN) administration, therefore, requested that people come in and *volunteer* this information, a nearly impossible task in a context of fear, destruction, and intimidation. Marriage, however, is still according to Catholic (canonical) law.

7. Portugal has 150 police, a full battalion (roughly 900 men) of military forces in East Timor (both now being reduced in size) and, along with Australia, constitutes a major part of the peacekeeping forces. Because of the common language, the Portuguese forces have been intimately involved in the reorganization and retraining (including Portuguese-language training) of the East Timorese defense forces. This is a very sensitive and complicated issue which, among other things, involves rivalries among the several peacekeeping forces, lingering resentments over earlier Portuguese colonial rule and present influence, the conversion of unprofessional militias and gangs into professional forces, and political questions of whether East Timor wants or needs regular armed forces.

8. Earlier (summer 2001) articles (for example, in the weekly *Visão* magazine) suggested that Portuguese investment and businessmen were coming to East Timor, but in November 2001 the author was told there were "only three or four" Portuguese businessmen working there. That seems quite rational since the East Timorese economy is so depressed; there is little trade or commerce, including with Portugal; there are few resources and investment opportunities, and the overall climate is not hospitable to business.

9. One of the most interesting and important Portuguese influences in East Timor was in the writing of the new constitution. This is a fascinating issue that offers perhaps more opportunities for the advancement of Portuguese interests than any other listed. In November 2000, Almeida Santos as president of the National Assembly in Portugal and Xanana Gusmão (who was educated in East Timor Portuguese colonial schools and is Portuguese speaking) as president of the East Timor Council (now president of the country) had signed a protocol, later renewed, to provide technical assistance and cooperation to Timor in the writing of the new constitution. As a result of this accord, five Portuguese technicians from the Assembly, experts in constitutional law, were in residence in Dili helping to write the new basic law. The draft East Timorese constitution was very similar to the Portuguese constitution; many of the articles were taken word-for-word from the Portuguese constitution; the final document is very close to the earlier draft. It provides for a semipresidential, semiparliamentary system of government like Portugal's, a Council of State like Portugal's, a supreme court and judicial review like Por-

tugal's with a "corps of judges"; fiscal, administrative, and audit courts; a system of civil codes like Portugal's, and a system of local government like Portugal's. Furthermore, as in Portugal, the codes and the system of local government are to be set forth and elaborated in a series of separate, basic, organic laws. An amusing aspect of the constitution writing is that the degree of Portuguese influence is not widely known and was being kept purposely quiet so as not to antagonize other (UN, EU, U.S., Australia) actors involved in East Timor. This was a subtle, effective, successful "stealth" campaign to enhance Portuguese influence but not to advertise that fact publicly.

10. The new office of the Portuguese Oriente Foundation has only recently been opened in East Timor; it was housed, temporarily, in the offices of the Portuguese Mission in East Timor. The Foundation office is only beginning to diversify its activities. The Foundation was already assisting in some limited cultural activities and was helping provide for Portuguese-language training through the approximately 170 Portuguese educators, professors, and teacher trainers who are in East Timor. There are plans for a museum emphasizing Portuguese history and culture, a structure that is sorely needed given the fact that most Timorese were not yet born when East Timor was still a Portuguese territory and so the memory of the Portuguese past is quickly fading, helped along by the large-scale destruction of archives, records, and monuments by the Indonesian military and militia forces, and the absence of monuments, signs, and indicators of the nearly five-hundred-year Portuguese presence.

The Foundation's programs are just now getting started in East Timor. There is much the Portuguese government and Portuguese foundations could do to advance Portuguese culture and knowledge of Portugal; the question is, given East Timor's poverty, lack of resources, and multifaceted problems, whether such an effort could be sustained for what predictably will be a long, arduous effort.

East Timor, now independent, remains a sad, bedraggled, violent, chaotic, burned-out, and quasi-destroyed country. It is still one of the poorest countries in the world. Not only is it underdeveloped economically and socially in virtually all aspects, it also has almost no institutions on which to build: no government, no civil service, no public administration, virtually no civil society, and no tradition of self-government, democracy, or a civic political culture. It has almost no or weak agriculture, no commerce, no industry, no international trade. It is a pitiful ward of the UN, an adopted stepchild. In the language of political science, East Timor may be a "failed state," "ungovernable," a case of "morbific politics."

In such a poverty-ridden country with so little hope for the future, the questions become: What are Portuguese interests in maintaining or enhancing its presence there? Is *any* investment or commitment to East Timor worthwhile? What return can be expected, what national interest can be served? The issue is complicated both by the fact that East Timor is so poor and by the fact that Portugal has negligible commercial, trade, or economic interests there.

There is a wonderful, exciting, marvelous history here that needs to be told, but it is almost completely unknown. East Timor has no history museum, no archeological museum, no art museum, no photography museum, no public museum or history of any sort. In that sense, which is different from the Hegelian or Marxian sense of the same phrase, it has no history in the form of recorded, displayed, visible history. It has almost no monuments, no historical markers, no tourist sites, no maps, no brochures, no picture books, not even postcards. Because of the violence, destruction, and burning of the last decade, including the burning and destruction of all the archives and legal and civil documents, its history has, quite literally, disappeared and been obliterated.

In this context, it seems worthwhile for the Portuguese government and the private Portuguese foundations to invest some time and funds in the telling of East Timor's history, the Portuguese contribution, and the Luso-Timorese culture and society. Some of these activities (the planned history museum, historical building, and church restoration) will require considerable outlays of funds; others (postcards, brochures, maps, historical markers, picture books, publicity, photography displays, research and publications on the Portuguese role) can be accomplished quite inexpensively. It seems to me that all these activities are eminently worthwhile and merit support.

Larger considerations must also be kept in mind. These include Portuguese prestige, its efforts to make up for past neglect of East Timor when it was a colony, its desire to play a greater and positive role in international affairs, its continuing interests in a Lusophonic confederation of some kind, its desire and effectiveness in serving, because of the language and cultural background, as an interlocutor in recent East Timor conflicts and in peacekeeping operations. It may well be (although the issue raises questions in Australia) that Portugal also has a long-term interest in those oil and natural gas reserves in the Timor Sea.

But all this needs to be seen in perspective, in context, and with severe limits on what Portugal can and should do. East Timor is a very poor country; it will likely always be very poor; and little can be expected in the way of a return on Portugal's investment. As compared with Portugal's other foreign-policy priorities—the EU, France, Spain, Germany, Italy, Great Britain, the

United States, North Africa, Brazil, Angola, Mozambique—East Timor will have to occupy a rather low place. And all of this carries major implications in terms of the degree of investment—economic but also political, cultural, and psychological—that Portugal or the private Portuguese foundations will want to put into East Timor.

CONCLUSION

The two cases presented here—Spain in Latin America and Portugal in East Timor—are intriguing. They are intriguing for a number of reasons:

1. The common ties of language, history, and culture that exist.
2. That former colonial powers are making an effort to reassert influence in their former colonies.
3. The problems as well as opportunities that emerge out of the reestablishment of these ties, as well as the tensions between such foreign policy "newcomers" to these areas as Spain and Portugal and more established global or regional powers such as the United States, Australia, or, as in the case of East Timor, the UN.
4. Spain and Portugal have sought to reassert themselves into areas that they believe they know especially well or have a comparative advantage; but such reassertions are often expensive, involve tensions with local officials who often have long memories of past colonialism, and may not be worth the candle.
5. Intriguing also is the notion of niche foreign policy. If you are not a global superpower with vast resources and the capacity to readily project power and influence to all comers of the globe, you need to choose your spots, or niches, to exercise influence very carefully. Spain has chosen to do so in Latin America and Portugal in East Timor. But such a niche foreign policy involves risk as well as opportunity. It may be expensive; your relations with the former colonies are often fraught with both love and hate; you may come in conflict with other, even larger (U.S.) or regional (Australia) powers; and your investment in former colonies may result in greater loss than gain. As the Netherlands has recently found out in Surinam, you may go back into your former colonies with good intentions, but the former colonies are also manipulative and good at trapping you in guilt-inducing charges of colonialism, racism, and imperialism from which you cannot extricate yourself. A niche foreign policy, therefore, carries strong risks as well as opportunities; we await more comparative studies of this phenomenon.[5]

DISCUSSION TOPICS

1. Describe Spain's relations, as the former colonial power, with Latin America.
2. Why is East Timor interesting?
3. What is meant by "niche foreign policy?"

NOTES

1. Samuel P. Huntington, *The Third Wave: Democratization in the Late Twentieth Century* (Norman: University of Oklahoma Press, 1991).

2. Howard J. Wiarda, ed., *The Iberian-Latin American Connection: Implications for U.S. Foreign Policy* (Boulder, Colo.: Westview Press and the American Enterprise Institute for Public Policy Research, 1986); see also Fredrick B. Pike, *Hispanismo* (Notre Dame, Ind.: University of Notre Dame Press, 1971). For an overview of Spain's changing foreign policy, see Robert P. Clark and Michael H. Haltzel, eds., *Spain in the 1980s: The Democratic Transition and a New International Role* (Cambridge, Mass.: Ballinger, 1987).

3. This is part of a larger study on the legacy of Portuguese rule in Asia, including Japan, Macao, India (Goa), and Indonesia.

4. For the background, see Taro McGuinn, *East Timor: Island in Turmoil* (Minneapolis: Lerner Publications, 1998); For the larger study of which the East Timor section is a part, see Howard J. Wiarda, *The Legacy of Portuguese Rule in Asia: Reasserting Influence in the Post-Colonial Era* (Lisbon: Portuguese Center for Southeast Asian Studies, 2002).

5. The author has just returned from two trips (taken in 2004 and 2005) to the Dutch Caribbean, Curaçao, and Surinam, where he saw many parallels with his earlier studies of Spain in Latin America and Portugal in Asia. The research on the Dutch Caribbean will be written up in a future publication.

III

EAST/CENTRAL EUROPE
*From Communism to Democracy—
Or Something Less Than That?*

7

Marxist-Leninist Regimes in Transition

While the transition from authoritarianism to democracy in numerous countries of the globe is one of the great epochal events of the late twentieth century, surely the other is the collapse of so many Communist regimes. These two historic events are interrelated. While democracy undoubtedly had a subversive effect on various authoritarian regimes, it also had a destabilizing effect on Marxist-Leninist regimes. It took longer, however, in the latter case. Authoritarianism, as the weaker and less complete or institutionalized of the two forms, was more vulnerable and began to crumble in the late 1970s. Totalitarian Communism, stronger and more institutionalized, required another decade before it, too, began to crumble. But by the late 1980s Marxism-Leninism was also in full retreat, and the regimes established on those principles were either unraveling or undergoing profound changes, or both.

There remain, however, profound differences between the transitions from authoritarianism to democracy and the transitions from Communism perhaps to democracy but maybe to some as-yet-unknown system. For the purposes of comparative politics we need to know the distinct starting points between these two kinds of transitions (that is, the differences between authoritarianism and totalitarianism), the nature and processes of the transitions themselves (different in the two sets of countries), and the likely outcomes or end points of the transition process. Is one group of countries more likely than the other to produce democracy? If so, why?

We begin by discussing how the concepts and models developed in the field of comparative politics, if unmodified as events change and treated as permanent dogma, can not only blind us to new events in the world but can also have a major impact on foreign-policy foresightedness or the lack thereof. The fact is that we in the field of comparative politics all but completely failed to anticipate the profound changes occurring in the world of Communist nations, in large part because the models we used failed to alert us to such possibilities. That blindness also led U.S. foreign policy to flounder and improvise because it, too, was caught unprepared for the depth and profundity of the changes.

AUTHORITARIANISM, TOTALITARIANISM, AND MARXISM: HOW OUR INTELLECTUAL MODELS LED US ASTRAY

Authoritarianism, which encompasses most of the world's traditional dictatorships, is fundamentally different from totalitarianism. Caesarism, sultanism, monarchism, Bonapartism, caudilloism, and military juntas are all examples of authoritarianism. Authoritarianism is generally premodern and occurs in less-developed countries; its controls are usually limited to the military and political, and sometimes to a degree the social and economic arenas. Traditional authoritarianism lacks modern means of communication, technologically conditioned terror, modern methods of thought control, and modern systems of bureaucratic organization. Without these, it cannot become truly "total." Hence, in the contemporary context, authoritarianism is usually found in more traditional, emerging, less-mobilized societies that lack these modern systems of total control, whereas totalitarianism, which implies total domination of all areas of life, is only really possible in a modern, developed, highly technological society, such as Hitler's Germany or Stalin's Soviet Union.

The distinguishing traits of totalitarianism are as follows:

1. An official, all-encompassing ideology covering all aspects of existence and to which everyone living in the society must adhere
2. A single mass party, typically led by one man, combined with and inseparable from the governmental apparatus, and monopolizing all political activities
3. A system of terroristic police control employing modern torture and surveillance techniques
4. A technological monopoly in the hands of the party or the dictator controlling all means of mass communications, such as the print media, radio, television, and motion pictures
5. A similar monopoly, under the same control, of all means of armed combat

6. A central control and direction of the entire economy, including the bureaucratic coordination of all formerly independent interest associations, typically including all group and corporate activities[1]

In contrast, the distinguishing traits of authoritarianism, "softer" or "less total," defined systematically by Juan Linz to distinguish Franco's Spain from Hitler's Germany and Mussolini's Italy, are as follows:

1. A "mentality" (traditional Catholicism, discipline, order) rather than a full-blown ideology
2. A single party but without full-scale political mobilization
3. Leadership operating with ill-defined but often quite predictable limits
4. Limited pluralism (the church, the army) without total control of all groups
5. Dictatorship, but not total control over all aspects (culture, society, and the like)
6. Apathy, not mass indoctrination, as a way of keeping the population in check[2]

The authoritarian-totalitarian distinction is a very useful one for comparative political analysis. It enables us to distinguish clearly the more traditional forms of authoritarianism prevalent in much of the Third World from the even more nefarious totalitarianism of modern, industrialized states, of which we may have both right-wing (Nazi Germany) and left-wing (Communist Russia) examples. It also contains a dynamic factor (modernization, industrialization, technology, communications) that enables us to see how a traditional authoritarian regime (such as the Shah's Iran or Trujillo's Dominican Republic) may evolve into a near-totalitarian one. That is, by staying in power over a long period of time and turning the country's instruments of modernization (schools, media, communications, and so on) into agencies of totalitarian control, a regime may bridge the gap between authoritarianism and modern totalitarianism. We have presented authoritarianism and totalitarianism as two distinct types, but they can also be seen as constituting a continuum, with quite a number of recent authoritarian regimes seeking to use the instruments of totalitarianism and increasingly having the technological capacities to impose total control.[3]

The idea of a continuum between totalitarianism and authoritarianism also means that there are gray areas and, sometimes, mixed cases that scholars and policy makers will have to take into account. We do not have space to do a detailed, country-by-country analysis here, but we do need to be reminded that the models of totalitarianism and authoritarianism models suggested above are textbook types and that reality is always more complicated. For in much of Eastern Europe and even the Soviet Union there was somewhat greater freedom at the end and even a degree of limited pluralism that the "totalitarianism" label fails to capture. For example, in Poland, there was an underground press, the Roman Catholic Church had considerable autonomy, the opposition Solidarity movement had not been crushed, and the government was having difficulty enforcing its own will. All these factors suggest we need to be aware of the new trends and openings that were occurring even as we recognize still the utility of the totalitarianism-authoritarianism distinction.

Our main concern now, however, is with the totalitarianism phenomenon and set of traits as they continued to be practiced as matters of state policy in the Soviet Union and particularly as it was practiced in the Soviet Union and Eastern Europe. We are especially interested in how this and other interpretations prevalent in the field prevented us from accurately seeing or predicting the changes, the unraveling, implosion, and collapse of these Communist systems.

For a long time, the two major approaches to the study of Communist regimes—Marxism and the totalitarian approach—tended to disregard the inner dynamics of these societies. Scholars ignored their internal workings, the possibilities for change within these systems, and also their vulnerabilities. The Marxist ideology leads us to think that a Communist regime is the end point of the working out of the Marxist dialectical process; and once that point is reached, no further change is necessary or can even be contemplated. The dialectic, which proceeds from feudalism to capitalism to Socialism, is presumed to stop with the achievement of the highest form of Socialism: Communism. This attitude derived both from adherence to Marxist principles on the part of many intellectuals and from the widespread belief during the Great Depression of the 1930s and World War II that Socialism represented humankind's best hope. Influenced by these ideas, many Western scholars became convinced by the self-serving rationales of the Marxist-Leninist regimes themselves that they constituted the ultimate form of historical rationality. How could one talk of decline and disintegration in Marxist-Leninist regimes if the Marxist ideology posited these as the best and most progressive final conclusion of the working out of the historical dialectic?

The totalitarian model, which was the one most often used by Western political scientists, was also problematic. It suggested similarly that, once a dictatorship had fully achieved the six traits of modern totalitarianism listed earlier, no further evolution would occur. Totalitarianism was a useful model for describing the total controls of the Stalin era, but it was not as useful for describing post-Stalin changes. The totalitarian model posits that the controls are absolute and total in the society, which results in a very pessimistic forecast about the possibilities for change. Once the full gamut of totalitarian controls is in place in a Communist regime, no further development—and certainly no resistance—is thought possible. Adding to this static picture was the fact that, in the prevailing wisdom, there was no record of a Communist system, once established, ever being overthrown; that obviously made it difficult to even contemplate the possibility of a post-Communist transition.

That is why not just scholars but also policy makers were so surprised, dumbfounded, and disbelieving when the Communist regimes in Eastern Europe and the Soviet Union did in fact begin to disintegrate. It was not so much that our intelligence was faulty, although that may have been the case also, but that the basic models we use to interpret these Communist regimes failed to take account of the evolutionary forces already under way. We had little literature on the subject, no guidebooks, so to speak The models used had become reified, locked in place, ossified; they failed to take account of the dynamics within Communist regimes. Both the Marxian and totalitarian models can be faulted in this regard. Only a handful of scholars recognized the changes under way in the Soviet Union and Eastern Europe that were leading away from totalitarianism and would eventually undermine these regimes. But the changes often had little effect on policy makers, and *no one* envisioned the complete collapse of these systems. This is a good illustration of how the models fashioned by scholars of comparative politics, especially the totalitarianism model, can have a strong influence on policy, but also of how, if they become a fixed orthodoxy without constant attention to new factors, they can lead us to miss some of the most significant changes in the world.

CHANGE, VULNERABILITY, AND THE COLLAPSE OF COMMUNIST SYSTEMS

By the late 1970s and early 1980s, various cracks and fissures were beginning to appear in the Communist monolith. Some of these internal problems were beginning to show up in scholarly analyses and CIA intelligence data, but they were often discounted by higher-level analysts because of the powerful mindset underlying the totalitarianism model. We propose to discuss these changes under six headings: changes in ideological underpinnings, changes in society, the growing economic crisis, the crisis of culture, the crisis of political institutions, and changes in the international system. Taken together and cumulatively, these separate problems added up to a profound systemic crisis that led eventually to the collapse of the various Communist regimes.

Crisis of Ideology

The basic fact ideologically in these Communist systems was that almost no one believed in Marxism-Leninism anymore. Marxism-Leninism is in any case sufficiently vague that any number of interpretations of it are possible; but if the ideology is that vague and pragmatic almost anything can, and did, go. In any event, the ideology became softer and softer, and certainly among intellectuals it was increasingly rejected. Communist party hacks could still spout the ideology if it suited their purposes, and some of them still even believed in it, but it seldom served as a barrier to action or as a basis for decisions. Increasingly, as the economies of the Communist countries fell farther behind those of the West and the political systems proved inefficient and corrupt, Marxism-Leninism came to be seen as a cruel hoax. The once-utopian ideology appeared bankrupt. After a while, virtually no one adhered to the ideology; Marxism-Leninism came to be concentrated in such isolated outposts as Albania and North Korea, and among a dwindling handful of intellectuals, but it was all but forgotten in the Soviet Union and Eastern Europe. The legitimacy, ideological base, and sense that the Communist systems represented the wave of the future had eroded.[4]

Social Change

The societal changes Communist countries were going through by the 1970s were immense, and increasingly their stodgy ideology and political institutions were unable to keep pace.

First, there was a yawning generation gap between the old septu- and octogenarian rulers still in power and the younger generation of technocrats and bureaucrats who wanted to change the system *and* inherit their elders' cushy government positions. There was a second, perhaps even greater gap between this latter group and young people who had no interest in or use for the Communist ideology and who were mainly devoted to rock music (including its protest lyrics), blue jeans, Coca-Cola, consumerism (in contrast to the vision of a "new," sharing and caring Socialist man), and freedom, meaning freedom to travel to the West (prohibited under the Communist regime) or even within the country.

A second social problem was ethnic discontent, which began to be a growing issue in the 1970s and exploded in the 1980s and 1990s. The fact is that the former Soviet Union and Eastern Europe are torn by intense ethnic, religious, and nationalistic sentiments. These groups hate each other with a passion that may go back hundreds, even thousands, of years; the hatreds will not be resolved easily, if ever. Moreover, as these ethnic and religious enclaves began to pull apart, new minorities rose up even within these smaller units, and they also demanded autonomy. The Soviet Union and much of Eastern Europe ran the risk of fragmenting into ever-smaller, city-state-size units.

A third problem had to do with social change. A sizable middle class had grown up in these countries; the middle class enjoyed greater affluence and wanted greater freedom. Furthermore, the working class (remember, these are supposed to be workers' paradises) was also disenchanted, impatient, and going on strike to demand change, and strikes are not supposed to happen in Communist systems! The rigid, archaic political systems of the Communist countries were simply not equipped to handle the social pressures thrust upon them. Since these regimes had very little capacity to bend or to respond to change, they eventually collapsed in the face of popular pressures rather than adjusting and accommodating as democratic systems can do.

Economic Crisis

At the root of the Soviet Union's and Eastern Europe's troubles were their noncompetitive, nonperforming economies. Increasingly, they were falling behind the United States, Western Europe, and Japan, and they were fated to lag even farther behind. Their agriculture was inefficient and largely ignored by the central government, their industry was old-fashioned and inefficient, and their technology was the dreariest of all, which was why they kept falling still farther back. In addition, their workforce was plagued by a host of problems ranging from drunkenness to high absenteeism and low productivity.

The Soviet Union was an advanced, First World country in terms of its military structure but close to being a Third World country in other economic areas. Poverty, illiteracy, malnutrition, social backwardness—all problems identified with the Third World—were increasingly prevalent in the Soviet Union as well as in Eastern Europe. Moreover, the conditions were getting worse rather than better, and the economic gap between the Communist countries and the West was widening rather than narrowing. Something had to be done but, as with the mushrooming social problems, the Communist political systems were unequal to the task of revitalizing their economies. Something would have to give. And it did.

Crisis of Culture

The crisis of culture in the Communist states occurred at two levels. One involved the disaffection of the intellectuals—writers, artists, editors, journalists, academics, and cultural leaders in general—with the system. They became fed up and ashamed of their own countries, of the ideology and the political system. The cultural leaders grew increasingly disillusioned with the graft, the inefficiency, and, most importantly for their purposes, the lack of freedom within the system. Ultimately, they turned on it and, like Natan Sharansky, the physicist and dissident writer, led the protest and opposition movements against it.[5]

The second cultural crisis occurred at the mass level. We refer here to conditions in the Communist political culture experienced by the average men and women in the street: the disillusionment, the endless lines, the absence of goods of all sorts, the shoddy products, the depressed living standards, the resentments at the special privileges reserved for the Communist party elites, the unwillingness to sacrifice or even work for the system, the underlying bitterness and sense of powerlessness, the truly frightening rates of alcoholism, the growing desire to emigrate or else to opt out of the system. These sentiments at the mass level created a climate in which the system either had to reform itself from within or collapse.

Crisis of Political Institutions

Unfortunately, the Communist system could not reform itself from within. It had no mechanisms for doing so, or even for tapping public opinion to find out how it should change. There were no competitive elections, no referenda, no public opinion surveys on serious topics. The Soviet and Eastern European Communist parties, in addition, were old and tired bureaucracies; they consisted of unproductive time servers, old men who desired to hang on to their perquisites and privileges at all costs and who were incapable of reforming these systems from within. Similarly, the ministries and government agencies had become gigantic sinecure operations, resting places for party members and regime favorites who collected their salaries and other privileges but who seldom did any actual work. These are the hallmarks of a Third World bureaucracy and political system, not one aspiring to advanced or superpower status.

Soviet prime minister Mikhail Gorbachev tried to change these ugly features, to reform the system, while still operating within a Communist framework, but the old system was too deeply entrenched. Gorbachev faced opposition from hard-liners who thought his reforms were destroying the system (essentially correct) and from reformers who thought he was proceeding too slowly (also correct). Caught in the middle, and lacking a solid political base, Gorbachev lurched from one side to the other, appearing indecisive and ultimately failing and falling from power. The problems were so great, and the bitterness so intense, that no one leader, or even group of leaders over a longer period of time, could hope to solve the problem. Eventually, these Communist regimes, like the authoritarian regimes analyzed earlier, began to totter, unravel, or implode.

International Pressure

Adding to these domestic pressures were international ones. First came President Carter's human-rights campaign. The Carter campaign was directed more at right-wing regimes than left-wing ones, but eventually it had its effect on Communist regimes as well. Carter's message of human rights served to undermine the legitimacy of Marxist-Leninist regimes that were gross abusers of them.

Ronald Reagan's defense buildup also hastened the demise of Eastern European and Soviet Communism. Reagan's rhetoric in defense of freedom and democracy, his calling the Soviet Union an "evil empire," and his advancing the idea, through the "Reagan Doctrine," that Communism could be turned back added further delegitimizing ingredients. Perhaps most importantly, Reagan's defense buildup during the 1980s forced the Soviets to spend more on arms, reinforced the conclusion that technologically and economically the Soviets could not keep up with the West, and drove home to Soviet citizens the realization that they had a "Cadillac defense system and a dinosaur economy."[6] This pressure policy undoubtedly hastened the undoing of Communist states.

Finally, the examples of Japan, Western Europe, and the Newly Industrialized Countries (NICs) played an important role. The prosperity of Japan and Western Europe offered vivid examples of success to the Soviets, as contrasted with their own backwardness and shabbiness. Also tipping the balance was the experience of such NICs as South Korea, Taiwan, Hong Kong, Singapore, Mexico, Brazil, Argentina, and Venezuela. These examples demonstrated to the Soviets that the future of the Third World lay not in such underdeveloped, strife-torn, Soviet-sponsored, Marxist-Leninist basket cases as Cuba, Ethiopia, Angola, Mozambique, Afghanistan, and Vietnam, and not in Socialism, but in the newly prosperous NICs, which used capitalism, export-led growth, and the creation of Western markets to develop at unprecedented rates.[7]

PATTERNS OF POST-COMMUNIST CHANGE

The pressures just described, beginning in the late 1970s in such countries as Poland, Czechoslovakia, Hungary, and the Soviet Union, continued to build during the 1980s. Popular discontent began to rise, more cracks and fissures began to appear in these once monolithically totalitarian regimes, alienation grew, and the signs of a regime unraveling began to appear unmistakably. Such leaders as Lech Walesa (Poland) and Mikhail Gorbachev (Soviet Union) tried to exploit these new openings politically while also holding their nations together and taking them in new and altered directions. These were tightwire acts that ran the threat of the wire snapping, the artist losing his balance and falling off, or the entire tent coming down about their heads.

It is not our purpose here to trace the several national histories of these regimes in any detail; that can be done by following the specialized literature on Russia and Eastern Europe. Rather, our purpose is to suggest the patterns, parallels, and/or contrasts that may exist in these individual national experiences, and to compare these with other areas, to further genuinely *comparative* analysis.

The first comparison—virtually unexplored territory—is between the Russian and Eastern European experiences and the transitions to democracy in Southern Europe, Latin America, and East Asia. The Southern European comparisons are probably most instructive since Southern Europe (Greece, Portugal, Spain) and Eastern Europe (including Russia) are at roughly comparable levels of development, are both a part of Europe and therefore share certain common traditions, and have both long been considered to exist at the margins or periphery of Europe.

As a hypothesis, or, really, a series of hypotheses, Southern Europe would seem to have better possibilities for successfully making the transition from authoritarianism to democracy than Russia or some Eastern European nations do in making the transition from Communism to democracy.[8] All these propositions need to be tested empirically (by scholars of comparative politics), but let us here at least state the dimensions of the issue and the paths along which future research could be directed:

1. The political culture of Southern Europe had already shifted to support of democracy at the time, in the mid-1970s, when the political transition began; Eastern Europe lacked this long preparation time and the groundswell of change in attitudes that had occurred in Spain, Portugal, and Greece.
2. Greece, Spain, and Portugal all had considerable prior democratic traditions and institutions on which to reconstruct democracy; those features were either lacking or not so strong in Eastern Europe, which had to build democracy from scratch.
3. Spain and Portugal, and to a lesser extent Greece, bridged the transition to democracy during a time of relative economic growth and prosperity, which helped ease the transition process; Eastern Europe undertook its transition during hard economic times.
4. In its transition Southern Europe received major financial and political support from the United States and the EC; it is not certain if Eastern Europe or Russia will continue to enjoy the advantages of such strong international support.

5. At the time the transition began, civil society (trade unions, political parties, interest groups of various sorts) seemed to be considerably more developed in Southern Europe than in most of Eastern Europe.
6. In Southern Europe, social and economic welfare and safety-net features were also, compared with Eastern Europe, already quite well developed and in place at the time the often disruptive transitions began.
7. In Southern Europe the social pacts between labor, employers, and government enabled the *political* transition to be carried out successfully without disruptive labor strife (Portugal was a major exception); in Eastern Europe economic, social, cultural, and political transformations are occurring all at once rather than in sequence, overloading the circuits and creating the potential in some countries for major systems upheaval.
8. The Southern European nations, except possibly Spain, either had less ethnic or nationality strife or had largely solved these problems earlier in their histories. In contrast, ethnic strife threatens to tear some Eastern European nations and some of the new republics of the former Soviet Union apart and to undermine their possibilities for successful transition to democracy. Many scholars see ethnic nationalism not just in Eastern Europe and Russia but in the Middle East, Southeast Asia, and sub-Saharan Africa as one of the next major subject areas in comparative politics.
9. While Southern Europe often had autarkic, inefficient, or quasi-mercantilist markets and economies, at least they had markets. In contrast, Russia and much of Eastern Europe (Hungary, the Czech Republic, and Poland excepted) had virtually no experience at all with markets as a modern economy. This difference (without a functioning economy it's all but impossible to have a functioning democracy) may have been the most important.

These factors suggest that the transitions to democracy in Southern Europe will prove to have been smoother, easier, and more successful than is likely to be the case for Eastern Europe and Russia. Future research will have to confirm or disprove these hypotheses.

A second approach (in addition to the Southern/Eastern Europe comparison) is to compare the quite distinct experiences of the various formerly Marxist-Leninist regimes themselves. Six categories of regimes may be identified, although some subgroups may also be discerned.

1. *Russia.* The U.S.S.R. (now Russia) is sui generis, unique, because of its immense size, large population, vast resources, and long-standing great-power status. None of the other Communist or formerly

Communist countries (except possibly China, but more on that later) has these distinctive features. Thus, while we want to facilitate and encourage comparison, we must also recognize that on several dimensions Russia is distinct, a category all by itself. Both economically and politically, Russia's transition looks very precarious.

2. *The Commonwealth of Independent States (CIS).* Today's Russia is only one (the biggest) part of the former Soviet Union; other areas (Georgia, Ukraine, Belarus, Transaucusia, Central Asia) have broken away to form independent states. Many of these are less developed economically and less well institutionalized than Russia; their democratic prospects, therefore, are even more precarious.

3. *Central and Baltic Europe.* This category includes Poland, Slovakia, the Czech Republic, Hungary, Estonia, Latvia, and Lithuania. These are the countries that, it is hypothesized, have the best possibilities for successfully making the post-Communist transition. They are comparatively well developed, have a better infrastructure, have fewer ethnic divisions, and are geographically closer to and in a position to benefit from the powerful German economy and from broader European prosperity; also, their political culture is less fractious and divisive.

4. *Southeastern Europe.* This area, commonly referred to as the Balkans, includes Romania, Bulgaria, the former Yugoslavia, and Albania. The possibilities here for a successful democratic transition are, except in Slovenia, less bright. These are comparatively less developed countries economically; they have weak political infrastructure; they are torn by severe ethnic, religious, and political conflict; they are farther from the main centers of European prosperity; their Communist *apparatchik* and secret police have not been entirely eliminated; and their political culture is deeply divided and fractious.

5. *Third World countries that have abandoned Marxism-Leninism.* Examples include Angola, Ethiopia, Mozambique, and Nicaragua. The problems for most of these countries are that they are so poor, have so few developed institutions, have so few resources, are so deeply divided politically, and are so far from the main centers of economic prosperity that no matter what they do, or what *systems* (Marxism, democracy) they opt for, they will still be poor and backward. Successful transitions to democracy *may* occur in these countries but they will be very difficult processes.

6. *Marxist-Leninist countries that have not begun a transition to democracy.* This category includes China, North Korea, Vietnam, and Cuba. Of these four, North Korea and Cuba remain isolated and inward looking and have not yet begun the transition to either free markets or democracy. In contrast, China and Vietnam have in part abandoned

Marxism in the economic sphere even while retaining a Marxist-Leninist system of political controls. Both countries are changing, however, and it will be interesting to see if greater economic freedom also produces greater political freedom.

Utilizing these categories, at least three types of comparisons may thus be suggested: comparisons among countries within one of the given categories, comparisons among countries in two or more categories, and comparisons among non-Communist countries in Asia, Latin America, or Southern Europe undergoing comparable transitions.

POLICY REFORMS

At the macro level, most of the Marxist-Leninist regimes (actual or former) surveyed here are going through major changes. They are making fundamental systemic decisions: whether they will be Socialist or capitalist, authoritarian or democratic, or some combination of these. Even while engaging in these major, wrenching, system-transforming debates, however, they are also being called on by their populations to solve pressing, immediate social and economic issues. The question is: Can these countries, while deciding the major systems debates, also provide the basic goods and services for which their peoples are clamoring? And how do these two levels interrelate? The issues, we have already seen, are very difficult and complex; at this stage no one is certain if both levels of problems —macro and micro—can be resolved at once.

Social Policy

Under their old Communist regimes, leaders in the former Soviet Union and Eastern Europe would sometimes grudgingly admit that their peoples did not, by Western standards, enjoy complete political freedom and liberty. But, they would counter, these are only "bourgeois freedoms"; real freedom comes in the form of economic and social progress for the masses. And by these standards, they would argue, Marxism-Leninism has done very well.

However, now that the old Communist leadership has been ousted and we are gaining access to archives and information previously unavailable, we are learning more facts about these regimes. The truth is that many of the supposed social programs and accomplishments of these regimes were a cruel hoax. In education, housing, and health care—those policy areas in which Marxist-Leninist regimes had staked their claim to major progress—most of these countries were steadily falling farther behind rather than moving ahead. True, there were minimum levels of education for most people; few people starved to death; health care provided the basics; and there were relatively few homeless people. Above the barest minimum standards, however, Marxist-Leninist regimes failed to deliver; and in fact the condition of their people—their standard of living and life expectancy—have all been in decline. Moreover, in many areas, things have worsened since the collapse of Communism.

The housing shortage is acute in both Russia and Eastern Europe. Families must double, triple, or quadruple up in small rooms; the waiting time for apartments often stretches into years; the existing housing stock is of generally of shoddy construction and deteriorating; and there are few alternative sources of housing. Medical care has also slipped badly, particularly in rural areas often characterized by poverty, malnutrition, and declining life expectancy; but even in the cities hospitals are woefully overcrowded; medicine and trained personnel are frequently in short supply; and there are severe lags in technology and equipment.

The food situation was often similarly bleak, characterized by lagging production, backward agriculture, poor distribution, severe shortages, except when it came to the Communist Party elite. Virtually all goods—such as clothes, food, or hardware—were often unavailable, in short supply, or of poor quality. Now that many of the economic restrictions of the former communist regimes have been abolished, foods and other goods are available but prices are high, beyond the reach of most people. Similarly, the once-vaunted educational systems had also slipped backward under Communism, with rising illiteracy, shortages of educational materials, and a lack of the computer and technological equipment that holds the key to the future. A decade and a half after Communism's fall, the educational systems are still often in decline.

Evidence has poured in that the high literacy, housing, and health-care figures that the Soviets and East European Communist regimes presented to the outside world were "cooked." They were made up, exaggerated, or deliberately falsified. The statistics were often invented so as to make the Communist countries look better, both to their own people and to the outside world. By now, however, with Russia and Eastern Europe opening up to foreign visitors, the depressed conditions in many areas are visible for all to see. Many areas, particularly in rural regions of Russia and Eastern Europe, are closer to Third World living standards than to the prosperity of the West.

The Communist regimes also claimed that in their supposed workers' paradise there was no pollution, no nuclear contamination, no environmental degradation. But the reality is that there are many areas of Russia and Eastern Europe that are unlivable, environmental disaster areas. Much of the vegetation is dead or dying; the buildings are caked in poisonous soot; runoff from chemical and nuclear facilities mingles with the water supply; and the people—sometimes neglected by their own governments—are afflicted with severe lung diseases and cancers. Because of poor or nonexistent quality controls, bad planning, and shoddy building materials, dozens of Chernobyl-like nuclear disasters, where the reactor melts down and explodes, spreading nuclear pollutants for hundreds of miles, may be waiting to happen. In addition, Russian and many East European smokestacks are still pouring pollutants into the air in unregulated and irresponsible ways. It is pure myth that these Marxist-Leninist regimes were uniquely environmentally sensitive; indeed, their records on environmental issues were far worse than in the West.

Meanwhile, the social indicators that point to grave problems in Russia and some areas of Eastern Europe are way up: wife and child beating, alcoholism, crime, antisocial behavior, and, perhaps not paradoxically, church attendance. At the same time, life expectancy in Russia and Southeast Europe has fallen dramatically from 72 to about 55, as compared with near-80 in the developed Western nations and Japan. Clearly, these countries have a long way to go to solve their many social problems. And the difficult social circumstances also make the establishment of democracy and a functioning economy that much more difficult.

Economic Policy

It is now all but universally agreed that Marxist-Leninist economic systems are incapable of producing sustained growth in the modern world. Marxism-Leninism may be a useful system of establishing *political control* in countries in the early stages of development (China, Vietnam, the Soviet Union), but as a system of economic organization it is woefully inadequate, and as countries modernize and need to adapt to new technologies and overall globalization, the situation only gets worse. Marxist-Leninist systems cannot consistently product goods and services; they cannot distribute goods efficiently; they have no way of determining prices and wages rationally; they lead to shortages and inefficiencies as well as corruption; they have no way of telling what their own people want; and they are notoriously unable to adapt to new demands and technologies. Belatedly realizing these shortcomings, the former Marxist-Leninist regimes of Russia, Eastern Europe, and the Commonwealth of Independent States (CIS) have rushed to embrace capitalism. At the same time, the few remaining Marxist-Leninist countries like China and Vietnam have sought to instigate capitalist reforms even while retaining autocratic, Marxist-Leninist political controls. But we need to know what form this capitalism has taken, how complete are the changes, and whether it is possible to have free markets in the economic sphere but not political freedom.

The issues are as much political as economic. On the economic front, Russia, the CIS, and much of Eastern Europe lack the capital, the investment, the physical plant, the skills, the entrepreneurship, the technology, the banking system, the stock markets, the financial institutions, the know-how, and the overall infrastructure to make a market system work. Only a market mechanism has the capacity to adjust productivity, set wages, determine prices, mobilize capital, and adjust rapidly to make a modern economy function. These are the basics; of course, once you have the basics in place, you also need an efficient, democratic government to play a strong regulatory role and to provide for social welfare and equity issues. The problem is that Russia, the CIS, and much of Eastern Europe, a decade after the fall of Communism, still do not have these basics in place, so their regulatory and welfare roles also lag. Making the transition from Marxism-Leninism to a successful market economy thus involves a host of thorny issues. It is much more complicated than either the countries involved or those who have sought to assist them thought, and the transitions in all these countries are still not complete.

The problem is that the economic issues involve one rationality, the political processes involve another, and though both are logical they are at the same time directly contradictory. On the economic side, everyone agrees that the former or still existing Communist countries need to introduce market reforms and downsize and privatize their inefficient, bloated, often corrupt state industries. But from a political point of view, that is far less obvious. That is why economic reform, if it occurs too fast or too completely, could be the Achilles' heel of the transition process. A lot of powerful people in Russia, the CIS, and Eastern Europe have a strong stake in things as they are. The stakes include jobs, patronage, perquisites, spoils, access to wealth and money, and political power and support. Reducing or eliminating the state sector—and doing so is rational and reasonable in economic terms—would upset all that and undermine the basis of the leaders' political support. Hence, for many presidents, party officials, government bureaucrats, farm and factory managers, and regional or local officials, thoroughgoing economic reform is the last thing they want, since it undermines the basis of their patronage support and, hence, of their power.

The situation is parallel to that in Latin America and other developing nations, which are similarly under pressure to privatize and reduce the state sector. The difference is that, whereas in many developing nations the state sector may be only 30–40 percent of GNP, in Russia, the CIS, and Eastern Europe the state monopolized 80–90 percent of GNP. Hence, in Latin America and other developing areas not only is the problem of state downsizing, difficult though it is, smaller and more manageable than it is in the former Communist countries, Latin America and these other developing nations (South Korea, Taiwan, Indonesia, etc.) already had a small but potent private sector on which they could build. The former Communist countries, in contrast, had almost no preexisting private sector and, therefore, must start from scratch. For these ex-Marxist-Leninist regimes, the stakes (a *huge* public sector) are higher; the private sector base, almost nonexistent; and the risks to political leaders whose base of support and power lies in all those public-sector patronage positions, far greater. Not surprisingly, the pace of economic reform and state downsizing in the former Communist countries has been slower than expected and may, in some countries, prove unsuccessful. Economic rationality in these countries often runs head on into equally powerful political rationality.

Another problem is the type of capitalism that is emerging in the former Communist countries. It is called "robber-baron capitalism" and is reminiscent of early exploitive capitalism in the United States and other countries. Almost nowhere in Russia, the CIS, or Eastern Europe does one find small entrepreneurs opening up hardware stores and other small businesses, putting people to work, paying salaries, benefiting the economy, and eking out a small profit. Rather, capitalism mainly takes the form of present or former Communist party officials, government officials, and other insiders using their contacts and privileged position within the system to sell off former state-owned properties (again, 80–90 percent of the economy), to gain enormously advantageous government contracts, or to reap the profits for themselves of so-called privatization. This is not a free-market system that any of us would recognize; instead, this is rip-off capitalism in which a handful of individuals are becoming enormously rich through their special access to government wealth and favors but are creating few jobs and not benefiting the economy as a whole.

This is a harsh condemnation; we need, therefore, to distinguish carefully between countries. Russia fits this model, as do other countries of the former Soviet Union. The Balkan countries, Romania and Bulgaria, also fit this model. Poland, Slovakia (formerly part of Czechoslovakia, now independent), and Slovenia (formerly part of Yugoslavia, now independent) are more of a mix: part robber-baron capitalism and part entrepreneurial capitalism that is closer to what is generally found in the West. The Czech Republic, the Baltics, and Hungary tip the other way: mainly an emerging Western-style capitalism but with worrisome remnants of the robber style. Of course, *all* these economies are now a mix of old Communist ways and newer capitalistic ones but, as indicated, in varying degrees. Moreover, the trends seem to be toward entrepreneurialism and more open-market systems, but slowly and with great agony as jobs in the old statist economy shrink but before new ones in the private sector are created.

Given these conditions, the questions become: How much should the United States and Western Europe assist or invest in Russia, the CIS, or Eastern Europe if they know a sizable share of the investment funds will be lost or squandered on patronage deals? What is the capacity of these countries to use the aid and investment in useful, constructive ways? Can the Western nations assist the formerly Communist nations in this difficult transition period, or must these nations reform themselves first and then, with a stronger base to build on, look to outside assistance? The answers, if you are an investor, are: You try to distinguish between countries as above, looking for good opportunities rather than being stuck with bad ones; you want to get in on the ground floor so that, if things work out well, you have a head start; and you look for guarantees from the Treasury Department or the international lending agencies (World Bank, International Monetary Fund) that will protect your investment. And if you are a Western foreign-policy or government official, you may want to invest in Russia and the other formerly Communist countries even if the economic prospects are not good, because of overriding political and strategic considerations: an economically distressed, politically unstable Russia, Ukraine, or Belarus, with thousands of nuclear weapons, could be dangerous.

Political Change

In some aspects, the formerly Communist regimes of Russia, the CIS, and Eastern Europe are facing the same issues of political transition as the countries analyzed in the previous chapters that evolved from right-wing authoritarianism. Should they be federal or unitary systems? Should they be presidential systems, parliamentary systems, or some combination of both? How much freedom should be allowed to dissident groups? How much to former or present Communists who want to turn the clock back to older, repressive, but what are widely thought of as stable, more settled ways? Should there be an established religion or complete freedom for all groups? How big a role should the state play in the economy? In social issues? How much autonomy can be allowed to ethnic or nationality enclaves who may push for complete independence?

None of these is an easy issue, and some of them have the potential to derail the possibilities for successful democratic transitions, as for example on the issue of federalism versus unitarism. In the United States, Australia, and other well-established federal systems, the issue between central and state or regional power—always a dynamic relationship—has been largely settled in the sense that no state or region wants to break up the Union, as in the American Civil War. But in countries like the former Soviet Union, the former Yugoslavia, and the former Czechoslovakia (the use of the word "former" gives the point away), where ethnic, religious, nationality, and regional tensions and conflicts abound—and frequently all of these combined—and where the long-simmering tensions have produced rebellion, civil war, and powerful separatist movements, these are hot, burning issues. Much is at stake, including the very survivability of the nation itself. In the previous decade, the former Soviet Union has split up into separate nations consisting of Russia and the various entities of the CIS, and in many of these the process of ethnic and national disintegration may well continue. The former Yugoslavia has also split up into at least four independent nations, at least two of which are wracked by conflict and civil war. The former Czechoslovakia has peacefully (but not without anger) divided into the separate states of the Czech Republic and Slovakia. In many of these, as well as in countries not yet mentioned such as Romania, Hungary, and Ukraine, there are other separatist movements that have not succeeded in splitting the country but are nevertheless divisive and make successful transitions to democracy difficult.

Since Marxism-Leninism, on one side of the political spectrum, and authoritarianism, on the other, have largely lost their legitimacy, democracy is the only acceptable form of government. But in many of the former Communist regimes, "democracy" sometimes takes strange forms, and its institutions are not yet well institutionalized. Democracy is often seen as a patronage system or as a means of using public office or access for private gain. As a result, political parties remain weak; pluralism is only in its early stages; and government agencies serve more to benefit those who work in them and those willing to pay to gain special favors than they do the general public. Russia, the CIS, and Eastern Europe have now all had elections that could be called democratic, but the institutional infrastructure of democracy is still quite weak.

Below these institutional issues may be an even deeper problem: changing the values and political culture of these former Communist countries. Some of their institutions are now formally democratic, but what about fundamental underlying attitudes? Have Russia, the CIS, and Eastern Europe developed the "civic culture" (see the introduction of this book) that is the only basis on which democracy can survive? Have they yet acquired the sense of tolerance, the respect for other opinions, the willingness to give as well as take, the basic trust, the sense of responsible government and loyal opposition, the widespread respect for human rights, the willingness to listen and take advice as well as give it out—in short, all the elements of a "political culture" of democracy? Often the nastiness, divisiveness, and personal character of the debates, to say nothing of high levels of corruption, brutishness, and orchestrated political violence, leave observers with the sense that basic attitudes have only marginally changed since the fall of Communism. Recall that in Southern Europe the underlying society and political culture had changed even while the old regimes were still in power; but in Russia, the CIS, and Eastern Europe the fall of Communism was abrupt and is still undergoing a slow transformation. And until the political culture changes, which may require two or three generations, changes in institutions are likely to remain quite superficial.

TOWARD THE FUTURE

The collapse of Marxism-Leninism and the disintegration of the Communist systems of the Soviet Union and Eastern Europe constitute one of the epochal changes of the late twentieth century. These transformations have ended the Cold War, fundamentally altered the face of the globe, ushered in some truly pathbreaking events, and forced the United States as well as other nations to rethink virtually every previous assumption of foreign policy. They have also undermined Marxism-Leninism as a possible alternative political system. Scholars of comparative politics at one time suggested that there are three worlds of development: a First World of modern, industrial, democratic nations; a Second World of industrialized Communist nations; and a Third World of developing nations. But now the Second World is dead and gone, and so comparative politics must rethink its categories as well.

Communism may be dead as an ideology and form of political system, but in most of the former Communist countries democracy is not yet well established. Their transitions are not yet completed, their new democratic regimes not yet consolidated. So far, democracy and free markets appear to be the only options open, but these newer systems are only weakly established and not yet well institutionalized. In Russia, the CIS, and Eastern Europe many necessary structural reforms have yet to be made—of the educational systems, of agriculture, of government institutions, of finances, of political attitudes, and so on—before democracy can be said to be effectively functioning.[9]

Once again, the contrast with Southern Europe is striking. In Greece, Portugal, and Spain, no one doubted that, once authoritarianism ended, democracy would be the preferred option and outcome. No other alternative was possible, certainly not one with the legitimacy and popular support to govern. But in the former Communist countries the outcome may be less certain. Any one of a number of possibilities remains. In countries lacking established democratic institutions, with little or no experience in democratic government, absent democratic political culture, and with immense social and economic problems, a variety of outcomes is possible. Uncertain and sometimes violent political conditions can produce a wide range of types of regimes.

Hence, in the formerly Communist countries of Russia, the CIS, and Eastern Europe, what can we expect? The answer is not clear, which in itself is worrisome. Five distinct possibilities as well as various combinations of them seem possible. First is a successful transition to Western-style democracy and integration into European economic and political organizations. Though not without continuing problems, the Czech Republic, Slovakia, Hungary, Poland, Slovenia, and the Baltic Republics (Estonia, Latvia, Lithuania) seem likely to continue moving in this direction. A second option is the *formal* adoption of democratic procedures but only limited implementation of genuine democracy: Russia, Romania, Bulgaria, Belarus, and the Ukraine, may fall into this category. A third option is a reversion to full-scale Communism: no country has yet gone this route, although some have elected "reform" Communist governments, and in many countries the nostalgia for the stability and certainty, especially of jobs and wages, under Communism is strong.

A fourth possibility is a new authoritarian regime, different from the old Communism but with the army, secret police, and old Communist Party apparatus and bureaucracy continuing to rule in an authoritarian fashion. Most of the states that were once a part of the Soviet Union but are now loosely organized as the CIS fall in this category. Fifth, and finally, is the possibility for national breakdown, disintegration, civil war, and/or such widespread violence that effective government is impossible: Serbia, Bosnia, and Chechnya (a part of Russia) are the major candidates in this category. Keep in mind there could also be a succession from one to another or an alternation between these several types of regimes.

The outcome in regard to the former Communist countries is thus far less certain and predictable than it was in Southern Europe. In Russia, the CIS, and Eastern Europe there are still major *system* issues that need to be decided. The often unsettled conditions make predictions harder; moreover, the predominance of the totalitarianism and Marxist models for a long time made it difficult for scholars of comparative politics to see the changes occurring in these Marxist-Leninist regimes or to construct new models to help us understand the processes of transition. The result is that the field of comparative politics lacks both a model of post-Communist change and a set of categories to help us understand the often mixed, frequently turbulent, crazy-quilt patterns and halfway houses (between Communism and democracy) that are emerging. There is obviously room for a great deal of research yet on these post-Communist transitions.

DISCUSSION TOPICS

1. Describe totalitarianism.
2. Describe authoritarianism.
3. Why is it harder to transition from totalitarianism than from authoritarianism?

NOTES

1. This is the classic model of Carl. J. Friedrich and Zbigniew Brzezinski, *Totalitarian Dictatorship and Autocracy* (New York: Praeger, 1962); see also Hannah Arendt, *The Origins of Totalitarianism* (New York: Harcourt, Brace, Jovanovich,1951). It should be said that I use the totalitarianism-authoritarianism distinction in the classic political-science sense, not in the more ideological, political, and foreign-policy sense later employed by UN ambassador Jeanne Kirkpatrick.

2. Juan Linz, "An Authoritarian Regime: Spain," in *Cleavages, Ideologies, and Party Systems*, ed. Erik Allardt and Yrjo Littunen, 291–342 (Helsinki: Westmarck Society, X, 1964).

3. Howard J. Wiarda, *Dictatorship and Development: The Methods of Control in Trujillo's Dominican Republic* (Gainesville: University of Florida Press, 1968).

4. Vladimir Tismaneanu, *The Poverty of Utopia: The Crisis of Marxist Ideology in Eastern Europe* (New Brunswick, N.J.: Transaction Press, 1988).

5. See "The Vulnerabilities of Communist Regimes," special issue, *World Affairs* 150 (Winter 1987–1988).

6. The analysis, language, and assessment of the Reagan presidency in this light comes from former Arkansas governor and Democratic President Bill Clinton, in *The Washington Post* October 17, 1991, A4.

7. Once when we were participating together in a conference in Singapore, Soviet expert Jerry Hough made national headlines by stating that Singapore had actually won the Cold War. By this he meant that NICs like Singapore had demonstrated to the Soviet Union that capitalism, not Socialism, was the wave of the future in the Third World. Naturally, it was flattering to small Singapore to be told that it had determined the Cold War.

8. For a general discussion, see Howard J. Wiarda, "Transitions to Democracy in Comparative Perspective," *PAWSS Perspectives* 1 (December 1990): 25–31.

9. Nicholas Eberstadt, "Health, Nutrition and Literacy under Communism," *Journal of Economic Growth* 2 (Second Quarter 1987): 11–22.

8

Defining the Borders of the New Europe

Question: "Where does Europe end?"
Answer: "Somewhere south of Vienna."

—Old Austrian saying

A new curtain, a "Golden Curtain," is being drawn across the heart of Europe. It stretches from the Arctic Circle in the north, thus including Finland and the Baltic countries, to the Adriatic coast in the south, thus incorporating Slovenia and Croatia but not for now the other countries of the former Yugoslavia. The new curtain may be more flexible and permeable, with less barbed wire, than the old Iron Curtain—and there are a number of "halfway houses" as well as some "disputed territories" along the border—but of the fact a new kind of wall is going up, whose barriers as well as "crossing guards" (the Schengen immigration rules) may be almost as strict, there can be no doubt. The drawing of this new curtain is giving rise to cries that a "New Yalta" is being created, one that includes some but freezes out other countries and condemns them to a future of backwardness and underdevelopment.[1]

This new curtain may be defined as incorporating into the European community those countries that are "making it," most obviously via NATO and EU enlargement but encompassing other criteria as well, and those that are not. The *stated* criteria sound institutional and perhaps rather dry, and there are all those NATO expectations of military interoperability and the eighty thousand (!) requirements of the EU's *Acquis Communautaire* to which aspirant countries must conform. But the final decisions on who gets in and who does not depend, ultimately, on political criteria. And, increasingly, those are being defined, informally if not yet spoken of publicly, along cultural, religious, ethnic, linguistic, and political-cultural as well as socioeconomic and strategic lines. Now that the old and somewhat artificial barriers of the Iron Curtain have fallen, Europe is once again wrestling with the question of where "Western Civilization" begins and, even more importantly for our purposes, where it ends. In theory, no one is left out; in practice the hurdles and barriers are again becoming harder.

In the process, all the old cultural, geographic, religious, historical, and ethnic reckonings, sentiments, biases, and dividing lines of the past are again coming into play. The end of the Cold War *might* have inspired a reappraisal of what Europe once was and could become—and perhaps it did in the heady, hopeful years of the early 1990s—but at this stage the process seems to have run its course and the gates are being closed once again. Europe cannot admit this openly, of course (and slaps down Austria's Jorg Haider when he has the effrontery to do so), but concerning the fact that such attitudes are being resurrected, we should not have illusions. History may have "ended" in terms of the great ideological and "systems" debates of the past, but it is also alive and well and being resurrected in the debate over where Europe's new boundaries are to be drawn. Both the elites (as exemplified by the EU) and the public have their views (not always exactly corresponding) on these matters, and the result is a dynamic political process that often has only limited relation to the formal requirements of memberships in the twin European "clubs" of NATO and the EU.

As Europe rediscovers its pre–Cold War and even ancient history, old and venerable debates and conflicts are being resurrected, often in new, sometimes shockingly new, forms. Where did the ancient Greek and Roman influences (the earliest definition of "Western civilization") end? How far did Christianity extend to the east and south, and where does Western Christianity, in both its Protestant and Catholic forms, bump up against Eastern Orthodoxy on the one hand and the Islamic borders of the old Ottoman empire on the other? Where are the outer limits of historic, "Western," German, Scandinavian, Polish, and Hapsburg (in the form of the old Austro-Hungarian Empire) influence, and where do these start impinging on the similarly historic Russian, Serbian, and Muslim or Ottoman lands? The questions being asked include: Are the Easterners (Russians, Georgians, Ukrainians, Belarussians) and "Southeasterners" (the Balkans, Turks) like us, do they share our values, are they "civilized"? Can they assimilate; can we absorb their immigrants; will they drag us down? In other words, beneath the formal and often arcane discussion about who will be invited to join NATO and the EU in the next rounds is an even more fundamental, ancient, and venerable question of how far east and south Europe goes and Western "civilization" extends. And who, therefore, in modern national terms, is included or excluded: Belarussians, Ukrainians, Hungarians, Georgians, Croats, Serbs, Montenegrans, Bosnians, Poles, Kosovars, Macedonians, Moravians, Romanians, Bulgarians, Georgians, Turks, Czechs, Slovaks, Slovenes, Croats, Russians, Estonians, Latvians, Lithuanians, whom?

The old Iron Curtain has been dismantled; I even have a piece of it in the form of a strand of barbed wire, a gift from a Hungarian general and former graduate student at the National War College. But "the wall" remains; it has just moved a ways east, and different criteria are being used to define it. It is a cultural wall, a religious wall, and a socio-psychological wall as well as an economic and strategic one. In this chapter, therefore, we seek to identify where and how these new lines are being drawn, what criteria are being discussed at street level or de facto being used in addition to the formally stated ones, and, ultimately, where the new, often informal, boundaries of Europe are being drawn.

DEFINITIONS OF EUROPE

The definitions of "Europe" and its distinguishing characteristics have varied over time and in terms of the criteria employed.[2] Defined purely in geographical terms, the continent of Europe stretches all the way from the Atlantic Ocean easterly to the Ural Mountains, thus cutting Russia in half and causing immense confusion, not least in Russia itself. North and south, its borders are often said to be the Arctic Ocean and the Caspian, Black, and Mediterranean seas, but that also leaves a lot of uncertainty regarding the Balkans, Moldova, Georgia, and Transcaucasia, and the southern (and Islamic) members of the CIS.

But there are other definitions of Europe besides the geographical. Recently, Greece, which thinks of itself as the font of Western civilization, has raised a storm of protest in the EU over that body's decision to found a Museum of Europe whose exhibits begin not with antiquity but with Charlemagne's empire in the ninth century, which presumably set Europe on the path of unification, the main theme of the museum. The Greeks argue instead that Ulysses is European culture's founding myth and are supporting an alternative exhibit sponsored by the Council of Europe that promotes that view. Meanwhile, EU officials at the Museum of Europe respond that (1) Greek civilization failed to promote a larger *European* consciousness, and (2) both ancient Greece and Rome discriminated sharply between citizens and slaves as well as outsiders ("barbarians") and, therefore, were not inclusionary or multicultural. One can imagine the politically correct arguments to which this dispute gives rise and the divisions (elites versus masses, EU officialdom versus man on the street, intellectuals versus Joe citizens, and leftists versus rightists) that will form. Meanwhile, though, the Greeks threatened to veto the museum project, and Italy remained silent.[3]

In Roman times the line between "civilization" and "barbarism" was roughly the Danube and Rhine Rivers; anything north and east of that was considered uncivilized. Hence, we have another division across Europe, a north–south one, that persisted into more recent times in the division between the Catholic, Mediterranean, and less-developed south versus the Protestant, developed, and industrialized north.

It took several centuries after the fall of Rome for "Europe" to be reconstituted, this time in the form of Charlemagne's (crowned A.D. 800) Holy Roman Empire. Charlemagne had bridged the Rhine and Danube to extend civilization both north and east; his kingdom encompassed a territory roughly coterminous with that of the original members of the EEC (France, Germany, Italy, the Benelux countries) which was also seen in a sense as constituting "Europe": certainly that's how Museum of Europe officials see it. The empire was really a decentralized collection of states (recall Voltaire's much-later quip that it was neither Holy nor Roman nor an empire) and its borders fluctuated over the centuries; nevertheless, even in medieval times there was a sense that the empire and its domains constituted Europe" Western Christendom or, for short, "the West."

Meanwhile, other, not necessarily just territorial, dividing lines had been and were being strung across Europe. There was the split between the Western Catholic Church centered in Rome and with Charlemagne, his successors, and the Holy Roman Empire as its leaders and territorial base, and the Eastern Orthodox Church centered in Byzantium. By the ninth and tenth centuries, Catholicism had spread north and east into Central and Eastern Europe (Croatia, Slovenia, Austria, the Czech lands, and Germany had been Christianized earlier)—Hungary (A.D. 1000), Poland (A.D. 966), and Lithuania (A.D. 1386). Meanwhile, orthodoxy had virtually contemporaneously spread north from Byzantium into Serbia (A.D. 850), Bulgaria (A.D. 865), Moldova and Ukraine (A.D. 972), Georgia, Belarus, and Russia (A.D. 996).

Religion was at this time the main carrier of culture and civilization; from this time, Central and Eastern Europe[4]—Catholic, historically conservative, eventually nationalistic (remarkably similar to Spain and Portugal in their political-cultural aspects, on the other "periphery" of Europe)—looked mainly to the West for its political, economic, religious, and cultural guidelines, even while recognizing what we would call its increasingly "less developed" socioeconomic status. At the same time, "the East" (Eastern Orthodoxy) took its spiritual lead from Constantinople but its political leadership (including—relevant to modern times—Serbia) from

Kiev/Russia. The rise and spread of Islam would provide still a third religious dividing line across southeast Europe, and in the sixteenth century the Protestant Reformation provided yet another divisive element. By the end of the century, however, most of Eastern/Central Europe had been restored to Catholicism via the Counter-Reformation, which had been successful in Central Europe but not in northern Germany, the Netherlands, and Scandinavia. Over time, the différences between Protestant and Catholic Christianity in East/Central Europe would fade but the Catholic-Orthodox, Catholic-Muslim, and Orthodox-Muslim chasms would remain wide.

War, invasion, and empire provide still other ways of defining (and dividing) Europe. Historically, Eastern and Central Europe have been subject to repeated invasions from east and west: Huns, Mongolians, Magyars, Tatars, Russians, Ottoman Turks, among others from the east; Germans, Swedes, Poles, French, Italians, Danes from the west. Meanwhile, although their histories are largely unknown to students of Western history, several indigenous empires were established in Eastern/Central Europe: the vast Polish-Lithuanian empire of the fourteenth and early fifteenth centuries that covered much of Eastern and Central Europe (including large swathes of Belarus and the western Ukraine), the Magyar empire of the later fifteenth century also encompassing much of Central Europe, including western Ukraine and northwestern Romania (Transylvania), and then the rise of the Austro-Hungarian empire in the fifteenth and sixteenth centuries, which encompassed most of the present-day, acceding countries to NATO and the EU, including, for our purposes, Hungary, the Czech Republic, Slovakia, Croatia, Slovenia, and parts of Romania and Serbia, to say nothing of Spain, the Low Countries, large parts of Italy, and Latin America too.

These empires mainly identified themselves with the West and Western Christendom; they saw their role in part as "civilizing" the peoples and migrants from the east; and they also came to view themselves as "on the frontiers of" and as the bulwarks and the "defenders of Western civilization" against the Tatars, Ottomans, Russians, and others. Meanwhile, as the best book on the subject makes clear, Eastern/Central Europe began to develop a self-identity as part of the West but also as a buffer, "Middle Europe," to use the German term, lying between, territorially, its two great and sometimes threatening neighbors: Germany to the west and Russia to the east.[5] This self-identity was submerged for a time under Soviet occupation; it resurfaced for a brief period immediately after the collapse of the Soviet Union, and it now seems to be fading once again as East/Central Europe is drawn inexorably into the Western (EU, NATO) orbit.

In more modern times, Renaissance Europe included, although belatedly in the case of some countries, most of the Western, Northeastern, and

Central European countries but excluded Russia and much of the Balkans. However, both Peter the Great and Catherine the Great sought, only partly successfully, to "Westernize" Russia. Napoleon abolished the Holy Roman Empire and, in an effort to extend his own power and Europe's frontiers, sent his armies deep into Russia, where they were eventually overcome by distance, vastness, and inadequate supply lines. Hitler's Third Reich similarly sought European domination both in the West and the East and was likewise bogged down and turned back in defeat in the vast expanse of Russia. In short, not only are there distinct definitions of Europe based on geography, religion, culture, politics, economics, sociology, and ethnicity, but the boundaries and parameters of Europe's influence and outer reaches are constantly shifting as well due to war, empire, and the mass migrations of peoples and ethnic groups.

The most recent dividing line in Europe was the Iron Curtain, which, incidentally, roughly corresponded with the selfsame eastern border of Charlemagne's Carolinian Empire in the ninth century. Although the Iron Curtain was a defining reality of most of our lifetimes, it was also thought of by historians (viewed as naive by many national-security experts who thought the Curtain would never come down) as an artificial and temporary dividing line. For over the previous one thousand years, Eastern/Central Europe had not only come to have its own identity but had also identified itself far more with the West than with the East. Then, when the Berlin Wall actually fell, the Warsaw Pact dissolved, the Iron Curtain disappeared, and the Soviet Union disintegrated, the idea—often romantically expressed—became widespread that "Europe" might finally fill its geographic parameters, encompassing the CIS and perhaps Russia as well—"Europe," in President George H. W. Bush's words, "whole and free."

Let us conclude this part of the discussion of Europe's alternative definitions and fluctuating, overlapping boundaries by reference to what in Europe became known, somewhat derisively, as "Madeleine's Map."[6] This was a map of Europe that former U.S. Secretary of State Madeleine Albright handed to the Europeans in May 2000. It contained a series of confusing, overlapping boundary lines in different colors that appeared to the Europeans to represent the efforts of a child with crayons run amuck. The first circle (in blue) showed the then-fifteen members of the European Union (EU). The next circle (in red) was for the nineteen members of NATO, while the next circle (in green) showed the seven NATO aspirant countries. The fourth circle (in brown) encompassed the eleven countries that had adopted the new single currency, the *euro*, while the fifth (in yellow) was for the six countries of East/Central Europe thought to be on the fast track to EU membership. A sixth circle (in orange) showed the other later, and presumed slower-track, EU aspirants, and a seventh (in violet) indicated the twelve countries that had agreed to the Schengen (border control) Accord. The eighth, ninth, and tenth circles, each with its own color, seemed to almost disappear into the far eastern horizon: one was for the forty-three countries (including Russia) of which the Council of Europe (which also runs the European Court of Human Rights) is composed; the next was for the Organization for Security and Cooperation in Europe (OSCE), which incorporates no fewer than fifty-five countries; and the final circle was for the twenty-seven countries making up NATO's Partnership for Peace (PfP) and also including Russia and the countries of Central Asia. This was "Europe," as Secretary of State James Baker once called it, stretching "from Vancouver to Vladivostok." It was also enormously confusing, and not just to the Europeans, leaving open, at least officially, the question of Europe's farthest borders. The map also seemed, in its confounding and overlapping circles, to echo former U.S. Secretary of State Henry Kissinger's earlier and similarly derisive question: "When I want to speak to Europe, whom do I call?"

Europe is not yet "whole and free" and there is presently much confusion and concern about where its borders lie. The definition of where Europe begins and, more importantly, ends, and what criteria to use, is again open to question. New lines, new curtains, new walls are being drawn across Europe. Significantly, these lines correspond almost exactly to the historic boundaries, fault lines of empire, and political-cultural-civilizational-religious boundaries suggested briefly here. The historians have proved to be correct; with modification and nuance, the ancient dividing lines have reasserted themselves, often to the frustration of U.S. political and strategic planners who must deal with such relatively recent phenomena as peace and security in Eastern Europe and NATO and EU enlargement. So let us begin peeling back the layers of this onion to see where Europe does, in fact, now begin and end.

HISTORICAL, CULTURAL, AND DEVELOPMENTALIST FAULT LINES

A variety of factors—geographical, religious, linguistic, strategic, ethnic, historical, socio-psychological, and developmental—have shaped the dividing lines, both historic and contemporary, in Europe and, particularly for our purposes, the frontier between Europe and its outside perimeter.

Geography

Hardly anyone, to our shame, studies geography anymore, or thinks it important, let alone takes a geographic determinist position.

Nevertheless, three points need to be made in consideration of the geographic factor.

First, what we now call Central Europe—defined provisionally as those lands located between Russia on the one hand and the borders of the German-speaking lands on the other—lies athwart Europe's primary invasion route, the great northern European plain that reaches from France and the Low Countries in the west to the Ural Mountains in the east. Historically, this has been what Adrian Hyde-Price calls the "crunch zone" between Europe and Asia, the route by which marauding, conquering Central Asian tribes—Huns, Magyars, Tatars, and others—have invaded Europe.[7] This was also the route by which, it was feared, Soviet armies would invade Europe, across Poland and through the Folda Pass. It should be said that there was also a reverse process: this was the route by which Western armies—those of Sweden's Gustavus Adolphus, Napoleon, and Hitler—attacked and sought to expand east into the Russian heartland. The point to be made here is that this is the area that nineteenth-century geostrategist Harold Mackinder (or, more recently, Zbigniew Brezezinski) called the Euro-Asian "heartland" or "pivot area." Whomever controlled this territory, in his view, controlled the world.[8] The result is that Central Europe was repeatedly subject to invasions from east and west; many of the great and most disruptive battles in history were fought on its territory; its nascent agriculture and cities have repeatedly been destroyed by battle and marauding bands; and, as a further result of all these invasions, Central Europe has the most complex ethnic makeup, often of small groups insufficient to constitute a separate nation-state, of all of Europe.

A second point has to do with distance. Central/Eastern Europe is on the periphery of Europe. If one's theory or conceptual framework is center-periphery relations, then Eastern or Central Europe is a marvelous laboratory. In this sense, Central Europe is much like Southern Europe. If London, Paris, Amsterdam, and now Brussels, Strasbourg, and Berlin are at the heart of modern or modernizing Europe, then Central (or Southern) Europe, especially in premodern times, is a very long way from the European centers of progress and development, not only physically or in travel time but social-psychologically as well. Central/Eastern Europe, like Southern Europe, missed out on the early stirrings of the Enlightenment, the Industrial Revolution, and the movement toward limited, representative government. Central and Eastern Europe for a long period thus remained feudal and two-class, and economic development and industrialization came slower, later, and more unevenly than in Europe's core.

Distance and underdevelopment bred resentments and complexes. Western Europe looked down patronizingly and condescendingly on the

East (witness the line in *My Fair Lady* when Professor Higgins proclaims that "she was born *Hungarian*," which always brings down the house with smirks and derisive laughter) while Eastern and Central Europe resented the West's superiority: desperately wanting to join the West culturally and economically (as in today's effort to integrate into NATO and the EU) but prepared to resent the West and go its own way (independently or back to Russia?) should the West reject it. Again, there are parallels with Southern Europe, where Greece, Portugal, and Spain in the mid-1970s were similarly prepared to follow their own Mediterranean, Atlanticist, or even Third World strategies if they were ultimately rejected by Europe. To sum up: almost in the form of a "law" of European development, the farther east toward the periphery one goes from Europe's center or core, the less developed and less democratic the country is likely to be and the deeper the resentments. By the same token, the closer one lies to Europe's center, the higher the correlation with development, democracy, and national self-confidence.

The third point has to do with the internal geography of these regions. In general, the farther east one goes, the worse the farming becomes—until one gets to the great Russian steppes, but that is another story. Unlike France, the Low Countries, or Germany, which are wealthy in terms of geography, resources, and agriculture, many of the countries to the east, and especially in the southeast, have poor soils, rocky terrains unconducive to large-scale agriculture, chopped-up geographies that make internal communications and transportation difficult, and poor or limited resources generally. The Czech lands (Bohemia, Moravia) are relatively rich and prosperous in mineral wealth and agriculture, but Slovakia, except for the Danube Plain, is mostly poor and mountainous. Austria and Hungary have rich, intensively utilized resources but Romania and Bulgaria, comparatively speaking, do not. As one travels southeast through the Balkans, Slovenia is a relatively rich country, including agriculturally, and is tied into the wealthy economies of Austria and Italy; Croatia is a mix of some good agricultural land and the beginning of a mountainous terrain; and much of the rest of the former Yugoslavia is mountainous, with some good but scattered agriculture in the valleys but little of it amenable to mechanization. Moreover, the farming in these areas is less well organized, is more primitive, and seems (despite the Socialist and post-Socialist changes) quasi-feudal. And without good agriculture and the surpluses derived from it, industrialization would also lag in this part of the world.

Obviously, these considerations cannot be taken as ironclad law. Poland is a major exception. It contains a rich agricultural area that nevertheless remained underdeveloped, in part because Poland's agriculture was organized inefficiently and was periodically destroyed by the invading armies that ravaged the countryside, and in part because Poland all but disappeared as a country during the formative nineteenth century when it was partitioned between its three more powerful neighbors, Austria-Hungary, Prussia, and Russia. Despite these qualifiers, the underdevelopment of East and Central Europe may in part be accounted for by their geographic location, characteristics, and resources, or the lack thereof. And that has also helped shape their social, political, and cultural orientation.

Religion

Americans are not used to talking about religion anymore, especially about religion's political ramifications, and are often uncomfortable doing so. Having incorporated notions of the strict separation of church and state, Americans tend not to inquire too closely—at least publicly—into a person's religious beliefs; nor do we seek—again, at least publicly—to explain public-policy preferences and outcomes by the religious or ethnic beliefs and backgrounds of those who advocate them. These may represent blinders on America's part to what is still a useful explanatory paradigm (particularly, as we shall see, in Eastern Europe); but Americans seem to have concluded that the costs in social and political terms of talking about religion or using it as an explanation are greater than the benefits to be derived.

But this is not necessarily the case in much of the rest of the world where (1) religion is often more strongly felt and internalized than in increasingly secular America and Western Europe; (2) religion is part of the political culture, often closely identified as in Poland with nationalism and nationhood; (3) religion is a part of *public* discourse in contrast to the "separation" concept of American public policy; and (4) religion is a powerful explanatory factor in understanding both conflict within the Eastern/Central European area and the relatively greater or lesser development of the countries of the area. One is almost in Eastern and Central Europe at the point of a "law of physics" comparable to the earlier "law" stated reflecting geography: tell me the predominant religion in a particular country and I will tell you whether that country is likely to be (1) developed, (2) democratic, and (3) a serious prospect to be integrated into broader European counsels (EU and NATO).[9]

One of the fundamental divides in Eastern and Central Europe is that between Roman Catholicism on the one hand and Eastern Orthodoxy on the other. An even more fundamental and deep-seated division is between Christian Europe (both Catholic and Orthodox) and Islamic Europe. These divisions are particularly prevalent and powerful in the Balkans. Indeed, in many respects the Balkan wars of the 1990s can be seen as a resurrection of these age-old religious animosities between

Christians and Muslims, with the Bosnian, Kosovo, or Albanian Muslims being assigned the role of "Turks" or "Islamic aggressors" and the Serbs (mainly in their own eyes) playing the role of defenders of Christianity and civilization. National missions in this part of the world have often been defined in religious terms ("chosen people," "bulwarks of Christendom," "defenders of the faith or of Western civilization") and directed against "The Other": "infidels" or "schismatics" or "heretics."

Beginning in the ninth century, missionaries from the Greek Orthodox Church centered in Byzantium had fanned out northwesterly and northeasterly to neighboring territories in the Balkans, Ukraine, and Russia, leading to the conversion of their leaders and ultimately their peoples, and to the establishment of national Orthodox churches. At approximately the same time (give or take a century!), Roman Catholic clerics mainly originating in Germany began the conversion of rulers and peoples to the east, including present-day Poland, the Czech Republic, Austria, Slovakia, Hungary, Slovenia, and the lower Baltics (Lithuania). In some cases, Christianity reached farther east and south, including the western provinces of Ukraine and Romania (Transylvania) and the northernmost province (Vojvodina) of Yugoslavia, which remain divided today and often, because of these distinct traditions, have strong separatist tendencies. The Protestant Reformation of the sixteenth century divided a number of these countries internally as well as producing international conflict mainly in the German lands, but by the end of that century the Catholic Counter-Reformation had recaptured most of East/Central Europe for the Roman Church, leaving only minority Protestant groups in Czechoslovakia, Austria, and Hungary. The basic divide, therefore, between Catholic and Orthodox Europe persisted and was even reinforced.

The conversion of much of Eastern and Central Europe to Christianity was far more important than just a religious change, however. In these historically underdeveloped and uncivilized lands, converting to Christianity symbolized progress and culture, and Eastern/Central Europe came to see itself as enforcing a civilizational dividing line, the defender of Western Civilization against the "barbarians" to the east and southeast. The conversion to Christianity also marked a turning point from preliteracy to literacy, from barbarism to culture and civilization, from primitive tribal forms of organization to more sophisticated feudalism. At this stage, in Hegelian or Marxian terms, Eastern and Central Europe entered "history," writ large. Being Christian meant being modern, developed, Western, a chance to catch up to the rest of Europe and overcome those historic inferiority complexes noted earlier. Eastern and Central Europe might still be on the periphery of Europe but at least it was now part of Europe, which meant progress and advancement. In later centuries, moreover, the particular religious or denominational form that religion took in various countries helped provide national identity in that nation and, for good as well as ill, a means of determining who "belonged" as part of that nation and who might be excluded as "the other"—again, Jews and Roma but other religious schismatics and minorities too.

The religious orientation of the various countries also had a profound effect on their political cultures and developmental possibilities. Religion in Eastern and Central Europe, in other words, is not neutral, nor is it confined just to the religious realm. For example, the Hapsburg rulers in the vast Austro-Hungarian empire, like their sixteenth- and seventeenth-century cousins in Spain and Portugal, used the authoritarian, hierarchical, top-down, and fatalistic (accepting one's station in life) feature of traditional, medieval, Thomistic Catholicism as a way of enhancing and reinforcing their absolutist authority and of keeping their peoples submissive and locked in place. But that authoritarian structure faded over time, enabling such predominantly Catholic countries as Austria to become successful both as a democracy and as one of the world's richest societies. Moreover, Hapsburg authoritarianism was as nothing compared with the Eastern Orthodox Church, which was even more hierarchical and top-down, entirely subordinate to state power, and without the slightest bow to limited, representative, responsible government. However authoritarian for a long time was the Roman Catholic Church, it was nevertheless strongly influenced by the Renaissance, the Enlightenment, the French Revolution, and, eventually, modern liberalizing currents in ways that the Eastern Church was not. The Eastern peoples remained passive and submissive far longer than their Central European and Catholic counterparts, "medieval," according to the best book on the subject, rather than modernizing.[10] The history of the Roman Church, not always exactly glorious, was thus intertwined with Westernization and modernization in Eastern and Central Europe, whereas the church at Byzantium and the lands where its influence held sway was not.

The religious divide separating Catholic from Eastern Orthodox Europe was reinforced by language criteria as well as alphabet. Language, literature, and alphabets also provide a means to measure political culture, as do religion, music, and art. Here again, the divisions are sharp. The Orthodox countries of Bulgaria, Russia, Belarus, the Ukraine, Serbia, and, until the nineteenth century, Romania (unusual because, as a remnant of the Roman Empire, it was Orthodox but not Slavic) all use the Cyrillic alphabet, historically looked to Byzantium for spiritual guidance, and after Constantinople's fall generally relied on Russia for political and military leadership. In contrast, Roman Catholic or "Latin" Eastern/Central Europe, including Slovenia, Croatia, Hungary, the Czech lands, Slovakia, Poland, Austria, and the lower Baltics, used the Latin alphabet, looked to Rome and the West for spiritual guidance, and took the culture and nation-state of the West as their model. Dare it be said at this early point in the discussion that the latter group of countries were all leading candidates for admission to NATO and/or the EU in the first or second round, while the former group of countries were all distant candidates, if they had any chance at all?[11] It is not that language or use of alphabet is a qualifier or disqualifier per se but they are parts of a larger package or bundle of cultural, social, economic, and political traits that *do* serve as qualifiers.

From the fourteenth through the sixteenth century and beyond, a new political-religious divide appeared in Eastern/Central Europe, and that involved the crusading conquests of the Islamic Ottoman Turks from their base in Asia Minor, up through the Balkans, through Hungary, and on up to the gates of Vienna where they were twice repulsed, in 1529 and 1683. The Ottomans did not make a concerted effort to convert, by persuasion or force, the Balkan peoples whom they conquered but they did rule the area for four centuries, imposed their law and absolutist imperial administration on the area, destroyed Southeastern Europe's emerging feudal institutions which must be seen as progressive at the time, and cut off Southeast Europe even more than other Central or Eastern areas from the modernizing currents of the West. Moreover, even though they failed to take Vienna, the Turks occupied Hungary for 150 years (forever "tainting" that country in the eyes of some of its neighbors) and most of the Balkans until the nineteenth century, when these states were able to liberate themselves. Again, it was Slovenia, Croatia, and the province of Vojvodina in northern Serbia that were longer and more fully liberated from the Ottomans and more quickly rejoined Christianity; Romania and Bulgaria less so; in contrast, present-day Serbia, Montenegro, and Macedonia that were mixed; and Bosnia, Kosovo, and Albania that converted to Islam.

Now if one thinks about it for a minute, this is almost exactly the pecking order by which the Eastern and Central European countries have been integrated, or are about to be, into Europe (defined as admission to NATO and the EU) and are considered fully European. That is, Austria first as Christian, developed, and fully European; then (Christian) Poland, the Czech Republic, Hungary, Slovenia and probably the Baltics, Slovakia, and Croatia; next (Orthodox) Bulgaria and Romania as less well-qualified countries; perhaps eventually (Orthodox) Serbia, Montenegro (if it becomes independent), and Macedonia; far down the pecking order (Orthodox) Ukraine, Belarus, and Russia itself; (Islamic) Bosnia, Kosovo (as part of or independent from Serbia), and Albania so far away as to be almost invisible; and perhaps one day Turkey, but that is a special case. Indeed, in informal (and certainly not spoken, or at least not in polite or politically correct company) European circles, as well as in public opinion, that is the informal and shorthand lineup for integration: Christian countries first, Orthodox countries maybe, and Islamic countries, do not even bother to apply. In other words, Christianity, as a part or indicator of "Western civilization" is informally being used as a hidden or disguised criterion for admission to Europe as much as any other factor, but one should not speak about that publicly for fear of being branded "racist" or "culturally insensitive."

Ethnicity

From time immemorial, Eastern/Central Europe has been a mixing bowl of migratory groups, some stimulated by peaceful movements and others by war and conflict. As historian Lonnie R. Johnson has written, it is "the most ethnically heterogeneous and religiously heterodox region in Europe."[12] Moreover, as Johnson's comment implies, religion and ethnicity have often reinforced each other, thus solidifying difference, division, and conflict over consensus and what Tocqueville called "the art of living together."

We cannot begin to analyze in detail all those ethnic movements, changes, and displacements here; we mention only some of them here for illustrative purposes. Thus, as early as the Middle Ages, ethnic Germans were already moving eastward into Poland, the Baltics, Ukraine, Bohemia, Russia, Hungary, Slovenia, and Croatia—which helps explain Germany's advocacy even today of a number of these nations' entry into the EU. Meanwhile, a Polish presence was also established in the Baltic countries, Belarus, Ukraine, and present-day Slovakia, helping to give rise to the vast Polish-Lithuanian kingdom of the fourteenth and fifteenth centuries. Ethnic Russians moved into border areas such as the Baltics, Belarus, Ukraine, Georgia, Poland, and Slovakia, thus complicating some of these nations' efforts to join NATO or the EU. Present-day Hungary was similarly a melting pot of Magyars, Slovaks, Ruthanes, Romanians, Germans, Gypsies, and Jews. The former Yugoslavia consisted not just of Slovenes, Croats, Serbs, Montenegrans, Albanians, Kosovars, and Macedonians but also of Turks, Greeks, Italians, Romanians, Germans, Magyars, and Bulgarians. Today, Slovakia, Romania, and the Ukraine have sizable Hungarian (and Christian) populations that still yearn for reunification with Hungary, while Bulgaria has a sizable Turkish minority not fully assimilated into European ways.

We should not necessarily think of these migrant groups as we think of immigrant groups today as consistently poor nomads looking for a better life. Instead, there was often an economic or political purpose to these migrations other than simply escaping poverty. Many German burghers were valued for their commercial skills and were recruited to found new towns and cities in the East so that entrepreneurialism could flourish. The Germans were also valued for their farming skills and technologies, so that all over Eastern and Central Europe, one finds German agricultural communities that may or may not be assimilated into local cultures and whose presence helped serve as rationalization for German military aggression eastward in World War II. Throughout Eastern and Central Europe, Serbs had often been employed as mercenaries who then settled in separate communities in the areas where they had served. In Hungary, Southern Germans were brought in to reinforce Catholicism and supplement and presumably provide new energy and know-how for the local Magyar aristocracy. In this way, not only did the immigrants often settle in their own, often unassimilated territories or communities, they also frequently reinforced existing, or established for the first time, class and social divisions. It was not unusual in this part of the world, because of the many ethnic changes and migrations over the century, for the towns and cities to speak one language and to be of one (or several!) ethnic groups, and the countryside of another; or for the gentry to speak one language and be of one ethnicity, and the peasants or middle class of another.

It is often said of the Balkans, for example, that they are basically tribal societies that had the bad fortune to be organized on that traditional basis at a time, still in the nineteenth century, when Western European–style nationalism and national boundaries were inappropriately imposed on them largely from the outside. In this sense, the Balkans in the nineteenth century (and perhaps continuing in some respects today) were comparable to Africa in the 1960s: basically tribal or ethnic societies with ill-fitting, Western-designed national borders and the trappings of the European nation-state imposed upon them. But in our analysis the situation is even more complex and difficult. Not only is much of East/Central Europe, and especially the Balkans, still tribally based, but the differences between towns and countryside, between educated and uneducated, between elites and masses, all tend to reinforce and perpetuate the sharp ethnic and religious differences that already exist.

Nor should we assume that *any* of these relations just analyzed are stable or permanent. Instead, war, revolution, invasion, plague, migratory movements, ethnic "cleansing," and the comings and goings of empires have all affected the social makeup, ethnic composition, and class structure of Eastern and Central Europe. For example, the Ottoman conquest of the Balkans from the thirteenth through the sixteenth centuries sent many Serbs, Croats, and Slovenes fleeing north, where they either served as mercenary troops employed against the Turks or settled in new locations in Bohemia (the Czech Republic), Slovakia, Austria, Hungary, or previously ethnically Hungarian Vojvodina. To make the discussion relevant to today, as the Serbs moved north, recently converted Muslim Albanians moved into the depopulated territories such as Bosnia-Herzegovina and Kosovo. In turn, as the Turks were pushed back into the

Balkans after their failure to capture Vienna, and eventually out of there as well, Germans, Austrians, Slovaks, Magyars, Croats, and Slovenes moved back into the territories they had vacated (while also leaving behind ethnic communities in other territories where their peoples had earlier settled), adding further to the ethnic mix—to say nothing of the frequent desire to settle old scores, gain revenge, or pursue policies of irredentism. For example, Hungary's continued talk about the plight of minority ethnic Hungarians in Romania, Slovakia, and Serbia is an irritant to other NATO members, for whom such border issues were supposedly settled and "forgotten" once Hungary joined NATO.

We have focused in this brief discussion on what we will call the Turkish-Austro/Hungarian frontier, but there were others as well as empires ebbed and flowed. These include the Swedish, Russian, Tatar, Polish-Lithuanian, Magyar, Ukrainian, Bavarian, Romanian, Prussian-German, even Danish (!) empires. All left behind in their wakes unassimilated or only partly assimilated ethnic communities, unsettled border issues, displaced and often resentful ethnic minorities, class and social structures that also reflected historic ethnic and/or religious backgrounds, peoples often uncertain or confused about their cross-cultural roots, and polka-dotted territories of such infinitely complex ethnic and social relations that one needs to combine a vast knowledge of history with a knowledge of cultural anthropology to figure them all out. Nevertheless, it needs also be said that, with the massive, unprecedented "ethnic cleansing" of World War II, and the redrawing of many national borders afterward, more of the Eastern/Central European countries are more ethnically homogeneous now than at any time in their history. The recent conflict and ethnic cleansing in the former Yugoslavia may in part be considered a continuation of that process.

Public Attitudes

Eastern/Central Europe is also defined by public as well as private attitudes. This may be expressed in a variety of forms: official designations, unofficial attitudes, jokes and stories (often ethnically based), and public-opinion surveys. But they all tend to reinforce the conclusions toward which we are already pointing as to where the new dividing lines in Europe are being drawn.

Official Designations. In 1994, president of the Czech Republic (1993–2003; previously president of Czechoslovakia [1989–1992]), Vaclav Havel, asked his fellow "Central European" heads of state to come together to discuss the future of the region. Those invited included the presidents of Austria, Germany, Poland, Slovakia, Hungary, and Slovenia. In addition to who was invited, note who was left out: Bulgaria, Romania, Belarus,

Ukraine, Russia, Serbia, Croatia. That is how the lines were drawn, at least in one official designation, in 1994. Significantly, all these heads of state posed in front of a life-size portrait of the Hapsburg monarchy in the eighteenth century, perhaps symbolizing the resurrection in new form of the old Austro-Hungarian empire.

When the European Union officially invited candidate countries to apply for accession, the first tranche of fast-track applicants included Poland, Estonia, the Czech Republic, Hungary, and Slovenia. All these countries are predominantly Christian, and all save Estonia are predominantly Roman Catholic. They are also the most economically and sociologically developed of the East/Central European countries. The next group of applicants, some of whom were making strenuous efforts and could catch up with some of the first group, consisted of Latvia, Lithuania, Slovakia, Romania, and Bulgaria. Turkey has been "recognized as a candidate." In contrast, Russia, Belarus, Ukraine, Moldova, and the other successor states of the former Yugoslavia were not even considered as possibilities. In short, the line drawn by the EU in terms of invited countries stopped at the border of the CIS and Yugoslavia (except for developed Slovenia). But now with the changes of governments in Croatia and Serbia, their new, more democratic leaders are regularly invited to meetings of European leaders, and preliminary steps are already underway to prepare them for possible future EU or NATO membership. But the leaders of Bosnia, Albania, Kosovo, Ukraine, Moldova, Georgia, Belarus, and Russia, often to their chagrin, still are not; they and their countries are being left out.

Unofficial Attitudes. Unofficial attitudes are probably as important as official invitation lists (with the two often mutually reinforcing one another) in determining who belongs in Europe.[13] Those who are all but universally accepted as Europeans include the Baltics, Poles, Czechs, Hungarians, and Slovenes. Those who are worrisome but nevertheless probably acceptable over time are the Slovaks and Croats. At a lower and marginal level are the Romanians and Bulgarians. Unacceptable are Belarussians, Russians, Ukrainians, Moldovans, Serbs (now changing), and Turks—although once again, because of strategic reasons and the presence already of millions of Turks within the EU member countries, the last listed may be a special case. In addition, almost all East/Central Europeans recognize that there are marginal or border areas, often the more developed, Christian, and/or Uniate (utilizing Orthodox rites but acknowledging papal authority) parts of countries that lie outside the currently acceptable borders of Europe but nevertheless "belong with the West": the western provinces of Ukraine, the northernmost province (Vojvodina) in Serbia, and Transylvania in Romania.

Central Europeans are often quite definite about these dividing lines. I have heard even highly educated Austrians say of those across that new

East-West boundary that we are describing, "They don't think like us; they don't act like us; they don't have the same values." It perhaps goes without saying that even more scathing and ethnically prejudiced are lower-class or popular attitudes toward those from the East, because of perceptions of job or security threats. Such attitudes—which are usually portrayed as anti-immigrant but are really much deeper than that, involving religion, culture, language, education, self-identification, and even the definitions of "civilization" described earlier, to say nothing of pressures on labor markets, taxes, and social services—formed the base of support for the rise of Jorg Haider and the Austrian Freedom Party. They also help explain why countries such as Austria, with one of the world's highest per capita incomes and almost literally surrounded by new EU applicant countries, wanted as a condition of its voting for EU expansion a seven-year "transition period" before the free movement of peoples from new EU countries into older members would be allowed. Wealthy Germany has many of the same fears: as one German high government official told me rather crudely, "Berlin is already the second largest Turkish city in the world. We do not want to become the largest Turkish city."

Attitudes such as these are hard to systematize or to deal with in a rigorous social-science way. But they are important nonetheless, maybe critical. For example, an EU official told me that when he went to Vilnius, Lithuania, for the first time, after an earlier posting in Kiev, Ukraine, he "knew immediately" that he was back in a "Western country." "The religion, the culture, the economics, the society, the architecture, the politics," he said, were "all basically Western." From this official's point of view, therefore, Lithuania's candidacy for EU admission was already assured, on the basis of informal attitudes formed early on rather than the formal, technical EU membership criteria. The *expectation* was already formed that Lithuania would qualify. The issue was no longer "if" but "when." I have found such informal attitudes on who "belongs" in Europe and who doesn't very firmly entrenched all around the continent.

In this respect, negative attitudes are as important as positive ones. Here the main targets are often the Turks, followed closely by Albanians, Kosovars, Bosnians, Russians, Belarussians, Ukrainians, Moldovans, Bulgarians, Romanians, Croats, even Serbs. There is, in short, a pecking order of negative stereotypes just as there is of positive ones. Serb hatred of Muslim Albanians, Kosovars, and Bosnians (and vice versa) is so intense, it is said, because they are so taught by their mothers! Ancient myths (child-snatching, ritual murder, blood feuds, family hatreds, clean and dirty business deals that go back for generations, past glories and defeats, revenge for old slights real and imagined) are resurrected, and often now fueled by alcohol, *machismo*, nationalism, religion, ethnicity, and more and bigger guns. Anyone who thinks that these deep-rooted hatreds, as in

Bosnia or Kosovo, will go away soon or can be papered over easily by such simple schemes as, for example, the Dayton Peace Accords doesn't know or understand the area.

Jokes and Stories. There are endless jokes and stories, many of them ethnically based and, therefore, unrepeatable here, that Eastern and Central Europeans tell about their even more easterly neighbors. Many of them, with variation, are the same kinds of ethnic jokes that Western Europeans used to tell about the previous "Easterners." Like everything else, the ethnic-joke line or "curtain" in Eastern/Central Europe has just moved slightly further east.

The jokes, as expected, tend to center on the alleged "dumbness," crudity, and corruption of those across the newly drawn European "border." Those across that eastern or southeastern frontier consistently do stupid things, like sawing off the tree limb on which they are sitting or self-destructing in often crazily romantic, and sometimes even humorous, ways. The "new Easterners" drive crazily, it is said; they are lazy and don't want to work; they only want to take advantage of the Western countries' social-welfare systems; they cannot organize stable governments; they are corrupt and dominated by mafias; and their women are all whores and prostitutes. Easterners (and Turks) are said to have strange sex and other habits so you would not want your daughter to marry one, and to ritually kill sheep in their living quarters and then wash the blood down the bathtub drains of public apartment complexes, and so on and so on.

Some of these stories are true, some partially true, others demonstrably false; but all of them are stereotypical and part of popular lore. Educated Americans and Europeans are appalled at the blatant prejudices these stories and stereotypes imply, but the United States often has the same popular attitudes toward blacks, Hispanics, and immigrants—in part because the immigrants we mainly see, like those in Central Europe, tend to be from the lower socioeconomic classes, not well educated, and not "civilized" into Western ways. From a distance we can easily denounce such attitudes as involving unacceptable ethnic prejudice, but for Europeans the problems they perceive are close by, right next door, or even clearly visible already within their own borders. And with all such stereotypes that are unfortunately reinforced by socioeconomic and sometimes even racial or ethnic differences, overcoming them will likely take three or four generations, not three or four years, as many EU and NATO planners envision.

Public-Opinion Surveys. The attitudes—often prejudicial—we have been informally reporting are bolstered by public-opinion surveys.[14]

First, Central and Eastern Europe remain strongly committed to democracy. In country after country, support for democracy as the only acceptable *system* of governance is in the 70–80 percent range. If and when there is slippage in these figures, it is because democracy is perceived as not delivering on its promised social and economic reforms, not because the public prefers some other governmental system. Support for democracy in Central and Eastern Europe is considerably stronger than it is in the countries of the former Soviet Union, Russia and CIS.

Second, and related, support for some other system of government is almost nil. Unlike the situation in Latin America, where the recent decline in the level of support for democracy has been accompanied by the parallel rise in support for "strong government" or an authoritarian "out," voters in East/Central Europe see no such alternative. They certainly do not want an authoritarian or "Fascist" solution, but neither do they want to go back to a Marxist-Leninist regime. The reasons are pragmatic as well as value based: to revert now to either a far right or far left regime would almost certainly mean the kiss of death for that country's chances for NATO or EU admission. When they do vote for Communist parties or candidates, it is not usually for ideological reasons but because these parties are seen as better able to govern, better administrators, or better at protecting the social safety nets of the old regime which many, especially older Easterners, still prefer to the uncertainties of the private marketplace.[15]

With regard to enlargement, the opinion surveys are interesting, controversial, and revealing. In East/Central Europe, the polls long showed strong (50–70 percent, depending on the country) support for joining the EU. Support for joining NATO was usually less than that for joining the EU (in the 30–40 percent range), although in most countries support rose after NATO stopped its bombing campaigns in Serbia and Kosovo. Most governments had not yet begun to make the case for NATO, and the public had not always seen, or wanted to see, the connection between EU accession, which implies benefits and privileges, and NATO membership, which involves costs and obligations.

More worrisome may be attitudes in the West, in the present EU member states. Immediately after the fall of Communism, there was considerable sympathy in the West for bringing the East, including Russia and CIS, into the fold. Western investment, especially German, Austrian, and Scandinavian, followed on a large scale, not only to help stabilize and democratize Russia but also on the assumption that Russia and the CIS got Socialism wrong (Stalinist) the first time, and now the West would help get it "right" (social-democratic) this time. But then disillusionment set in, the West began seeing Russia and the CIS as unreformable in the short term, and it began reallocating its funds to Europe's own "near abroad" (Eastern/Central Europe), which not only looked more hopeful economically and politically but also, because of close proximity, had the capacity to affect the West more strongly in the short term.

But there is considerable popular sentiment in the West against admitting East/Central Europe to the EU. The issues are complex, but they mainly have to do with fears of Eastern immigration that will cost jobs in the West, increased taxes that will have to be used to subsidize the less-developed East/Central European economies, fears that the Eastern countries lack the capacity to control their borders with those countries even farther east (Belarus, Ukraine, for example—hence, a huge push in the West to retrain the East in border patrol), and general trepidation that Eastern expansion of the EU will bring additional, often unspecified "problems" to the West: rising crime, disease, mafias, prostitution, and so forth. On the other hand, the benefits to the West in items of larger consumer markets for its products, and stability and security in the historically volatile East also provide powerful arguments that governments in the West have begun to emphasize. Plus, the EU is betting that it can assist the East in solving its labor and immigration issues, and reach compromises that will satisfy its own domestic constituencies, thus also allaying Western public opinion.

Socioeconomic Development

High levels of socioeconomic development and/or a major economic-reform program are, of course, required to be a part of the European "club" of developed countries and are widely thought to be required for the establishment and consolidation of democracy. In any case the East/Central European countries need to meet the *eighty thousand* requirements of the *Acquis Communautaire* if they wish to join the EU. But in this part of the world it seems to be political culture—combined with other factors—that often determines socioeconomic success, at least as much as underlying class or institutional factors.[16] At the least, political culture and socioeconomic development are closely correlated and appear to be mutually reinforcing. Thus, we may never be able to answer the chicken-or-egg question of which came first and foremost and was causative in East/Central European development, changes in political culture or structural changes; most likely it is some murky combination of the two, and it may no longer, except for historical determinists and true-believer ideologues, even be an important question.

Let us take the easy issues first. Number one, if we ask what explains the successful economies of Eastern/Central Europe in the last fifteen years, the clearest answer, to echo the real-estate agent, is: Location! Location! Location![17] By almost every criteria, Poland, the Czech Republic, Slovenia, and Hungary have been Eastern Europe's leading success stories in the last decade. If we ask why, the most obvious answer is their location next to some of the world's most prosperous economies, such as

Germany, Austria, Italy, Scandinavia, and the other EU countries. Not only has there been a rub-off effect from the wealthy Western economies, but a number of the Western countries are now devoting almost all their foreign aid and investment capital to their proximate neighbors in Eastern/Central Europe, with the expectation of far greater and more immediate results *and*, in terms of protecting their own self-interest, wanting prosperous neighbors so that those neighbors solve their own problems of poverty, unemployment, underdevelopment, and other social problems, rather than, through immigration and common borders, passing them on to the West. The situation, although somewhat less extreme in terms of economic disparities, is analogous to that governing U.S.-Mexican relations: it is far better, we have concluded, for Mexico to use U.S. aid and investment (hence the rationale for NAFTA) to solve its problems internally rather than pass them on to the United States through immigration.

Number two, and closely related to the first point, early in the analysis we suggested that the farther east you get from the European heartland (Paris, just to resolve any possible dispute), the less developed, the less modern Eastern and Central Europe becomes. But the reverse, of course, is also true: the closer you come to the core, the better your possibilities. This is true not just for concrete aid and trade but for other kinds of effects as well. By that we mean closer contact with Western culture, Western movies and television, Western roads, Western democracies, Western markets, Western ways of doing business, Western institutions ranging from ATMs to McDonalds, Western social and behavioral mores, Western tourists and (to come full circle in the argument) their dollars, francs, pounds, shillings, deutschmarks, and now euros. Again, are these cultural factors, structural ones, or, as seems most likely, some complex overlapping of both? Compare, for example, the present dynamism and "Westernness" of Warsaw, Prague, or Budapest to the changing but still relatively quieter pace of Bratislava, Sophia, Bucharest, or Zagreb, to say nothing of backward, dreary, gray, and discouraged Kiev, Minsk, Tirana, Chisinau, Tlbisi, or even Moscow for that matter. Clearly some parts of Eastern and Central Europe are doing far better than others.

Let us move now from impressionistic data to actual socioeconomic figures as in Table 8.1. The first thing to say is how poor many of these countries are. One expects to see shocking poverty in Africa, Latin America, and the Third World but not in East/Central Europe. But, in fact, parts of East/Central Europe *are* the Third World. Using year 2000 figures for GNP per capita, Moldova is down at the level of Haiti, which is one of the poorest countries in the world; Albania, Montenegro, and Ukraine are all under $1,000 per person per year, putting them at a level *below* Central America. None of these is a candidate anytime soon for the EU or NATO,

Table 8.1. Select Social and Economic Development Figures: Eastern and Central Europe (2000)

Country	Population Millions	Surface (Sq. km)	Population Density	Life Expectancy M	Life Expectancy F	Adult Literacy M	Adult Literacy F	% Urban	GNP ($ billions)	GNP Per Capita	Rank Among Nations	Measured at PPP GNP	Measured at PPP GNP Per Capita	Measured at PPP Rank
Albania	3	29	123	69	75	9	24	41	2.9	870	136	9.8	2,892	137
Belarus	10	208	49	63	74	0	1	57	26.8	2,630	92	66.5	6,518	79
Bosnia	4	51	79	73					(Data unavailable)					73
Bulgaria	8	111	74	67	75	1	2	69	11.3	1,380	121	40.4	4,914	99
Croatia	4	57	80	69	77	1	3	57	20.4	4,580	69	30.9	6,915	78
Czech Republic	10	73	133	71	78	0	0	75	52.0	5,060	65	126.3	12,289	52
Hungary	10	93	109	66	75	1	1	64	46.8	4,650	68	105.5	10,479	60
Latvia	2	65	39	64	76	0	0	69	6.0	2,470	94	14.4	5,938	85
Lithuania	4	65	57	67	77	0	1	68	9.7	2,620	93	22.5	6,093	83
Macedonia	2	26	79	70	75	0	0	62	3.4	1,690	109	8.8	4,339	108
Moldova	4	34	130	63	70	1	2	46	1.6	370	167	10.1	2,358	144
Montenegro*	—	—	—	—	—	—	—	—	—	900	—	—	—	—
Poland	39	323	127	69	77	0	0	65	153.1	3,960	73	305.5	7,894	73
Romania	22	238	97	66	73	1	3	56	34.2	1,520	117	126.8	5,647	89
Russia	147	17,075	9	61	73	0	1	77	332.5	2,270	98	928.8	6,339	80
Serbia**	10	102	104	—	72	—	—	—	—	1,800	—	—	—	—
Slovakia	5	49	112	69	77	0	0	57	19.4	3,590	78	52.9	9,811	63
Slovenia	2	20	98	71	79	15	16	52	19.6	9,890	49	29.8	15,062	47
Turkey	64	773	84	67	72	7	25	74	186.3	2,900	88	394.1	6,126	82
Ukraine	50	604	86	62	73	0	1	68	55	750	143	156.8	3,142	133

*Most data unavailable because Montenegro is still part of Serbia.
**Data incomplete because of war and destruction.
Source: World Bank.

nor is Macedonia, with a per capita income less than $2,000 per person per year and about at the level of Guatemala. Bulgaria and Romania are in the same economic category as Macedonia but, because of security reasons, they will be allowed into both NATO and the EU.

When we get up in the $2,000 to $3,000 range, including Latvia, Lithuania, and Turkey, whose per capita incomes are still only *one-tenth* that of the EU average (and roughly comparable to the situation of the U.S. and Mexico) we begin to see EU candidate countries—but not Belarus or Russia, which also fall within that economic range. In the $3,000 to $5,000 range, roughly comparable to Brazil, Chile, or Mexico, are the better-qualified countries of the Czech Republic, Croatia, Estonia, Hungary, Poland, and Slovakia. The upper end of the scale is represented by Slovenia, which, with a per capita income approaching $10,000, is getting close to the level of the poorest EU member at present, Portugal.

On the social indices—life expectancy, adult literacy, urbanization—Eastern and Central Europe come out higher than these Latin American comparisons. And if we employ the World Bank's PPP (Purchasing Power Parity) indices, which use a formula that builds in the free (or nearly so) housing, health care, education, utilities, and services that citizens of these former Socialist states received and often still receive, the rankings go up considerably. Nevertheless, even with these adjustments, the richest of the Eastern/Central European nations (Slovenia, Czech Republic, Hungary) are still only at about half the present EU average, and *most* of the present countries are still only at about one-fourth or one-fifth the EU average.

Clearly, these countries have a lot of catching up to do. Economic growth, already accelerating in a number of countries, is brightening their prospects. They will also be recipients of EU enlargement funds and thus a drag on the other EU economies for decades to come. The EU, and especially the taxpayers in its member countries, do not want to subsidize these weaker economies forever and certainly do not want to take on a series of "basket cases." The large income disparities also explain why the present EU countries remain fearful of the newcomers exporting masses of immigrant job seekers as well as other problems to them.

One of the curious paradoxes of the East/Central European transitions is that democratization has successfully occurred even while economic levels in many countries of the area have fallen. This is counterintuitive, since one would expect the prospects for democracy to be better in times of rising affluence rather than decline; or, as (I think) Billie Holiday once put it, "I've been rich and I've been poor; rich is better." The most recent figures, however, of the European Bank for Reconstruction and Development show that, of all the East/Central European countries, a decade after the overthrow of Communism, only Poland, Slovenia, and Slovakia had reached a level surpassing their 1989 levels. The Czech Republic, Hungary, and Estonia were within a few percentage points of that goal and have probably reached it by now. Elsewhere in Eastern and Southeastern Europe, especially Bulgaria and Romania, the shortfalls as compared with 1989 were between 20 and 30 percent. And in Russia, the CIS, and the war-torn lands of the former Yugoslavia, the figures were nothing short of catastrophic. Russia's GNP fell by almost 50 percent between 1989 and 1999, although subsequently, rising oil prices boosted Russia's economy. The moral (not a glorious one) of this story is that the countries of the area that are at least breaking even or beginning to show positive gains are also the ones in which democracy is most secure and have the best chances for NATO and EU membership. In countries where economic growth is still significantly negative compared to 1989, democracy is also insecure and NATO or EU admission is still in the future. However, in the catastrophic countries, neither consolidated democracy nor admission to either of Europe's two key clubs are in the offing anytime soon.

The final point to be made in this section is how closely these social and economic indicators correspond to the political culture and other variables already presented. Slovenia, the Czech Republic, Hungary, Slovakia, Poland, Estonia, Croatia, Lithuania, Latvia—in that order—are the wealthiest, most developed countries in Eastern/Central Europe. They are also the ones closest to the main centers of West European prosperity; all are Christian and "Western"; all are more or less unified ethnically or at least without serious separatist movements or the potential for civil war; all are democratic not just electorally but in terms of real substance, change, and reform as well. They are also, not coincidentally, the leading countries in terms of admission either to NATO or the EU or both. Perhaps not surprisingly, but seldom said publicly, high levels of socioeconomic development, Westernness, and acceptability within NATO and the EU all go together.[18]

Democracy and Human Rights

Democracy and human rights, along with economic reform leading to growth, have become the *sine qua non* for admission to both NATO and the EU. But democracy can be defined in a number of ways. At least four of these definitions come into play in assessing the countries of Eastern and Central Europe.

The first, easiest, and most widely accepted definition of democracy is regular, competitive, fair elections that lead to periodic, peaceful transfers of power. This is usually referred to as the institutional definition of democracy. It is widely used in academic as well as foreign-policy considerations because it provides the easiest way to call a country "democratic" and thereby to qualify it for aid and cooperation. By this criterion, since they have all had elections, all the countries of East/Central Europe (including Belarus, Ukraine, Georgia, Moldova, and Russia, and now Serbia and Croatia) may be called democratic.

This first definition is often referred to as "formal" or "electoral" democracy. The criticism is expressed that it is relatively easy to engineer elections (look at Belarus, Moldova, Ukraine) but real, meaningful, genuine democracy implies considerably more than that. Hence, the second definition, often called "real" or "liberal" democracy, emphasizes the actual practices and political culture of democracy *beyond* elections, including discourse that is civil, respect for the opinions of others, presumptions of equality, military subordination to civilian authority, free press and other classic freedoms, pluralism of interest groups, and respect for minorities. Countries that fall into this category include the Baltic republics, Poland, Czech Republic, Hungary, and Slovenia. Others (Slovakia, Bulgaria, Romania, Croatia) continue to struggle with these criteria; still others (Serbia, Bosnia) have so far made little democratic progress beyond formal elections; and some (Moldova, Belarus, Ukraine, maybe Russia) have slipped backward.

A third definition builds on these other two. It is not so much a distinct definition as an extension of the first two. Its most distinguishing feature is its focus on what are often called second-stage or second-generation reforms, such as judicial reform, anticorruption measures, police reform, transparency in the management of public accounts. These reforms are second stage or second generation in that they imply a long-term political/economic reform process that comes after the first stage involving elections and the initial granting of new political freedoms. Second-stage reforms may also involve the growth of civil society and the further *consolidation* of democratic reforms, continued economic reforms and privatization, modernization of education, bureaucracy, and so on. Significantly, *all* the EU and NATO candidate countries are now at various places in this stage, having already qualified in terms of the first and second definitions of democratic basics, and are now seeking to fill all the complex technical and reform criteria that the EU and NATO impose as conditions of membership.

A fourth and final definition involves human rights. Clearly, this issue is interwoven with the previous three, though it also stands by itself in both the NATO and EU criteria for admission. The human-rights criteria involve most, if not all, the classic human rights—press, assembly, speech, religion, and so on—and these are frequently used to criticize transgressions by applicant countries. Currently, the human rights criteria are employed frequently in East/Central Europe with regard to treatment of national minorities, especially the Roma. Cynical observers interpret this as

Table 8.2. Freedom House Ratings for Central and Eastern Europe (2001)

Country	Rating
Albania	4.5
Belarus	6.0
Bosnia	4.5
Bulgaria	2.5
Croatia	2.5
Czech Republic	1.5
Estonia	1.5
Georgia	4.0
Hungary	1.5
Latvia	1.5
Lithuania	1.5
Macedonia	3.5
Moldova	3.0
Montenegro	1.5
Poland	1.5
Romania	2.0
Russia	5.0
Slovakia	1.5
Slovenia	1.5
Turkey	2.5
Ukraine	4.5
Yugoslavia	4.0

Source: Freedom House website, "Freedom in the World: Table of Countries—Comparative Measures of Freedom," most recent update, April 3, 2001 available at www.freedomhouse.org/research/freeworld/2001/table1.htm. A lower number = greater freedom.

the EU countries telling the applicant countries to treat their minorities well and with respect so that, once enlargement occurs and border restrictions fall, these minorities will not flood immediately and en masse to the Western countries.[19] Once more it is the Baltic countries, Poland, Czech Republic, Hungary, Slovenia, and Slovakia that score the highest on human-rights criteria, with other countries rated less highly.

The criteria used here for classifying countries as democracies are the so-called freedom scores issued by Freedom House on a yearly basis for each of the world's countries.[20] The scores represent the averages of ratings on political and civil rights; scores range from 1 (best) to 7 (worst). There are drawbacks to this methodology, but it is a reasonably accurate way of assessing democratization. In accord with our definitions, it encompasses electoral rights and the meaningfulness of elections, real procedural rights and practices, second-generation reforms, and human rights. On this as on a number of the criteria raised here, hypocrisy is frequently involved.

Here, we sort our countries into four categories. Category 1 includes those countries that received the highest scores, 1 or 1.5, in the Freedom House surveys. In the mid-1990s (1996–1997), countries that received those scores (all at 1.5) were the Czech Republic, Estonia, Hungary, Lithuania, Poland, and Slovenia. These scores were the same as those received by Belgium, Germany, the United Kingdom, and Italy and, for comparison purposes, were one-half point ahead of Chile, Israel, and South Korea. While the possibility exists for backsliding or a reversion to authoritarianism in several of these countries, that possibility seems increasingly remote. Not only would such slippage violate domestic public opinion in these countries, it would definitely kill their chances for NATO and EU admission. By the year 2001, not only had these countries remained democratic, they had been joined by Latvia and Slovakia, the latter of which showed dramatic improvement after a change of government in 1998. On the basis of their progress and solid performance, the Czech Republic, Hungary, and Poland were invited to join NATO in 1999. The 2001 Freedom House ratings for Central and Eastern Europe are shown in Table 8.2.

Category 2 consists of countries that received scores of 2 to 4 in the mid-1990s Freedom House surveys. These countries seemed at that time to be improving, moving up in the rankings, toward greater democracy. These included Georgia, Latvia, Moldova, and Romania. Turkey also scored in this range. But since that earlier survey Latvia has, as indicated, moved up to a top position in the rankings; Romania stayed the same, at 2; and Georgia and Moldova have stagnated or slipped rather badly. Meanwhile, Bulgaria and Croatia had moved out of a lower category to join the good/improving group.

Category 3 consists of countries that by the mid-1990s, after earlier hopes, experienced an eroding democracy, ranging from mild to severe. Mild erosion (one-half point loss) occurred in Croatia, Macedonia, Russia, and Ukraine. Severe erosion (one full point) took place in Albania, Belarus, and Slovakia. But since that time, as we have seen, significant democratic improvement has occurred in Bulgaria, Croatia, and Slovakia; the others have stagnated or deteriorated further.

Finally, Category 4 consists of countries that, by the mid-1990s, had simply moved from one form of authoritarianism to another, without substantial democratization. These countries are Bosnia and the former Yugoslavia (Serbia and Montenegro). But with the Dayton Peace Accords and a massive aid program for Bosnia, and with Slobodan Milosevic now out of power in Yugoslavia, these countries are also moving up and may join the more hopeful group. Meanwhile, Albania (4.5), Belarus (6.5), Russia (5.0), and Ukraine (4.5), until the Orange Revolution of 2004, should probably be placed in this lowest category.

What is striking about this classification scheme is the increased division between countries that are "making it" to democracy and freedom and those that are not, and therefore the erosion of the middle categories. With Croatia, Latvia, and Slovakia moving up, the "democratic" category has been expanded. It now includes the Czech Republic, Estonia, Hungary, Latvia, Lithuania, Poland, Slovenia, and Slovakia. The only countries left in the middle are Bulgaria, Romania, Croatia, Turkey, and now, possibly, Bosnia and Serbia—and they are also improving. At the same time, Russia and the CIS countries Belarus and Moldova have stagnated or moved down. Georgia and Ukraine have had democratic openings. Significantly, this is precisely the lineup of acceding countries to the EU and NATO: the first or democratic group probably "in"; the second or intermediate group comes in under special conditions or else sits and waits as also-rans and potential candidates for future admission; the third group (both those who have slipped significantly and those who never really transitioned away from authoritarianism) are "out." Note how closely these categories correspond to the indicators for the other criteria of "Europeanness" that we have been considering.

Institutionalization

Another criterion for determining who makes it into the EU and NATO is levels of institutionalization, both political and economic. There is much that can be said on this subject; let us just make the major points, but briefly.

First, we need to distinguish between (1) those states that have had a considerable history as independent nations and, therefore, have some history of nationalism, national identity, and a national political culture, national bureaucracy, decision-making, policy implementation, and living and working together both as a state and a people and (2) those entities for whom these traits are either lacking or are so recent as to be non-institutionalized. Historian Lonnie R. Johnson has this distinction in mind when he categorizes states as either "historical" or "nonhistorical."[21] By "historical nations" he means those states that could identify their own historical origins in the form of a kingdom or state in the past, such as Poland, the Czech Republic, Croatia, Hungary, Serbia, and Bulgaria. "Nonhistorical" nations are those peoples who have had no, submerged, or, comparably very short records of independent national institutions, territory, or historical continuity, such as Slovaks, Slovenes, Bosnians, Macedonians, Belarussians, Ukrainians, or Georgians. "In-between" states, such as Albania, Romania, and the Baltic countries, have had "less history" than the former but generally "more history" than the latter. Recognizing that the point needs further elaboration and that the correlations are not one to one, we can nevertheless say that the "historical" and "in-between" states generally show greater prospects for political stability, democracy, institutionalization, and thus integration into Europe than those states who at present are struggling to create viable state structures and national institutions really for the first time.

Second, we come to the sphere of political economy. During the Cold War, policy analysts seldom differentiated sharply among the various Warsaw Pact countries, assuming that all Communist economies functioned more or less the same. But with the end of the Cold War we have become increasingly aware of the need to disaggregate among countries, and that the old assumptions of similarity were misleading. For example, Poland, Hungary, and Czechoslovakia, even with Soviet repression, were long known as countries possessing tremendous buoyancy and dynamism and a long and deep sense of rebelliousness characterized by small acts of protest and revolt (work slowdowns, sabotage, refusal to conform) and of a sense that "you can't keep us down forever." Politically, these three had powerful legacies of dissent, opposition, punk groups, and even a gay movement in otherwise repressive Slovenia—all as expressions of dissatisfaction with Soviet occupation and Communist rule. They also had partly decentralized and liberalized before the Berlin Wall fell, enabling groups like Poland's Solidarity and the Czech Republic's Civic Forum to organize and form a base for later democracy.

Economically, the Poles, Czechs, and Hungarians, along with Slovenia, drawing on their pre–World War II experience with markets, as well as the fact that they had been less completely socialized than other Communist countries, lost little time after the collapse of Communism in resuming entrepreneurial activities, opening shops and commercial ventures, hustling for money, devising new commercial codes, reorganizing banking and credit, and inviting in and effectively utilizing foreign investment. But in much of Belarus, Ukraine, Georgia, Moldova, to say nothing of Russia and Central Asia, there is neither a comparable historical legacy of free entrepreneurial activity nor the pool of skills for either grassroots democracy or a flourishing market economy. It is no accident that the former countries were the first to join NATO and among the first to be admitted to the EU, whereas the latter, still mired in political authoritarianism and economic distress, stand no chance of being integrated into Europe anytime soon.

A third institutional indicator is civil society. Here our markers are less clear. Poland's Solidarity is proverbially cited as *the* classic case of how a strong, popularly based civil-society organization can be the essential base both to oust a dictatorship and to establish democracy. The Czech Republic's Civic Forum is similarly cited, although its composition and the history and process of democratization there were quite different from Poland's. Hungary had already liberalized its regime from within, though it lacked a single, strong civil society movement at the time of the transition. But the evidence indicates that since the early 1990s, when these transitions began, the civil-society movements in these countries may have declined somewhat, atrophied, and fragmented. So the evidence leads us to speculate: Is a civil-society movement only necessary in the early stages of the transition, after which it disappears? Is American-style, pluralist, "Tocquevillian," civil society necessary for the maintenance of democracy, or are there other systems of state-society relations emerging in East/Central Europe and, if so, what are they? Meanwhile, we also know that those countries, especially in the Balkans, the CIS, and Russia, that lacked and still lack *any* well-established system of independent civil society, whether in the short or longer run, have had and will have a harder time securing and consolidating democracy.

CONCLUSION

Early in the 1990s, after the Berlin Wall had fallen, the Iron Curtain had come down, and the Soviet Union had disintegrated, there was a great deal of optimistic talk, in the West and East alike, of a free, unified Europe stretching from the Atlantic to the Urals: the geographic definition of Europe. It has not worked out that way.

A new divide, referred to here as the Golden Curtain, is stretching across Europe to replace the old and torn-down iron one. The new curtain has been designated "golden" because it separates the wealthier countries, or countries that are "making it" into the ranks of the affluent—Croatia, the Czech Republic, Estonia, Hungary, Latvia, Lithuania, Poland, Slovenia, and Slovakia—from those who are also-rans or mired in poverty and underdevelopment. The first group, with qualifications, is also democratic; in the present decade all or most of the countries are likely to be integrated successfully into the EU and NATO. The rest have not yet made it or, worse, may be condemned to seemingly permanent exclusion from Europe.

The new curtain being drawn across Europe seems, at least in theory, to be more flexible than the old one. There is a "wall" but not literally so; and there are no police dogs, barbed wire, or armed guards—although with Europe's strict new border (Schengen) rules and patrols, the differences may not appear so great. Theoretically, it is possible for Russia and the CIS states to qualify for admission to NATO and the EU; the EU *says* that it wants no new "artificial" barriers across Europe, and there are ongoing, though declining, cooperative programs. But the gaps between new and about-to-be member and nonmember states are widening rather than narrowing and are likely in the future to get wider still. Through its relations first with the new NATO applicants, then (moving eastward) with the CIS, then with GUUAM (Georgia, Ukraine, Uzbekistan, Azerbaijan, Moldova), then with the Black Sea Economic Cooperation (BSEC) project, next with Central Asia, and finally with Russia itself, NATO seems to have erected a formidable hierarchy of groupings, associations, and defenses aimed more at hemming in, isolating, and weakening Russia than at bringing new states into the fold (which may, in fact, all be part of the same overall strategy). While theoretically open to still further expansions besides those currently contemplated or already under way, the practical likelihood of bringing anymore than a handful of present also-rans (Croatia, Serbia) into the European fold, which would thus in effect "complete" the borders of Europe, seems remote. Russia, the CIS countries, and Central Asia are at present hardly even contemplated as potential members.

The theme that emerges most clearly, however, is not only the new fault line being drawn across Europe but how closely this line corresponds to the historic sense of Europe as encompassing Western, developed, Christian Europe. In the age of political correctness, these are not themes that are often expressed; but they are so obvious that they jump off the page. These dividing lines were more or less established a thousand years ago; even with all the fluctuations of history over the centuries, the wars and invasions and conquests, not much has changed since then. Christian Europe is part of the new Europe; Orthodox Europe is marginal; Muslim Europe is still out. Central Europe still lags economically and sociologically behind the West, but it is far ahead of the Russian or CIS East. The Baltic countries and Central Europe are in; Russia and its historic constituent units (Belarus, Ukraine, Georgia, Moldova) are out. The new lines being drawn in Central Europe are almost exactly the same borders as those of the historic Austro-Hungarian Empire, with Western Ukraine, Transylvania, northern Serbia (Vojvodina), and somewhere along the Bosnia-Croatia border being the farthest edges, or "military frontiers," of that empire.

My purpose in this chapter, in focusing on religious, political, institutional, developmental, and cultural fault lines, is not to be overly determinist. We need to keep our minds, and Europe's rules, open to the possibilities of Europe's continued expansion. For this is also, as British writer Martin Walker reminds us,[22] an existential question: not only what Europe is but also what it might be, and whether it can summon the political will to keep the enlargement process going. Many of the borders talked of here are vague, flexible boundaries, and countries and peoples, after all, can and do change: witness the dramatic economic growth and democratization in Eastern and Central Europe itself in the last decade and a half, in countries that we once considered forever "lost" to Communism. Moreover, it seems to me that the way to solve the manifold problems of the Balkans, Turkey, the CIS, and ultimately Russia itself is not to draw new "curtains" that forever exclude them from Europe, but to bring them in over time, to incorporate them into Europe in some fashion, though not necessarily the EU, to give them hope and a shot at democracy and economic development, to devise new halfway houses (associated rather than full membership) that offer the prospect at least of change and modernization. But that prospect is scary as well as costly to today's Europeans, which is why they are presently drawing the boundaries as portrayed here; but in the long run it is the only way to provide a measure of peace and stability in the areas farther to the east. For now, however, it is the closer border that is the realistic and operable one.

To that hallowed question of where Europe ends, therefore, the answer in 2005 is a little firmer in terms of national boundaries than it was in the past. It ends along the Golden Curtain we have been describing, which is as much cultural and historical as it is economic and strategic. But the shorthand and informal answer, "Somewhere east and south—or southeast—of Vienna," also still applies. It appears, therefore, that not all that much has changed over the last millennium. Do geography, history, and political culture, therefore, still count? Absolutely. Are these factors determinative or, alternatively, accommodative to new countries and ways of doing things? That is now the harder question that can only be decided in the future.

DISCUSSION TOPICS

1. Can you define where Europe ends? By what criteria?
2. How does Eastern Europe compare to Southern Europe or Latin America in terms of levels of socioeconomic development and preparedness for democracy?
3. What is meant by "the golden curtain"?

NOTES

1. The author resided in Vienna during part of the research period for this project, and in Budapest for another part. From these two home bases he conducted research, including interviews, in Poland, the Czech Republic, Slovakia, Romania, Bulgaria, the former Yugoslavia, the Baltic countries, Germany, Spain, Portugal, and Belgium (EU and NATO headquarters).
2. The distinct definitions of "Europe" may be traced in map books beginning in Roman times.
3. *New York Times*, January 29, 2000, A7.
4. Unless otherwise stated, Central/East Europe is here defined as those countries west of Russia and the CIS, and east of Germany-Austria. In turn, Central/East Europe is further divided into three subregions: the Baltic countries of Estonia, Latvia, and Lithuania; the Central European countries of Poland, the Czech Republic, Slovakia, and Hungary; and the Balkan countries and countries of the former Yugoslavia (Slovenia, Croatia, Serbia-Montenegro-Kosovo, Bosnia-Herzegovina, Macedonia, Romana, Bulgaria, and Albania).

5. Lonnie R. Johnson, *Central Europe: Enemies, Neighbors, Friends* (New York: Oxford University Press, 1966).

6. The analysis in this paragraph follows that of Martin Walker, "Europe's Existential Crisis," *Wilson Quarterly* (Winter 2001), 30–53.

7. Adrian Hyde-Price, "Patterns of International Politics," in *Developments in Central and East European Politics*, vol. 2, ed. Stephen White et al. (Durham, N.C.: Duke University Press, 1998), 255–75.

8. Recall Mackinder's famous dictum:

Who rules East Europe commands the Heartland
Who rules the Heartland commands the World Island
Who rules the World Island commands the world

A modern-day expression of this view is Zbigniew Brezezinski, *The Grand Chessboard: American Primacy and Its Geostrategic Imperatives* (New York: Basic Books, 1997).

9. Neither religion nor ethnicity is, of course, exactly coterminous with national boundaries—which is precisely one of the key problems especially in Southeastern Europe—and it also leaves out a number of groups (Jews or Roma [Gypsies], for example) who have no separate state in Europe. In addition, some nations are internally divided precisely on religious and/or ethnic lines, which again helps explain political conflict, lack of unity, and, often, underdevelopment in the countries affected.

10. Victoria Clark, *Why Angels Fall: A Journey through Orthodox Europe from Byzantium to Kosovo* (London: Macmillan, 2000).

11. Bulgaria and Romania seemed to be also-rans but, because of 9/11 and the war against terrorism, joined the acceding countries; see Chapter 9.

12. Johnson, "Eastern Europe," *Encyclopedia of Nationalism* (New York: Academic Press, 2001), 1:165–96.

13. The materials in this section are based on author interviews and participant observation in the countries and areas indicated. But see also Richard Rose and Christian Haerpfer, *New Democracies Barometer V: A 12-Nation Survey* and *Trends in Democracies and Markets: New Democracies Barometer 1991–98* (Glasgow: University of Strathclyde, 1998).

14. See the two studies cited in #9; also William Mishler and Richard Rose, "Learning Democracy: The Dynamics of Popular Support for Post-Communist Regimes" (paper presented at the Annual Meeting of the American Political Science Association, Atlanta, Georgia, September 1999); and Rachel A. Cichowski, "Western Dreams, Eastern Realities: Support for the European Union in Central and Eastern Europe," *Comparative Political Studies* 33 (December 2000), 1243–78.

15. Alejandro Moreno, "The Democratic-Authoritarian Cleavage in New Democracies: Eastern Europe and Latin America in the 1990s" (paper presented at the Annual Meeting of the American Political Science Association, Atlanta, Georgia, September 1999).

16. On the relations between culture and development in East/Central Europe, see Jacques Rupnik, "The Postcommunist Divide," *Journal of Democracy* (January 1999), 159–61; Ilya Prizel, "The First Decade after the Collapse of Communism:

Why Did Some Nations Succeed in Their Political and Economic Transformations while Others Failed?" *SAIS Review* 19 (Summer/Fall 1999), 1–15.

17. Jeffrey S. Kopstein and David A. Reilly, "Geographic Diffusion and the Transformation of the Postcommunist World," *World Politics* 53 (October 2000), 1–37.

18. Using the socioeconomic data alone, particularly the PPP index, Belarus and Russia might also be considered candidates for EU admission or possibly even NATO. But they have clearly been ruled out at least for now on cultural, political, and strategic grounds. As usual, Bulgaria and Romania are in an ambiguous intermediary category.

19. Belgium, France, the Netherlands, and Sweden have been quick to condemn Eastern/Central Europe's treatment of the Roma, but when the Eastern countries suggest to the West that it could help solve the problems by absorbing some Roma into their own countries, the answer is "absolutely not." On this as on a number of the criteria raised here, hypocrisy is frequently involved.

20. The information used here and in Table 8.2 is from the Freedom House website, "Freedom in the World: Table of Countries—Comparative Measures of Freedom," most recent update, April 3, 2001, available at www.freedomhouse.org/research/freeworld/2001/table1.htm.

21. Johnson, *Central Europe*; also Jacek Kochanowitz, "Leviathan Exhausted: Ideas on the State of the Post-Communist Transformation," *East Central Europe*, 27, Pt. 1 (2000).

22. Walker, "Europe's Existential Crisis."

9

The Politics of European Enlargement

Since the fall of the Berlin Wall in 1989, the pulling down of the Iron Curtain, the collapse of the Warsaw Pact, the disintegration of the Soviet Union, and the end of the Cold War, the main issues in Eastern and Central Europe, and in U.S. and European policy toward the area, have been in achieving peace and stability, building democracy, accomplishing economic and institutional reform, accelerating growth and modernization, and anchoring and integrating the countries of the area into Europe and its two great "clubs," the EU and NATO.[1] It could be said that three of the purposes listed—democracy, economic and institutional reform, and European integration—were all means to the end of achieving peace and stability in this critical area—which is not known historically for its stable, peaceful politics—and of securing a buffer zone on Europe's eastern frontiers that would also function as a means to hem in and limit any future Russian resurgence. But what may have begun in strategic planners' eyes as a means to an end has since taken on a life of its own, suggesting that purposes and motives which seemed quite reasonable at one time have a way of changing over time and acquiring a dynamic of their own.

The formal *technical* and general criteria for democratization, economic reform and modernization, institutional reform, and human rights for the accession of new aspirant countries to NATO and the EU are quite clear and have been set forth in summary form in numerous official documents.[2] In addition, the EU requires applicant states to conform to the extensive legal, regulatory, and financial stipulations of the *Acquis Commu-*

nautaire, while NATO also has a variety of technical requirements that include the restructuring of civil-military relations according to the Western model, reform of defense ministries and of equipment, armaments, and military systems to achieve interoperability, and the ability to be a net contributor to, not a drain on, NATO forces and functions, including, importantly, peacekeeping in Southeast Europe and, now, cooperation on counterterrorism.

In the early 1990s, it was often thought by analysts and policy makers alike that the processes of EU and NATO enlargement would go forward in tandem, on parallel tracks, mutually reinforcing each other.[3] To some degree that has happened, but the road has been bumpier than expected, and the two roads have often diverged. In addition, and a key argument of this analysis, is that while early on the technical criteria largely defined the enlargement process, in the final analysis it was political criteria that proved decisive. At least at the formal and institutional level, almost all the acceding countries now are at the stage, or close to it, of EU and NATO entry. Almost all the countries are now democracies, have undertaken economic and institutional reform, observe human-rights criteria more or less, have carried out military reforms, and have adapted their laws to the requirements of the *Acquis*. Part of this is charade, of course, since both Easterners and Westerners understand that full *implementation* of these changes will take three to four decades, if not generations, not just a few years. But as the acceding and hopeful countries now reach the end of this process, the question—and it is a political one—becomes, now what? Once they all qualify or come near to it, how is it possible to discriminate further among them, to allow some in even while keeping others out? Who gets in, who stays out, and on what basis? The answer is, increasingly, by the use of political criteria. In other words, what began as a process employing largely technical and formal criteria is ending, now that these have been largely met, using preeminently political criteria.[4]

In this chapter I focus on these political criteria, or what may be termed the politics of the "end game" of EU and NATO expansion. Now that the technical criteria have been for the most part satisfied, what comes next? Who decides who gets admitted, when, and on what basis? Four major actors or sets of actors are discussed: the Eastern/Central European acceding countries, the EU and the European allies, Russia, and the United States. In each case we examine the interests and the politics involved and try to reach some tentative conclusions as to how the process of enlargement will now proceed. A final substantive section, building on the earlier analysis, weighs both the technical and, increasingly, the political considerations operative as the enlargement process nears its final stages.

THE INTERESTS OF THE ACCEDING COUNTRIES

The interests of the acceding countries are perhaps the easiest to discuss: they want *in*, in almost all cases, to both NATO and the EU. They identify membership in these two "clubs" as essential to their aspirations to become developed, democratic, *European* states, tied to "the West," in all its dimensions, rather than pointing backward, in their view, to the East and what they identify as the past, with its backwardness, underdevelopment, authoritarianism, and oppression.[5]

In all of Eastern and Central Europe, the EU is viewed more favorably at the popular level than is NATO. Public support for the EU in most Eastern/Central European countries is in the 50–70 percent range while that for NATO is in the 40–60 percent range. The difference is largely due to the fact that for most East/Central Europeans, the EU means affluence, prosperity, rights, and opportunity, while NATO stands for obligations and expenditures, a formula certain to produce disparate popularity among the two organizations. In addition, NATO's bombing campaign in the former Yugoslavia frightened many East/Central Europeans, reminding them of past wars and instability in their own countries. But the leadership and *informed* public opinion in Eastern/Central Europe recognize that they cannot have the benefits of the EU without also taking on the obligations of NATO. Moreover, they believe that, as in Spain in the early 1980s, once their governments explain and present the case for NATO, they can succeed in bringing support up to over 50 percent in all countries. In *no* country of Eastern/Central Europe is there much doubt that they need and want to join both NATO and the EU.

In the early 1990s, and again recently as Russia puts pressure on members of the CIS and others to conform to its policies, protection from Russia was, and remains, one of the primary motives for the Eastern/Central European countries to join NATO and the EU. But in this respect one must discriminate between countries. While all of the Eastern/Central European nations are wary of Russia, those countries that actively border on the Bear, with no buffer states in between—Estonia, Latvia, and Lithuania—are the ones who fear Russia the most. Also, those states that were once members of the USSR—again, the three Baltic states, who also have sizable Russian populations within their borders—as distinct from those countries (Poland, the Czech Republic, Hungary, the former Yugoslavia) that were part of the Warsaw Pact but had at least some nominal independence from the USSR, feel more threatened by Russia. In addition, Russia made it very clear that, while it objects strongly to all eastward expansion of NATO, it particularly objected to NATO's expansion into those countries of the former USSR.

NATO means something different, furthermore, to the different countries of the region. The Eastern/Central European countries tend to see it as a collective security agreement that *guarantees* that the other European NATO members and the United States will come to their defense if they are ever attacked by their neighbors or, especially, Russia. Meanwhile, in seeking not to awaken and invite a drastic reaction from the slumbering, sorely wounded, and greatly diminished Russian Bear (how much Russia has disintegrated and reverted to Third World status is not fully known in the West), the United States sought for a time (prior to the September 11, 2001, terrorist attacks) to make the case to the Russians that NATO was no longer a collective security agreement aimed at them but more like a political club that even they could join, a sales pitch that the Russians never bought. Meanwhile, the debate goes on in academic as well as policy circles as to whether NATO's Article 5 really is a collective security agreement calling for an *automatic* response by the others if one country is attacked, or if it allows them discretion. Naturally, the Eastern/Central European countries, fearing Russia, emphasize the language that seems to support an automatic response, whereas the United States and the Western countries tend to stress the language implying discretion.

A second, major reason the Eastern/Central Europeans want membership is economic. The EU and NATO, especially the former, stand for affluence, prosperity, and the good life of which the Eastern/Central European countries wish to become a part. Recall that Eastern/Central Europe, like Southern Europe earlier on, has always been on the poor, underdeveloped, marginal, semifeudal periphery of Europe. Joining the EU is seen as a way of overcoming past underdevelopment and entering the rich-man's club, indeed, what may be the world's richest, most affluent area. Entering "Europe," writ large, makes them eligible for aid, transfers, loans, investment, and subsidies on a grand scale. Just as Greece, Portugal, and Spain benefited enormously in the 1980s and 1990s from joining what was then called the EEC and receiving massive infusions of investment and aid (cohesion as well as structural funds), so Eastern/Central Europe sees joining the EU as giving them an opportunity to leapfrog into the world of the developed, or First World, nations. Unfortunately for them, there is far less assistance money available for Eastern/Central Europe than there was for Southern Europe in the 1980s and 1990s.

Third, the Eastern/Central European countries see membership in the EU and NATO as securing, anchoring, and *guaranteeing* their often still-fragile democracies. These are countries that have had democratic elections, often several of them, thus qualifying them as "democracies" at least formally. But in terms of becoming solid, liberal, pluralistic, human-rights-observing democracies, most of the countries still have a considerable way to go. Only a few of them (the Baltic countries, Poland, the Czech Republic, Hungary, Slovenia, now joined by Slovakia) have begun the second-generation reforms (judicial reform, tax reform, budgetary and policy-making transparency, others) necessary to complete and consolidate their democratic transitions. They also need time to change their political cultures—their beliefs and ways of behaving—to conform to democratic understandings and practices. Because their transitions to democracy are still incomplete, the Eastern/Central European countries see joining the EU and NATO as both a "Good Housekeeping" badge of approval for accomplishments so far and an incentive, inducement, and even requirement to complete the process.

These are all pragmatic reasons to join the EU and NATO that Americans can understand; the fourth reason is harder. It may be called "civilizational" in the sense that, for the Eastern and Central Europeans, joining Europe is about more than butter quotas and military hardware. Historically underdeveloped and on the fringes of Western civilization, Eastern/Central Europe was the butt of endless cruel, ethnic jokes that portrayed it not just as backward but as barbaric and stupid. For a thousand years, Eastern/Central Europe was viewed as inferior, racially tinged (because of Hun, Tatar, Mongol, and Ottoman invasions), and incapable of European achievement. These patronizing, condescending, sometimes racist attitudes bred resentment in the East and some gigantic national inferiority complexes. So joining Europe is not just about wheat and military modernization, it is also a symbol that Eastern/Central Europe has joined *Western civilization*, that it is no longer backward and barbaric but as good as the rest, that it no longer should be the butt of cruel ethnic jokes, and that after centuries of isolation and underdevelopment its ties to the West have been cemented. Indeed, above and beyond all the practical reasons for joining NATO and the EU, I would submit that this sociopsychological motive may be the most important of all.[6]

This consideration also helps explain the ups and downs in the Eastern/Central European public opinion polls regarding joining the EU and NATO. The fact is, as we see in the next section, that Western Europe's enthusiasm, and that of the United States and NATO as well, for bringing more states in has waxed and waned over the years. And when the West is ambivalent, the Eastern countries have to salvage their pride by saying, "Well, we aren't really interested either."

Meanwhile, there are still some political uncertainties. While most of applicant Eastern/Central European states will soon be in conformity with EU and NATO requirements, some are lagging—especially Bulgaria and Romania—and there is no great expectation that they will catch up soon or enthusiasm for admitting them quickly even if they do turn around. Cyprus's candidacy, which once seemed assured, was hung up and may remain there on the seemingly intractable issue of still-bitter Greek-Turkish relations, an issue that may now be resolved. Slovakia's internal politics may also be problematic.

Russian Interests

Russian interests in EU and NATO expansion have been almost entirely negative, or at best cautious, though it is obvious Russia is far more opposed to NATO expansion than to the EU.

It is not fully appreciated in the United States, perhaps because U.S. officials and reporters mainly visit Westernized and relatively developed Moscow and St. Petersburg, how far Russia has disintegrated since the collapse of the superpower Soviet Union in 1989–1991. Instead of being the leader of the so-called Second World of *developed* Communist states, Russia has sunk to near–Third World levels. Virtually everything has disintegrated: the economy, the armed forces, the educational system, health care, institutional infrastructure, transportation, social welfare, housing, public services, everything.[7] At this stage, therefore, Russia is not in a position to be a threat to any serious power, although it does have a nuclear arsenal (also rusting and disintegrating) that policy makers need to keep under control. It sometimes blusters and threatens in ways that frighten Europeans and remind them of the Cold War and, with its economy now recovering somewhat because of higher oil prices, it is able to put pressure on its smaller neighbors, mainly those in the CIS that have historically been a part of Greater Russia, but also those in the near abroad, which includes the Central and East European states.

Russia's interest in Europe and the EU is in the prosperity, affluence, and aid that it would like to acquire and have access to. Russia also desires acceptance by the West, though for political and nationalistic reasons it cannot say this publicly. But both Europe and Russia know that it cannot possibly qualify for EU admission anytime soon, or maybe ever. In the early 1990s, the vision of a Europe "whole and free," stretching from the Atlantic to the Urals or perhaps all the way to Vladivostok, had some resonance both in Western Europe and in Russia and may still have some future possibilities. However, Europe has its hands full with its present, limited, eastern enlargement, and Russia often has been ambivalent about "joining Europe." That, of course, is a centuries-long and hotly contested issue in *internal* Russian politics, and it remains divisive today. Russia wants to be known as a "civilized" country and, to some extent, that means becoming "Western," but what precisely that means and how far to go are questions that are intimately tied to Russian pride, nationalism, and sense of uniqueness or distinctiveness. Russia is divided over these issues and not a little bit complex (rather like Central and Eastern Europe, only worse) over them. Meanwhile, as Russia has stuttered, declined, and proved enormously corrupt, Europe's aid, investment, and enthusiasm for assisting Russia have also dried up. Europe is still casting about for some halfway-house or associated status for Russia (not an EU member but offering some hope for future possibilities), but even that limited relationship is greeted with ambivalence and considerable opposition on both sides.

Although Russia has been vigorously opposed to NATO expansion eastward, it knows at this stage it is all but powerless to prevent it.[8] During its decade of disintegration in the 1990s, Russia saw its borders and, hence, power progressively reduced and is at this stage surrounded and hemmed in by American influence. First it lost its Warsaw Pact allies in Eastern Europe; then it saw U.S. influence expand in the CIS states of Belarus, Ukraine, and Georgia; now there is a Black Sea Cooperative Council (BSCC), as well as an expanded U.S. and Turkish presence in Central Asia; and, finally, (not really "finally" because there are other layers as well) U.S. efforts to influence what is left of Russia itself through its invitation to join the Partnership for Peace (PfP, the Organization for Security and Cooperation in Europe (OSCE), and NATO itself through the Permanent Joint Council (PJC), signed in 1997 as a way of deepening Russia-NATO cooperation. Moreover, in May 2002, Russia and NATO agreed to form a joint NATO-Russia Council. Central and East Europe, meanwhile, continued to view NATO as a collective security agreement; the U.S. tried to convince Russia that it was now more like a peaceful political association for cooperation and democracy, a line Russia never quite bought into.[9] Nor have the U.S.-sponsored efforts to seduce and civilize Russia by luring it into these joint military cooperative arrangements been very successful; in fact, they have so far been fraught with tension, misunderstanding, and the absence of Russian cooperation.

Although Russia is a weak, decimated power, it is now somewhat rejuvenated by new, vigorous leadership in the person of President Vladimir Putin as well as by a suddenly, more expansive economy, thanks to swelling oil revenues. For these reasons it has been able to bully, intimidate, and expand its leverage against its neighbors. The CIS countries in Central Asia, as well as Belarus, Ukraine, and Georgia, have been the main recipients of this pressure, which chiefly takes the form of threats to restrict energy supplies and seeks to draw them closer into Moscow's orbit both economically and strategically. The United States has sought, not very vigorously or vociferously, to counter these Russian pressures; Europe has been largely silent. In part it already has a full plate with the currently ongoing EU enlargement, in part it prefers not to get involved in what seem to most Europeans to be distant squabbles bearing on internal Russian affairs, and in part, despite the Soviet Union's disintegration and Russia's decline, it remains fearful of Russia. Russia has played on these ancient fears by sounding bullyish and tough (despite its weaknesses), by trying to divide the United States from its European allies on various issues, and by threatening to introduce nuclear weapons into Kaliningrad, that odd, unsupportable, potentially unstable bit of Russian territory on the Baltic (and thus "within" Europe in ways that Russia is not) that is separated from the main Russian territory by Belarus and Lithuania.

The main issue for purposes of this discussion is Russian reaction to the possibility of NATO expansion into the Baltic republics of Estonia, Latvia, and Lithuania. While Russia is opposed to *all* NATO expansion eastward, it has been especially opposed to a NATO enlargement that would include these three countries. First, because, alone among the NATO candidate countries, the Baltic states were *part of the USSR*, not independent countries, and so far Russia even in its weakened condition has not been willing to concede *any part* of the former Soviet Union to the West. Second, there are significant Russian minorities in each of the Baltic countries (30 percent in Estonia, 34 percent in Latvia, 8.5 percent in Lithuania), and even though the Baltic republics have moved to regularize the legal status of these citizens, Russia continues to raise the issue of minority rights as a way of inhibiting the Baltics' EU and NATO candidacies. Third, Russia, as well as those Russians living in the Baltic republics, still often harbor visions of a restored "Greater Russia" that would include the Baltic countries and perhaps serve again as an Eastern alternative to the West. While the Baltic states themselves continue to lobby Washington and European capitals strenuously on behalf of both "club" memberships, the Europeans, still worried about the dormant Russian Bear and unwilling to risk arousing its wrath, remained negative toward the Baltics' NATO membership. The Americans, at the same time, continued to debate whether one Baltic country should be invited to join, on the logic that only one country would not antagonize the Russians overly, versus admitting all three at once, following the logic that having Russia react vociferously once is preferable to having it react three separate times. Once the three Baltic states were, in fact, admitted to NATO, Russia continued to object even at that stage to the possibility of NATO troops being stationed there.

EU/European Interests

The European Union and the European member states (whose interests do not always exactly correspond) also have a strong stake—cultural, social, political, economic, strategic—in the enlargement of the EU and NATO.[10]

First is the idealism and glowing vision of the early 1990s of a Europe "whole and free," stretching from the Atlantic to the Urals and beyond. This implies, after the two terribly destructive World Wars of this century, Hitlerism and Stalinism, the Cold War, the Holocaust and ethnic cleansing, a Europe at peace, stable, prosperous, and democratic. In many quarters this vision still holds sway, although more recently it has been tempered by the realization of the time and costs involved. Central/Eastern Europe, especially Russia and the CIS, is increasingly seen as a two- or three-*generation* project, not one of two or three years. It is especially significant that the EU's plans and criteria for expansion were drawn up during this earlier and more hopeful stage rather than during the more tempered and realistic one that followed. The EU agencies in Brussels still believe that their expansionist plans can be carried out through their own and member governments' positive publicity programs, despite declining support in European public opinion. Moreover, the EU as a central bureaucracy remains committed to the enlargement process, argues that the entire process is nearing completion and can't be stopped now, that the wheels are constantly turning and that positive closure needs to be reached on this issue. Others are skeptical that a Europe that proved so indecisive on Yugoslavia can ever get its act together sufficiently to carry out and complete the enlargement process.

Second, and related, European enlargement, economically through the EU and strategically through NATO, is driven by a desire to achieve peace and security in Central/Eastern Europe. At the end of the Cold War, two major problems were seen: what to do about Russia and what to do about Eastern/Central Europe, that area in the heart of the Eurasian land mass lying between historic Germany and Russia that had for centuries been a source of instability and conflict. One solution was to think of this area as a buffer between Europe and Russia, another was to integrate it into the West. And we now know from former National Security Advisor Brent Scowcroft's statements that a conscious decision was made to opt for solution two, to solve the historic problem of Eastern/Central European instability by integrating it into Europe by expanding the EU and NATO eastward, knowing that would necessarily come at the expense of antagonizing and isolating Russia.[11] Russia correctly saw European enlargement, particularly NATO, as a hostile act, exacerbated by the near-neuralgic rejection of Russia by the Eastern/Central European countries. Attempts to ease Russian fears through the PfP, assurances that NATO is nonthreatening, and creation of the PJC within NATO for Russia and of the NATO-Russia Council did not achieve the desired end and may have *increased* Russia's sense of isolation. However, under President Putin, Russia began to warm to its role in NATO, and NATO moved to open its arms wider to Russia. Russia at this stage cannot hope to join either the EU or NATO anytime soon, and they see this negativity as perhaps permanently closing the door on their integrating into Europe. Meanwhile, as much of Eastern/Central Europe seems poised on the verge not just of joining the EU and NATO but of being integrated into Europe in a "civilizational" sense, the buffer talked of earlier has moved farther east to encompass all or parts of the CIS states:

Belarus, Ukraine, Moldova, Georgia, maybe (in the security sense) Armenia, Azerbaijan, and parts of Central Asia as well.

Europe wants protection from the Russian Bear but at the same time it sees the bear as resting, dormant, hibernating, and, given its size, resources, and nuclear weapons, does not want to arouse the bear's hostility. Because of its proximity to Russia and the experience of the Cold War divide, Europe feels this issue more intensely than the United States does and, therefore, is more sensitive about which countries to include in NATO. The United States does not want to resume the Cold War, but it has also been more aggressive about hemming Russia in through a variety of new eastward-oriented alliances and cooperative programs (not just NATO expansion, but also PfP, OSCE, Council of Europe, the BSCC, GUUOM, others) than has Europe. Both of these views may overstate Russia's current or future threat potential, for if the country is viewed from a comparative-politics perspective rather than an international relations one, it is a disintegrated, quasi–Third World state that, apart from the careless use of its nuclear weapons or their fear potential, is not really a serious threat at present.

Third, Europe is also in favor of expanding democracy, human rights, and, in some of the more ideologically driven countries, and *social democracy* to Central/Eastern Europe. Quite a number of the Western European countries sought to assist Russia as well as the Eastern/Central European countries in their transitions to democracy. Aid, investment, and much political advice (not all of it wanted), therefore, followed. But afterward Russia and much of the CIS proved to be a "black hole" into which aid and investment would go, never to be seen again. On this score, the Europeans have largely come around to the American view, although without acknowledging this evolution publicly. Like the Americans, the Europeans now view democracy in Eastern/Central Europe both as a good in itself and as a means to an end: peace and stability in a contiguous territory not well-known historically for these traits. Russia and the CIS countries are viewed less hopefully and, in any case, too large and too poor for Europe to take on at this stage.

Fourth and continuing in this positive vein, Central/Eastern Europe has begun to prove profitable for West European investments. That was not always the case. In the early 1990s, for instance, when Western investment was going into Russia for the first time and Lufthansa Airlines was opening up regular service to Russia's interior cities, assuming that businesspeople would soon follow, the expectations of quick or at least eventual profits were high. But, for the most part, Russia and the CIS have not proved very profitable, and, consequently, Western investments have been quietly redirected toward Eastern/Central Europe, Europe's near abroad. The result is that Scandinavian investments in the Baltics,

German investment in Poland and the Czech Republic, Austrian investments in Hungary, and Italian investment in Slovenia have turned around and started to show a profit—in some cases, a considerable profit. These investments plus, of course, ties of culture and history also help explain why some West European states are more interested than others in some Eastern/Central European states' accession to NATO and the EU. Meanwhile, the redirection of investment to Eastern/Central Europe means that Russia and the CIS have largely been left holding the bag.

But there are strong negatives as well, especially at the popular level, to Europe's expansion to the east.[12] First and foremost, West Europeans fear the loss of jobs, security, and lower wages that eastward expansion implies—comparable to fears in the United States over competition from cheap Mexican labor. Simply put, Western Europe fears it will be overrun by Eastern European immigrants willing to work for less and, therefore, taking Western Europeans' jobs, because, under the EU's Schengen rules, labor as well as capital is free to move about within the EU borders once a nation joins, but immigration from outside the EU borders will be tightly controlled. Austria, for example, which is surrounded by potential new EU members, is particularly worried because a number of Eastern/Central European urban/industrial centers, such as Slovakia's capital of Bratislava, are located right on its border; Austria fears what it calls "commuter immigration" from these centers that will cost Austrian jobs. While there is abundant sociological evidence showing that most Central and East Europeans prefer to stay put in their own communities even if given a chance to move,[13] West European popular opinion nevertheless fears a large influx; moreover, this finding of likely lower-than-expected immigration does not help Austria's commuter-immigration problem.

Hence, Austria, with strong German backing, proposed a "seven-year transition" period before the free movement of labor is allowed. Actually, under a provision of a white paper on immigration that was circulated among EU members, there would be a two-year *EU* prohibition on the free movement of labor (so individual members can let in as many immigrants as they want), followed by a three-year period in which the free movement of labor is provided for but not necessarily in the whole of EU territory, followed by another couple of years of "exceptions." In this way, Austria and Germany could claim for domestic political reasons that there is a "seven-year" transition, while the EU can say it stands for the "free movement of labor," and those prosperous countries who actually want more immigrant labor can also claim victory.

Immigration is the key issue, but Western Europeans also harbor other fears about eastward expansion. Among the most important is taxes, which Western Europeans see as inevitably going up if the requirement is, through aid, grants, and subsidies, to bring the Eastern economies up to

EU levels. If you're already paying 40–60 percent of your income in taxes, the last thing you want is to see taxes skyrocket to 50–70 percent. In addition, West Europeans worry greatly about assimilating the Easterners, whom they often refer to indiscriminately as "they" or "the other," and whom they often think of as different, less developed, and less "civilized." The result is some quite clear new dividing lines across Europe: to simplify only a little, "Christian" and "Western" countries are acceptable, Eastern Orthodox may be considered, while Islamic countries are out. In practical terms, that means the Baltics, Poland, Czech Republic, Hungary, Slovenia, Slovakia, and probably Croatia (eventually) are "in" Europe; Romania and Bulgaria are marginal; and Belarus, Ukraine, Moldova, Georgia, Russia, and Turkey are out.

In addition to the issues of immigration and higher taxes, Western Europe also sees the East as a source of potential "problems." Such problems are often vague and undifferentiated in the popular mind, and they sometimes evoke national and cultural stereotypes and even racism. Eastern Europe is thus often perceived as a source of crime, violence, instability, racketeering, prostitution, drugs, abused children, and more. And, of course, since the Easterners "don't work very hard" (a contradiction, if one of the arguments against expansion is that they take Westerners' jobs), they will be a drag on Western Europe's already financially strained welfare and pension systems. It is certainly convenient and comfortable, however inaccurate, on cultural and nationalistic grounds to believe that one's fellow citizens are entirely faultless in causing all the problems outlined here and that all the blame should be attributed completely to eastern immigrants, a position which demagogic politicians such as Jorg Haider of Austria (which really does have a rising crime problem that is linked to immigration) have been able to exploit. And even though the racism and culturalism involved in such stereotyping is misplaced and off the mark, such ideas do have powerful popular appeal; and we know that it is what people believe more than what is objectively true that often counts politically.

These are the main *overall* European worries but there are also concerns that are specific to individual countries. First, there are what we might call front-line states (Germany, Austria, and Italy): those countries that are closest to Eastern Europe and, therefore, most strongly affected by it, by immigration, refugees, and "problems." Second are what we will term the human-rights sensitives (the Netherlands, Belgium, Scandinavia): countries that while often far from Eastern Europe are nevertheless especially vigilant about human rights abuses there, particularly with regard to treatment of the Roma (Gypsies). Third are those countries we call net EU recipients (Greece, Portugal, Spain): countries that have been receiving EU grants, loans, and subsidies since joining the organization in the 1980s and are now faced with the prospect of seeing many of those subsidies redirected to Central and Eastern Europe. Finally, it needs to be said that support for EU expansion into Central and Eastern Europe is not uniform across Europe, with opposition strongest in Austria, Germany, Ireland, France, and Great Britain. Hence, the politics of dealing with the issue of enlargement, itself preeminently political, will vary from country to country as well.

The polls tell us that there is declining interest in EU and NATO enlargement, both in the West among member states and in the East among aspirants. The Western countries tend to see Eastern/Central Europe as less potentially explosive than fifteen years ago, possessing greater stability and more viable economies than expected, and Russia as more disintegrated and less of a near-term danger than earlier thought. But they also see expansion as very expensive and as a threat to their jobs, cultures, and ways of life. Therefore, there has been declining Western Europe interest in enlargement, with the favorable ratings going roughly (depending on the country) from 60 to 70 percent to 50 to 60 percent. Both the Brussels bureaucracy and the Western governments believe they can turn this negative trend around with a large-scale publicity and educational campaign.

In the East, sentiment is more favorable because the Eastern countries will be the chief beneficiaries of enlargement. But they also recognize that small, "mom'n'pop" businesses and agriculture will go under as a result of enlargement; patronage and opportunities for graft will be reduced; budgets must be kept under control; and that the capitalistic world out there is often mean and unforgiving. Hence, East European sentiment favoring enlargement has dipped from 80 to 50 or 60 percent. Polls about NATO membership tend to show 10–20 percent less support than for EU membership, in part because of the NATO bombing campaigns in the former Yugoslavia being seen as excessively militaristic, in part because it makes little sense to Eastern politicians to expand military budgets when there is no threat and when popular social programs are threatened by austerity, and in part because the Easterners, naturally enough, would rather focus on the advantages of EU membership rather than the costs (in terms of new military training, equipment, etc.) of NATO. When the chips are down, however, all the Eastern countries can be expected to opt for membership in both the EU and NATO because for them this is a matter of joining Western *civilization*, not just an economic or military affiliation.

One final point needs to be made in this section, and that concerns the *differences* between the EU and NATO enlargement processes. Contrary to earlier expectations, these are not entirely congruent processes on parallel tracks proceeding (to mix a metaphor) hand in hand. First, the EU extended formal invitations to the aspirant countries to apply for membership (implying that once they meet the requirement, the EU will have no further reason to turn them away); NATO only asked aspirants to improve their military situation, meaning that an invitation might come later on. Second, with its PfP, OSCE, Council of Europe, and other programs, NATO developed a flexible system of halfway houses for aspiring members; the EU had little such flexibility or partial solutions. Third, the criteria for NATO, because they are highly subjective, can be relatively easily fudged or glossed over; with the EU, since we're talking *real money*, the requirements are much harder to fudge. And fourth, there is a political/financial tradeoff operating here: the United States preferred to see the EU expand as quickly as possible so as to modernize the Eastern/Central European societies overall and thus assist them in preparing for NATO membership, whereas the EU first wanted to see NATO expand to the east to provide a kind of "training ground" for EU enlargement. In the end, both processes, with these differences built in, did proceed more or less in tandem.

U.S. Interests

U.S. interests in Central and Eastern Europe are of long standing, having to do with the Cold War, NATO, the sense for many years that Eastern Europe was likely to be the Cold War's main venue and the potential invasion route into Western Europe for Warsaw Pact armies, repeated U.S. assurances over the years of support for Eastern European freedom and democracy, and, more recently, Bosnia, Kosovo, and the problems of the former Yugoslavia, and terrorism.[14]

In 1989–1991, as the Berlin Wall fell, Eastern Europe asserted its independence, the Soviet Union disintegrated, and the Cold War ended, the United States perceived two key problems in this critical strategic area. The first was what to do about Russia; the second was what to do about those historically unstable states of Eastern Europe lying between Russia and Western Europe. The decision could have been that Eastern/Central Europe would continue to serve as a buffer between East and West. Instead, the decision was made by the administration of George H. W. Bush, pushed along by its NATO allies, to solve the Eastern/Central European problem by incorporating these countries into NATO and the EU, which could only come at the expense of Russia.[15] Russia would be hemmed in at one level through an expanded NATO, and at others through the PfP extended to CIS members as well as to Russia itself, plus a range of new U.S. aid and cooperation measures with Central Asia, Caucasia, and the Black Sea area; meanwhile, the United States would seek to manage and control internal Russian political developments through its democratization program, aid and investment efforts, market reforms, programs to control nuclear weapons, IMF and World Bank assistance, and so on. The United States, in short, sought not just to democratize Russia but also to surround it, shrink it, limit its options, maintain its dormancy, and prevent a new Russian threat from arising. EU and NATO expansion into Eastern/Central Europe was one of the primary means of accomplishing these goals.

A second goal of American policy was and is to democratize Russia. The issue can be looked at in one of two ways: either the United States values democracy in itself (which is useful for rhetorical purposes; in addition, most Americans subscribe to that view), or democracy can be seen as a means to an end; that is, a stabler, less bellicose Russia (note the literature demonstrating that democracies do not go to war with each other). In the long run, however, it doesn't matter which motive is predominant; the fact is, both are undoubtedly operating at the same time. That is, democracy is advanced whether we value it as a good in itself or as the best available means to ensure stability in Russia. In addition, by promoting the democracy agenda, the United States can stand for high moral purpose, rally congressional, media, and domestic support, and serve U.S. national interests at the same time.

Much the same arguments apply to economic development. The United States clearly prefers an economically developed, modernized Russia integrated into EU, U.S., and world markets, seeing that as preferable to a poor, underdeveloped, unintegrated, isolated Russia. But once again the questions can be raised: Why do we prefer that solution? Do we value economic development for its own sake or because we wish to expand investment and trade with Russia? Or is it because we see economic development, trade, and European integration as a means to stabilize Russia, help it build a stable middle class, bring peace and security to the area, reduce nationalistic and jingoistic sentiment by diverting popular preoccupations to economic self-advancement, defuse a potentially bellicose Russia by channeling its energies to peaceful economic goals, and "civilize" it by incorporating it into the main European agencies, the EU and NATO? The obvious answer is that both of these sets of goals may happily be served at one and the same time. And again, like democracy, the goal of economic development/trade/integration serves a combination of purposes at the same time: high moral purpose, domestic agreement, and U.S. interests.

A third goal of U.S. policy, at least initially after the end of the Cold War, contemplated a string of buffer states across Central and Eastern Europe, from the Baltics in the north to Yugoslavia and the Mediterranean in the south. The aim, once again, was to deprive Russia of its former Warsaw Pact allies, or satellites, and to shrink its size, power, potential, and forward presence. Many Eastern/Central European politicians and intellectuals, such as Vaclav Havel, contemplated the same vision of an independent and culturally distinctive Central or "Middle" Europe, lying between Russia and Germany-Austria, a bridge between East and West but no longer a pawn in Cold War machinations, a vision that stretched back a thousand years into the area's misty (and idealized) past. But many Central and East Europeans reacted emotionally against further ties with Russia, failed to see any advantages in serving as a "bridge" to the East, and, especially as Russia's debility and impoverishment were realized, wanted little to do with it. Instead, it was the West that was attractive: its affluence, its freedom, and its "civilizational" influences in an area that was long considered, and considered itself, on the margins of Western civilization. Recognizing these pent-up aspirations, and in some cases anticipating them, U.S. and Western European policy also shifted away from the notion of Eastern/Central Europe as a buffer area and toward integrating them into the EU and NATO, with the consequences for Russia already noted. Hence, rather than a separate and independent Central Europe, we now have a group of Eastern/Central European states clamoring for admission to "Europe," writ large. Meanwhile, the "buffer" has moved east, encompassing Belarus, Ukraine, Moldova, Georgia, Central Asia, and Transcaucasia.

Not only did the Eastern/Central European states wish to be included within NATO, the EU, and "Western civilization," but their application to join NATO became, after the Cold War ended and the organization's purposes were now openly questioned, a way to resurrect and even save that potentially irrelevant organization. NATO's purpose in Europe had long been, in the popular expression, "to keep the Russians out, Americans in, and Germany divided." But the first objective had been accomplished with the disintegration of the Soviet Union, the third had become moot with Germany's reunification, and that left only the second purpose; but clearly America's continuing military-strategic presence in Europe—absent the Soviets—required a new rationale. NATO (and EU) enlargement provided a part of that rationale, and then came Bosnia and Kosovo—justified not so much by hard-headed American national interests in Southeast Europe (recall Secretary of State Baker's dismissive comment early in the Yugoslav conflict, "We don't have a dog in that fight") as, after the intervention had already begun, that the *credibility of NATO* was at stake, which, of course, meant it had to be supported regardless of whether or not any other important interest was at stake. Central and Eastern Europe, in a sense, thus gave NATO something to do, a new mission and objective, at a time when the organization's continued usefulness and even existence was being questioned.

Over the years, however, as Russia more or less democratized and most of Central/Eastern Europe (even the former Yugoslavia) continued on the democratic, economically reformist path, Eastern/Central Europe as well as European (NATO and EU) enlargement garnered fewer headlines and, therefore, less official attention or public interest. The stakes seemed to be smaller and no longer so important as they had been in the early 1990s; in the fickle, here-today-gone-tomorrow way that American foreign policy deals with most issues, Central/Eastern Europe faded from the headlines, came near to dropping out of public sight, and received less high-level attention than in the past. Poland, the Czech Republic, and Hungary entered NATO in 1999 but, other than the celebratory headlines and pictures (of Secretary of State Albright dancing for joy), there was almost no public debate about the merits (and demerits) of these three cases and the implications of the decision for U.S. policy. The decision, as even NATO and Department of Defense officials readily acknowledge, was made exclusively on political grounds: the U.S. administration decided that it wanted these countries *in*. Future enlargement decisions will similarly be made on the same kinds of political grounds.

But today the conditions are different: Central and Eastern Europe has stabilized, attention has waned, there appear to be no large or immediate crises in the area, and they are lower on the list of American priorities. In addition, the political conditions are quite different: whereas Poland, Hungary, and the Czech Republic all had sizable constituencies in the United States and in critical swing states that could be mobilized for political action (recall that in the heat of the 1996 election campaign both Bill Clinton and Bob Dole called for these countries' admission to NATO), that is not so true of the present applicant countries. There are sizable and activist communities of Slovaks, Slovenes, Estonians, Latvians, Lithuanians, and others in Pennsylvania, Ohio, Michigan, and Illinois (all swing states), and their ambassadors in Washington, just like other ambassadors with important U.S. constituencies, have been busily mobilizing their communities for the showdown vote; but it was predicted to be a close call and there were many uncertainties as to whether Congress, in its treaty-ratifying as well as power-of-the-purse roles, would go along.

Interviews by the author at NATO headquarters in Brussels, at the Department of Defense office of European affairs in the Pentagon, and with political officers, ambassadors, and military attachés in U.S. embassies in the capitals of the applicant countries were revealing. First, they showed a quite sharp split between the civilian officials who almost to a person favored NATO enlargement as a desirable political goal, and military officials, generally with a narrower view, who saw applicant countries skeptically as "not yet ready" or as "recipients but not contributors" to NATO, and who, therefore, were laying the groundwork to blame civilian officials (the mantra was well-nigh universal that it will be a "political" and not a "military"—presumably more rational or merit-based—decision) if anything went wrong or enlargement proved more expensive (almost certain) than contemplated.

Secondly, and this applies mainly to Department of Defense officials who must testify on Capitol Hill and make the case for enlargement, they saw themselves as having three main constituencies: Russia, the European allies, and Congress. With regard to Russia, these officials said the Bear is presently dormant and in hibernation, and we do not want to do anything to rouse its ire or provoke a bellicose attitude, let alone a renewal of the Cold War. But that ignores both how much Russia has changed and how far Russia has disintegrated and that it is not in a position now or anytime soon to cause big trouble—although it can still sound bullying and threatening and cause some degree of a problem. As far as the European allies are concerned, they are far closer to Russia than is the United States, still worried about it, and even more inclined than Department of Defense officials to let sleeping dogs (or bears) lie—once again ignoring or perhaps not fully apprised of Russia's weak and disintegrated state or not willing politically to risk even the slightest tremor out of Moscow. These worries about Russia, whether exaggerated or not, have major implications for some of the candidate countries, particularly the three Baltic states.

The biggest unknown, however, was the U.S. Congress, both the House and the Senate, which must approve new NATO enlargements: (1) Congress had not yet focused sharply or specifically on the issue (one congressman, on a junket in Vienna, told me he had never been to Eastern Europe and wanted to know if I was in favor of NATO enlargement —obviously not yet a well-defined, discriminating, or carefully considered question); (2) neither Congress nor the public saw NATO enlargement into Eastern/Central Europe as the same critical issue it was a decade ago; (3) Congress was not yet sure how the politics and political constituencies will play out on this issue; (4) Congress, knowing the costs involved with and the continuing problems of the three most recent members, was very worried about the expenses in bringing new NATO members up to even minimum levels of military interoperability; (5) it was worried about whether the United States, under NATO's collective security Article 5, will be called on to police every border skirmish, ethnic clash, or signs of instability in Eastern Europe; and (6) Congress could well have gone along with the Pentagon's assessment that *none* of the applicant countries was yet "ready" for NATO admission. In the end, however, Congress approved enlargement overwhelmingly.

ENLARGEMENT PROCESSES

The criteria for admission to the EU and NATO are of two kinds, technical and political. In general terms, the criteria for both organizations are similar and parallel: what a country accomplishes in attempting to qualify for the EU will also help it get into NATO, and vice versa. But there are subtle and interesting differences that help explain why the enlargement processes in these two large European organizations have not run exactly parallel. In addition, while the technical criteria are important and must be met by an applicant country in order to qualify for admission, it is the political criteria that are more interesting and that ultimately will be determinative of who gets admitted and who not. Hence, we will devote more attention to the political factors involved, although before doing so we need also to have an understanding of the technical processes.

Technical Criteria

The collapse of the Warsaw Pact and the disintegration of the Soviet Union were the triggers that unleashed the process of integrating Central and Eastern Europe into the EU and NATO. Fearing instability and/or chaos in the Central European area and wishing to prevent the countries of the area from falling back into the Russian orbit, the U.S. and the European Community sought ways to integrate these nations into the stable, affluent, democratic West. Enlargement of the Community and of NATO was seen as a key means to achieve that goal.

As early as 1991 the EU had signed European Association Agreements (EAA) with Czechoslovakia, Hungary, and Poland.[16] EAAs were signed with Bulgaria and Romania in 1993, the Baltic states in 1995, Slovenia in 1996, and Slovakia in 1998. Cyprus and Malta also signed EAA agreements, bringing the total to twelve. Turkey has been declared "eligible" for EU membership but is still viewed as problematic by the EU. The EAAs established a framework designed to support the gradual integration of these countries into the EU through harmonization of regulatory structures, technical standards, competition laws, opening of services, free trade, and so on. Criteria for social, political, and cultural convergence with the EU were also adopted. At its 1993 Copenhagen summit, the European Council, which was put in charge of managing enlargement, defined the political and economic criteria to be considered for EU accession. In 1994 in Essen, the Council requested the design of a strategy for the accession of new members. In 1995 at Cannes, the Council identified the key legislative, regulatory, and institutional aspects required for accession. Under the PHARE (originally *P*oland and *H*ungary: *A*ssistance for the *R*econstruction of the *E*conomy, but later extended to include twelve more countries) program, the EU designed a plan to bring EU members and applicant countries together to provide information on community matters, to assist the reform efforts, and to provide preaccession assistance funds. In 1996, the Council meeting in Luxembourg required regular reports from its staff reviewing the progress of each applicant according to the Copenhagen criteria. In 1997, *Agenda 2000* provided a comprehensive statement of accession criteria, obligations of membership, and the strategy of enlargement. This document, together with the EAAs, constitute the core of the institutional requirements for enlargement. A subsequent meeting in Nice reopened what appeared to have become a stalled enlargement process.

The criteria for EU enlargement now included the following: at the political level applicant countries must establish democracy and the rule of law, must respect human rights, and must demonstrate respect for minorities. The economic criteria include the existence of a functioning market economy and the capacity to withstand competitive pressures and market forces within the Union. Other obligations of membership include acceptance of the aims of political, economic, and monetary union, adoption of the *acquis communautaire*, and the administrative and judicial capacity to apply the *acquis*. Each of these main categories is then broken down into further subcriteria or "chapters" to which the applicant countries must also adhere.

To help promote as well as to monitor the process of conforming to these criteria, the EU had established an office in each of the EU candidate countries. The offices were well staffed with professional technicians and observers whose role was to assist the applicant countries in meeting the requirements but also to oversee the process and issue some sharp and often quite critical periodic reports on the progress being made.[17] The applicant country is then invited to respond to these reports, offer its own point of view, and make corrections if necessary. Several conclusions emerge from a systematic examination of these offices: (1) they are staffed by highly competent EU officials who are independent of and objective toward the countries to which they are assigned; (2) their reports are detailed, exacting, perceptive, and surprisingly frank (for an international agency) about their specific country; (3) the criteria used and reports issued are more exacting and systematic than the parallel NATO reports on candidate countries (perhaps explainable by the fact these EU offices are largely staffed by lawyers, social scientists, and trained observers, whereas NATO reports are mainly done by military attachés whose analyses tend to be more impressionistic); and (4) one cannot conceive that the EU would staff these offices with thirty or forty persons in each country unless the EU was dedicated to and convinced their candidacies would in the final analysis be successful.

In 1996, the so-called first wave countries (the Czech Republic, Estonia, Hungary, Poland, and Slovenia) were invited to begin negotiations for accession. These were the countries already considered by the EU to be "best prepared." At the Helsinki Council meeting in 1999, Bulgaria,

Latvia, Lithuania, the Slovak Republic, and Romania were also invited to begin accession negotiations. Outside of Eastern/Central Europe, Cyprus and Malta were similarly invited to begin negotiations. Among several of those in the second group, a race began to catch up with those in the first group, since the EU has determined that merit and the meeting of the EU's enlargement criteria are to be the measures used, not the order of the invitations issued to apply. Turkey was added to the EU "eligible" list mainly at the insistence of the United States, which was thinking more in strategic than in economic terms.

Of course, there is a world of difference between the enactment of all this legislation (relatively easy) and its actual implementation, which certainly will take two or three generations, not years. Herein enters a political problem, for the EU could not hold the applicant countries at bay for that long, and the candidate countries were impatient and could not wait that long. In addition, once a country meets all eighty thousand criteria and completes negotiations on all thirty-one chapters, what additional criteria could the EU use for keeping it out? The EU said that the chapter negotiations are completed only "provisionally," but denial of admission to an applicant country on the basis of that formality would constitute a lame excuse at such a late stage of the game that it would be almost impossible to sustain politically. The process worked its way out: in December 2002 the EU states agreed on an admission package, and in April 2003 the accession treaty was signed.

NATO's criteria for admission were never so formally, elaborately, and mechanistically set out as were those for the EU, which gives NATO maximum flexibility in either accepting or rejecting new members; nor did NATO ever issue formal invitations for countries to become candidates, thus avoiding the trap just identified that the EU fell into that once a country meets all the criteria, the EU has no further basis for excluding them. NATO may eventually find itself in the same position of "inevitability" (not "if" but "when") as the EU, but at least for now NATO maintains the posture that, through the PfP and other programs, it is asking countries to bring themselves up to NATO standards, *after which* a membership invitation *may or may not* follow and, in any case, the country in the meantime will have vastly improved its economic, political, and security structures.

As with EU enlargement, the conception and criteria for NATO enlargement have evolved over time.[18] As early as July 1990, with Mikhail Gorbachev still in power and the Soviet Union still intact, NATO heads of state extended a "hand of friendship" to the East. Later that year, the first eastern "enlargement" took place through the unification of East and West Germany, the latter a NATO country. Then, with the collapse of the Soviet Union, the United States and its NATO allies, not wanting to dilute NATO by expanding it, focused on strengthening the Conference on Security and

Cooperation in Europe (CSCE, renamed the Organization for Security and Cooperation in Europe—OSCE in 1994), whose membership soon grew to fifty-three members. The OSCE included Russia and the new CIS countries as well as NATO members, but without an enforcement mechanism it was recognized as essentially toothless. Hence, in late 1991 the United States created the North Atlantic Cooperative Council (NACC), also including Russia and CIS, as a further institution for consultation and cooperation on security issues. But the NACC was similarly conceived as a consultative rather than decision-making body and thus also lacked teeth.

As these early, partial steps indicate, initially there was little support in the U.S. government or among the allies for NATO enlargement. A handful of U.S. strategic thinkers supported expansion of the organization to the east,[19] but it was really Germany's initiative in early 1993, aimed at stabilizing its eastern border as well as the economies of the Eastern/Central European countries, that triggered the NATO enlargement process. U.S. senior officials at the State Department and the National Security Council (not the Department of Defense) acknowledged that a U.S.-led NATO enlargement process could stabilize the eastern countries, demonstrate that the United States and not Germany was the key driving force, also demonstrate the continuing relevance of NATO, and, not coincidentally, serve some politically important ethnic constituencies in the United States in the run-up to the 1996 election. But because there were still many reservations (costs, worries about Russia's response, whether an enlarged NATO could still be an effective NATO, and the preparedness of the potential new members), the United States and its NATO allies in 1994 produced a new compromise, the PfP.

The PfP agreement said that NATO would "expect and welcome NATO expansion that would reach to democratic states to our east, as part of an evolutionary process, taking into account political and security developments in the whole of Europe." NATO invited CSCE and NACC countries to participate in PfP, defining *their own* role and scope in the program in negotiations with the sixteen (later nineteen when the Czech Republic, Hungary, and Poland joined) NATO members. NATO would establish sixteen-plus-one, later nineteen-plus-one (the PfP country), consultations with individual countries concerning reform of their military institutions through permanent partner offices (like a small, self-enclosed embassy) at NATO headquarters in Brussels and at a military planning unit in Mons, Belgium. In other words, countries (including Russia and CIS) were free to join PfP or not and could participate more or less in accord with their own capabilities, wishes, and interests; at the same time, NATO was in a strong position to link partnership and eventual membership with specific reforms and norms to which the country had to agree if it aspired to membership. PfP was an inspired, even ingenious idea that has worked out better than expected—rare in policy making; some of my interviewees suggested its authors should get the Nobel Prize.

Although NATO's rhetoric still proclaimed it a collective security organization, and that is how the aspirant Eastern/Central European countries seeking guarantees against Russia's future or potential expansionist proclivities continue to see it, in fact the processes of the first enlargement to manifestly militarily unprepared countries tended to minimize the strategic purpose in favor of vague and less-strict political criteria. This posture in turn alienated U.S. military officials who want to maintain the strategic emphasis within NATO, who recognize the severe limitations militarily of the three new member states, and who emphasize that further enlargement would impose additional costs and immense organizational efforts, in a time of generally declining defense budgets, personnel, and public support, on the alliance. However, the Eastern/Central European countries' cooperation in the war against terrorism will boost their chances of NATO admission: Romania and Bulgaria, especially, benefited from this consideration.

While NATO's criteria for admission of new members are nowhere near so detailed and elaborate as the EU's, there *are* criteria; moreover, and parallel to the EU, they have been more clearly spelled out over the years, making it politically more difficult to deny an invitation to membership to a country once it meets the criteria—unless NATO is willing to risk the fall of the elected, democratic government that worked hard to meet the criteria and thus to precipitate the very instability and conflict in Central and Eastern Europe that NATO wants to prevent. The basic criteria are:

- democracy (although not clearly defined)
- a market economy (but, again, without clear definition)
- civilian control of the military (but without degrees and gradations recognized)
- a responsible foreign policy toward its neighbors (i.e., no post-NATO membership claims on its neighbors' territories)
- a credible PfP track record of upgrading and reforming the armed forces and the defense ministry
- building NATO-compatible military forces and interoperability (which may mean only a single elite unit)
- a willingness to participate in NATO activities (such as assisting in Bosnia or Kosovo or in the war on terrorism)
- being a net *contributor* to NATO and not just a recipient of NATO assistance
- strategic importance

These often vague standards were, as with the EU, soon supplemented by more detailed criteria. The first step in the PfP program was thus for the applicant countries to sign "framework agreements," similar to the EU's EAAs. The country would then prepare "presentation documents" that identified its objectives, particularly if it sought NATO membership or a more limited role. Each "partner" would next submit an Individual Partnership Programme (IPP) identifying its assets and how it would work with NATO. The PfP countries were subsequently required to list steps taken toward meeting these goals, again similar to the EU's closings of "chapters." A Partnership Work Programme (PWP) was also established to indicate NATO activities undertaken to meet their partnership goals, as well as a Planning and Review Process (PRP) to guide PfP states toward NATO compatibility. These and other steps indicate that the NATO enlargement process has become approximately as formalistic and stylized as the EU accession process, leading in addition to elaborate bureaucratic procedures and mountains of paperwork to a certain inevitability of expansion because, once the great wheels of the process start turning, it becomes almost impossible politically and bureaucratically to reverse them since the negative consequences (instability, government failure, chaos, Russia stepping into the vacuum of a NATO veto on membership) would be far worse than admitting a country even if its strategic performance by NATO standards was far from perfect. Most of the new NATO members came in under these criteria, but Romania and Bulgaria largely bypassed the processes indicated and were invited to join NATO on the basis of their strategic importance in the war on terrorism.

At first the countries that were serious about joining NATO saw the PfP as another strategy of postponement, to which NATO was forced to respond that participation in PfP *would* indeed lead to NATO membership. If it did not, what would be the logic of a country going through all the reforms and expenditures of improving its military (including raising the defense budget at a time of both budgetary austerity *and* pressing social needs) only to be turned down in the end? These assurances to the applicants from the East that their quest would eventually be successful in turn had the effect of alienating the Russians still further, who subsequently reduced their PfP cooperation and for a time all but stopped participating in the Joint Council at NATO headquarters that had been especially created for them. And as Russia's uncooperative attitude, bellicose posturing, and blatant pressures on its CIS neighbors increased, the desire of the Eastern/Central European countries to achieve protection under the NATO umbrella increased. Meanwhile, the technical and procedural wheels of their efforts to meet the NATO criteria kept turning, ultimately making it harder and harder either to turn them down or keep them on the string indefinitely. President Putin's cooperation with the West in the antiterrorism campaign reduced the tension over NATO and its enlargement to the east, though there may/will be a cost to pay for Russian cooperation.

Political Considerations

We are now nearing the endgame of the enlargement processes.[20] Decisions could not be put on hold or postponed forever without jeopardizing the very purposes of the twin EU and NATO enlargements: peace, stability, prosperity, democracy, reform, and security in Central and Eastern Europe. Both the EU and NATO preferred to draw out the process, both because the applicant countries are, in fact, not yet fully prepared and because they knew, once admission was finally granted, all incentive for further reform from the applicants is lost. Although the final results of both processes are still unknown and unknowable, here are some political variables presented in summary form that will help shape the outcome:

1. Both EU and NATO enlargement, once begun, acquired a momentum of their own; once that momentum gained force, it would be very hard to reverse it again. Moreover, as the process moved further along, the possibility of turning countries down was further complicated. The events of September 11, 2001, accelerated the enlargement process. Because Russia seemed to be more cooperative, the terrorist threats helped to bring more countries closer together, and the United States reemphasized its strategic and international interests.
2. Both the EU and NATO had a record of encouraging the new prospective members and of promising enlargement; given that record and the expectations raised, it would have been difficult to change course. In his June 2001 speech in Warsaw, President George W. Bush went on record as favoring NATO enlargement from the Baltic to the Black seas, thus encouraging a large number of potential new members; ultimately, the United States and Europe *had* to deliver.
3. There was always a certain economic and security logic in enlargement to include the Eastern/Central European countries as a way of "completing Europe" up to the CIS/Russia (in the case of the Baltics) strategic border, or to the socio-cultural-economic-religious-political border of "Western civilization." This seems to conform to what most European publics currently see as the "natural" border of Europe.
4. The applicant countries were *invited* to apply; once they then met the criteria, by what additional reasoning could their admission be further postponed or denied? Recall, this logic applied more strongly to the EU than to NATO, but it was not absent in the latter. Decisions could still be postponed, but not indefinitely. Once a country was invited, it proved hard to then turn it down.

5. By the end of 2002, almost all the applicant countries had more or less met the criteria for EU admission—at least formally. But once nearly all qualified in this way, how could the EU further discriminate among the qualifiers? The answer: It couldn't, not without severe damage being done to the organization and the applicant countries. Therefore, in regard to EU enlargement, the "big bang" in which nine or ten countries were admitted at once was predictable. (The EU all but said as much in its November 2001 report on the progress of the candidate countries.) Among the twelve countries then candidates for admission, Romania and Bulgaria could not fully qualify; their admission was put off until 2007. Cyprus was a question mark because of lack of progress on the island's internal divisions, but in 2004 came a breakthrough on those negotiations that enabled Cyprus to qualify. NATO had more flexibility and could be expected to be more discriminating in selecting new members, but the war on terrorism altered that calculation and obliged NATO to admit some new members that, on the merits, would not have qualified.
6. While the decision to enlarge was fraught with difficulties, the decision *not* to enlarge would have been even worse. Most of the Eastern/Central European countries' governments had put enormous time and resources into their efforts to join NATO and the EU, making it their number one priority. If they should then fail or be turned down after so much effort, several of the governments of the area would undoubtedly fall, producing the very chaos, instability, and threats to democracy that enlargement was designed to ensure. In other words, admitting countries that were still admittedly incompletely prepared would be better than not admitting them and risking even worse consequences. To which NATO hard-liners retorted, if they're that unstable, they shouldn't be in NATO in the first place. That is a macho answer, but it does not solve the dilemma posed.
7. While the logic of enlargement was compelling, there remained numerous *large* practical problem areas still to be settled (the common agricultural policy, the issue of regional development funds and whether access to these by current EU members will be transferred to the new members, the question of immigration and borders, whether capital and labor can move freely, the internal organization and voting within the EU, the costs involved, the effectiveness of a significantly enlarged EU or NATO, etc.). But enlargement advocates argued that these problems, or at least many of them, did not all need to be settled conclusively before enlargement occurs.
8. Some of the EU applicant countries had already established bilateral or multilateral customs unions and other agreements among themselves. Admitting one part or one country of an

already-existing such arrangement could not be done without admitting the other(s).
9. Slovakia proved to be a pivotal country for both the EU and NATO. While its democracy was still uncertain and its preparedness for NATO incomplete, it brought other assets to the table that enabled it to enter both of the European clubs regardless:
    a. For NATO, Slovakia provided a land bridge (around neutral Austria and Switzerland) linking the north and south of Europe, it completed the previously postponed Visegrad process (named after the town where representatives of Poland, Hungary, the Czech Republic, *and* Slovakia had met to plan their incorporation into NATO, but intially Slovakia didn't qualify), it completed NATO's borders up to the CIS, and it provided a logical defense perimeter: that is, it would be far easier to patrol a seventy-mile border with Ukraine with Slovakia *in* NATO than a nine-hundred-mile border with Slovakia still outside NATO.
    b. For the EU, much the same logic applied: admitting Slovakia completed both the Visegrad Four and Europe's expansion to its easternmost limits, Slovakia was already strongly integrated culturally and economically into Europe, and it would be far easier in terms of border patrols enforcing the Schengen immigration controls to have only a seventy-mile rather than a nine-hundred-mile border.
10. The terms of reference kept changing: in the early 1990s several West European governments thought the Eastern countries would be economic "basket cases" they would have to continuously bail out; now quite a number of countries are making large profits from their trade with Eastern/Central Europe, and they anticipate even more.
11. The United States had long favored European enlargement eastward, as a way of stabilizing the area and keeping Russia in check. Although there is less attention to the area now than in the 1990s, less sense of crisis, this was *NATO*, after all, the foremost collective security agreement of the last fifty years and maybe of all time. NATO had impressive political support in the Congress and among the public, and it is doubtful that the United States could at this stage go back on its commitments.
12. For a considerable period, there had been a little "dance" going on over enlargement between the United States and its European allies. The United States wanted the EU to expand faster and first because the economic development, political democracy, and governmental reforms the EU insisted on for admission also helped prepare countries for NATO and ultimately made NATO enlarge-

ment less costly for the United States to bear. At the same time, in this "after you, Alphonse" two-step, the EU wanted NATO to expand first because the same conditions NATO insisted on (democracy and economic and administrative reform) for enlargement were, as in the cases of new NATO members the Czech Republic, Hungary, and Poland, also the requirements for EU accession and, again importantly, made enlargement less expensive for the EU. While this dance provided for an interesting political dynamic and rivalry between the United States and EU, both entities eventually had to come to terms with the fact that the reason they went to the dance in the first place was to integrate new partners.

13. The three Baltic countries provided a special dilemma: they had been part of the Soviet Union; Estonia and Latvia have large Russian ethnic minorities; and Russia had in the past said it would draw the line to prevent NATO expansion here, a threat that Europe often viewed more seriously than the United States did. But the Baltics are also predominantly Western; they wanted to join the EU and NATO and were among the most eligible candidates; the United States could not allow Russia—particularly a weak, enfeebled Russia—to dictate the borders of Europe; the United States had a certain long-standing moral obligation to the Baltics to help preserve their independence, and the constituencies of the Baltic countries in the United States are influential. Various formulae were being discussed: one "Balt" at a time (so the Russians scream three times), all three at once (so the Russians scream once, but loudly), and some kind of grand compromise in which the Baltics withdraw their application to NATO in return for guaranteed admission to the EU. The latter is just the kind of compromise, however, that gives veto power to Russia that the United States earlier had said it could not allow. Meanwhile, Russia's "mellowing" toward NATO coupled with U.S. insistence resulted in all three Baltic countries coming in at once without major opposition.

14. The rhetoric and mythology in this process suggests that, on these parallel paths to European integration, the United States can largely dictate NATO expansion while the European countries decide on EU enlargement. But that is a polite fiction: in fact, the United States is also extremely influential on EU enlargement and, while it was reluctant to put pressure on Europe to expand, its views in favor of enlargement were well known to European foreign ministries. That is why, at U.S. insistence and over European objections, NATO member Turkey became an EU candidate—although its actual accession may still be far off or never happen. Nonetheless, the United States wanted Turkey listed as a potential member to help

stabilize that divided nation and to offer it hope for the future. Similarly, if the United States had insisted on some countries or all being admitted to either NATO or the EU, it is unlikely that Europe would be able to say no.

15. The result was as follows: in regard to EU enlargement, the three Baltic states, Poland, the Czech Republic, Slovakia, Hungary, Slovenia, and Malta were all admitted to the EU. Romania and Bulgaria were admitted at U.S. insistence, but their actual accession was postponed to 2007. Cyprus was admitted, but on the condition it solve its internal Greek-Turkish conflict. Croatia and Serbia have become candidates; Russia, the CIS states, Bosnia, Croatia, and Albania will stay out at least for the foreseeable future; Turkey's candidacy will be postponed but nevertheless encouraged at least rhetorically; and new prospects Israel and Morocco are likely to be eventually given some form of associated status.

    NATO admitted Poland, the Czech Republic, and Hungary in 1999; in a second round, it admitted the Baltic countries, Slovakia, and Slovenia. But, on security criteria (as distinct from merit or qualifications) stemming from 9/11 and the war on terrorism, it (actually, the United States) insisted that Bulgaria and Romania be brought in, and that they would go through the PfP or reform process *after* admission rather than in preparation for it. The same logic led the United States to seriously consider Albania's admission even if it was woefully unqualified at the time. Croatia and Serbia would also be brought in and maybe Bosnia and Kosovo. In short, the NATO admissions process changed in midstream, with immediate and short-term security considerations coming to overwhelm all other qualifying criteria.

16. Two quite distinct sets of logic were operating here. In regard to NATO, the first way of thinking was that, since NATO is primarily a defense alliance, a military collective security arrangement centered on Article 5, no unqualified or not fully prepared candidate, or one that fails to contribute substantially to the collective defense, should be taken in. Much the same logic applies to EU enlargement, but substituting EU criteria for NATO's strategic criteria. The alternative logic suggests that the present situation provided a unique opportunity for enlargement to the east. There are no credible threats in that region and few risks, the potential gains are large, and the costs are modest. So the West should seize this unique opportunity to expand both NATO and the EU, guarantee and monitor their development, and assist and envelop them in the Western European community, as a means of serving candidate countries' interests as well as those of the West. The second way of thinking appears to be the more compelling.

CONCLUSIONS

We have already presented quite a number of specific conclusions about the candidate countries and the processes for EU/NATO accession. Here let us review some of the more general conclusions.

First, it is striking how political the enlargement process was and is. Both the EU and NATO had quite specific technical criteria that they applied to candidate countries, but in the end it was preeminently political criteria and political decision making that were decisive.

Second, it is striking how the logic of EU/NATO enlargement changed over the years. The fears—and rationale for enlargement—of the early 1990s, of a resurgent Russia and a destabilized Central and Eastern Europe requiring massive bailouts, did not materialize. The later, early-twenty-first-century logic and justifications for enlargement (consolidating democracy, profits on investments, immigration controls and, hence, border patrolling, drug and crime control, etc.) were quite different from what they were a decade before.

Third, even though there was less of a sense of crisis about Eastern/Central Europe by the accession year of 2002 and, hence, declining interest in the area in both Europe and the United States, the wheels of the accession process continued to turn. At that stage, to follow the doctrine of lesser evil, the negative consequences of *not* moving ahead with enlargement were graver than the obvious problems of moving ahead with states that were not meeting all the criteria.

Fourth, one is repeatedly struck by how much EU/NATO enlargement was tied up with cultural and "civilization" issues rather than strictly technical economic or political criteria. From the beginning, the Europeans had a quite clear definition of where Europe ends (at the borders of the CIS); developments since the early 1990s only confirmed and reinforced that they drew the dividing line almost precisely where European and Western "civilization," regardless of the criteria used, terminates. Significantly, in our research, these "softer" criteria of where Europe ends turned out to correspond almost exactly with the empirical and technical criteria reported here.

Fifth, even with enlargement, Europe will not be "whole and free." The political and economic situation (democracy, free markets) in Eastern/Central Europe is much better than before, but we must also recognize that new barriers, new "curtains," are going up in the East. Although change is in the air, Russia, the CIS, parts of the former Yugoslavia, Transcaucasia, Central Asia, and Turkey are still being excluded. But it is precisely because they are being excluded from Europe's—and the globe's—powerful economic engines and trends toward democracy, prosperity, and social justice that these countries are dangerous. (Ukraine may now be the crucial state in the area, no longer Central or Eastern Europe; the fact that the locus of political crisis has now moved farther east may tell us more than anything else about Eastern/Central Europe's progress in the last decade.) There is a crying need to offer the excluded countries hope, possibilities, aid, future affluence, democracy, and security lest they be drawn back into the pit of poverty, instability, authoritarianism, foreign domination, and even terrorism. For unless our attention is now drawn to this new eastern frontier, the United States and Europe will be inviting the very instability, chaos, and economic and political hopelessness that EU and NATO enlargement was designed to alleviate. We have seen with horrendous consequences what poverty combined with alienation, frustration, and hopelessness have led to in some Middle Eastern countries; let us ensure that we avoid the same or similar outcomes in Russia and the CIS.

DISCUSSION TOPICS

1 Compare and contrast the interests of the older EU and NATO countries regarding enlargement, and those of the new members.
2. The author makes the case that the EU and NATO were enlarged for political reasons and not based on a country's merit. Discuss.
3. What are U.S. interests in enlargement, and why?
4. What would be the arguments for and against bringing Ukraine, Belarus, and Russia into the EU and NATO?

NOTES

1. The information and materials in this and subsequent sections were based in considerable part on interviewing of NATO and EU officials in Brussels and Washington and of government, foreign ministry, and U.S. embassy officials in Spain, Portugal, Estonia, Latvia, Lithuania, Switzerland, Germany, Austria, Poland, Slovakia, and Hungary.

2. *Agenda 2000: For a Stronger and Wider Union* (Brussels: European Commission, 1997) is the key document spelling out the rationale and criteria for enlargement; see also the detailed and remarkably frank (for an international organization) reports by the EU assessing individual applicant country progress. For NATO the best studies are edited or authored by Jeffrey Simon, *NATO: The Challenge of Change, NATO Enlargement: Opinions and Options,* and *NATO Enlargement and Central Europe* (Washington, D.C.: National Defense University Press, 1993, 1995, and 1996, respectively).

3. Martin A. Smith and Graham Timmins, "The EU, NATO, and the Extension of Institutional Order in Europe," *World Affairs* 163 (Fall 2000), 80–9; Ronald Tiersky, "Europe Today: The Integration-Security Link," in *Europe Today*, ed. Ronald Tiersky, 427–99 (Lanham, Md.: Rowman and Littlefield, 1999); Sabina A. M. Crisen, ed., *NATO and Europe in the 21st Century* (Washington, D.C.: Woodrow Wilson Center, 2000); Sean Kay, *NATO and the Future of European Security* (Lanham, Md.: Rowman and Littlefield, 1998).

4. This conclusion, as will become clear, is based largely on my interviews.

5. Richard Rose and Christian Haerpfer, *Trends in Democracies and Markets: New Democracies Barometer, 1991–98* (Glasgow: University of Strathclyde, Center for the Study of Public Policy, 1998); Christian Haerpfer, Cezary Milosinski, and Claire Wallace, "Old and New Security Issues in Post-Communist Eastern Europe: Results of an 11 Nation Study," *Europe-Asia Studies* 51, no. 6 (1999), 989–1011.

6. See especially Lonnie Johnson, *Central Europe: Enemies, Neighbors, Friends* (New York: Oxford University Press, 1996).

7. Based on the author's field research in Russia in 1992 and 1996.

8. Hans Binedijk and Richard L. Kugler, "NATO after the First Tranche: A Strategic Rationale for Enlargement," *Strategic Forum*, 149 (October 1998), 1-4; Sean Kay, "NATO's Open Door: Geostrategic Priorities and the Impact of the European Union," paper presented at the Woodrow Wilson Center, Washington, D.C., January 17, 2000.

9. I was once asked by the U.S. government to tour Russia to present this picture in a series of lectures. Naturally I accepted the invitation to tour Russia, and I actually gave the Russians a more honest assessment than the U.S. government wanted. But nevertheless I had the experience of being shoved aside, my lecture interrupted, the microphone seized, and even roughed up by Russian (mostly older, Communist Party, secret police, and military) officials who objected vigorously and at times violently to even a balanced, even-handed discussion of NATO.

10. The information and materials in this section are based on the interviews cited in note 1 as well as participant observation and living as a Fulbright scholar in Vienna and Budapest in 2001.

11. Brent Scowcroft, "Whither the Atlantic Community," *Issue Brief*, No. 01-02 (Washington, D.C.: The Forum for International Policy, March 21, 2001).

12. See the data presented in Rose and Haerpfer, *Trends*.

13. See the results of the research carried out by Claire Wallace and her colleagues at the Institute for Advanced Study, Vienna.

14. The author's Washington research institute, the Center for Strategic and International Studies (CSIS), has had a longtime research and action agenda for EU and NATO enlargement. Some of the materials in this section are based on my involvement in these programs as well as interviews at the Department of Defense, with U.S. embassy officials and military attachés, and with NATO and OSCE officials in the field.

15. Scowcroft, "Whither the Atlantic Community."

16. The history is traced in the EU's *Agenda 2000*.

17. Based on interviews with EU officials in these "field offices."

18. One of the best studies, maybe *the* best, is by Erich Reiter, *The Effects of NATO and EU Enlargement* (Vienna: Landesverteidigungsakademie/Militärwissenschaftliches Büro, 1999).

19. See George Grayson, *Strange Bedfellows: NATO Marches East* (Lanham, Md.: University Press of America, 1999).

20. The materials and analysis in this section rely heavily on the interviews described earlier.

Conclusion

Toward a New Europe

The changes that have occurred in both Southern and Eastern Europe since the mid-1970s are nothing short of phenomenal, maybe even miraculous. In Southern or Mediterranean Europe we have three countries—Greece, Portugal, and Spain—historically poor, undemocratic, underdeveloped, and isolated for centuries from the mainstreams of European civilization, that have now, in a relatively short period of time, become affluent, democratic, on the forefront of advanced European civilization, and closely integrated into the mainstreams of modern Western life. The changes have been both rapid and thoroughgoing, so thoroughgoing as to render these countries almost unrecognizable from what they were three decades earlier. It is said that neither Greece nor Portugal nor Spain is your grandfather's country anymore, but I would argue the changes have been so complete and so rapid that they are not even your father's countries. Indeed, as a scholar who has been studying, visiting, and traveling in these countries for some forty years by now, I find the pace of change there sometimes dizzying, not a little bit overwhelming, and incredibly impressive—and that is within a single lifetime.

If anything, the changes in Eastern Europe have been even more impressive. That is because they involve complete *system* changes and within an even shorter time period, since the collapse of the Soviet Union, the fall of the Berlin Wall, and the dismantling of the Iron Curtain occurred in the 1989–1991 time period. The Eastern European countries still have farther to go to catch up than do the Southern European countries, but that is because they started at a far lower base and beginning point. In the late 1980s these were still countries under the thumb of the Soviet Union, with low standards of living comparable to those of the Third World, and with *none* of the institutions of a modern, democratic, free-market system. But since 1989 the countries of Eastern Europe have thrown off their Soviet shackles, undertaken democratic reforms, opened up new opportunities economically, and joined the two great European "clubs" of the EU and NATO. They still have, as this book makes clear, a long way to go both politically and economically; nevertheless, the changes in Eastern Europe in only a fifteen-year (as compared with thirty in Southern Europe) time span are incredibly impressive, and we now have every reason to expect that the changes and forward motion will continue.

COMMON FEATURES

There are many common features of Southern and Eastern Europe. The commonalities are even more striking if one takes a long historical view going back, let us say, a thousand years. Since history has often marched slowly in these two parts of Europe, such a long view is necessary for our analysis. Among the common features of Southern and Eastern Europe are the following:

1. Historically, these have long been the poorest parts of Europe. For at least a thousand years, these areas have lagged behind the wealthier areas of Europe.
2. The countries of the South and East had particularly long-lasting forms of feudalism and such rigid, two-class, social structures that they were prevented from developing into modern states and societies.
3. Both these areas were unsettled for long centuries of time, beset by war, repeated foreign invasions, and internal civil conflict that left them unable to achieve the peace and stability necessary for growth and development.
4. Both areas were on the periphery of Europe, isolated from the mainstreams of European civilization, bypassed by the Renaissance, the Protestant Reformation, the Enlightenment, the Industrial Revolution, the movement toward limited representative government, and all the great changes that we associate with the making of the modern world.
5. Both areas were torn by ethnic strife that was often also religious and racial; these conflicts, many of which persist today, prevented the

South and the East for a long time from developing into stable, modern nation-states.
6. Both areas experienced for a thousand years or more a form of religion and religious organization (Roman Catholic, Eastern Orthodox) that was particularly rigid, unchanging, orthodox, and authoritarian—traits that supported and reinforced rigidity and authoritarianism in the social, political, cultural, and intellectual spheres.
7. Both areas were beset by feelings of inferiority vis-à-vis the core and wealthier areas of Europe. They were looked down on by the core for their instability and underdevelopment; at the same time, when they were, as often, rejected by core Europe, they withdrew into themselves, became even more isolated, and set forth a defensive nationalism (as in Serbia) that was ultimately self-destructive.

In short, both Southern and Eastern Europe started off with a lower, more underdeveloped base than did core or central Europe, and both areas for long centuries tended to remain locked in that position.

If we now move ahead to the twentieth century, we again see some fascinating parallels and commonalities between Southern and Eastern Europe:

1. Both areas remained poor and underdeveloped as the twentieth century dawned.
2. Both had such rigid and old-fashioned social structures that they seemed incapable of reform.
3. Both tried democracy in the early twentieth century, but with weak institutions, weak civil society, and no prior experience with representative government, these experiments ended in failure.
4. Both areas were particularly hard hit and devastated by the depression of the 1930s, which not only wrecked their economies but swept away existing political systems as well.
5. Both areas were attracted to corporatism in the 1920s and 1930s, since Communism was unacceptable and democracy had already failed.
6. Both areas were particularly hard hit by World War II, either in the sense of war and more devastation being wreaked on their territories or by the economic privations of that time period.
7. Both areas were attracted by authoritarian solutions for providing a way out of their problems—Franco, Salazar, and the army in Southern Europe; other forms of authoritarianism in the East.
8. Both areas experienced polarizing periods, with Southern Europe going to the right for long decades and Eastern Europe under the thumb of Communism and Soviet occupation armies.

Bringing this analysis right up to the present, we can say that there are also parallels and commonalities between Southern and Eastern Europe even in the contemporary period:

1. Both areas have undergone in the last few decades enormously impressive transitions to democracy.
2. Both areas have recently experienced vast social changes and considerable economic reform and development (far more in Southern than in Eastern Europe) that have increasingly transformed them into modern nations.
3. Both areas have largely repudiated their former ideologies of authoritarianism and Communism and have embraced freedom, pluralism, and open markets.
4. Both areas (again, far more in the South than the East) have begun to develop political-party systems, civil society, and government institutions that identify them as Western countries.
5. Both areas have recently joined and become increasingly integrated into the two great "clubs" of Europe, the EU and NATO.

With all these commonalities and parallels, it would appear as though Southern Europe and Eastern Europe would provide particularly interesting and fertile areas for comparative political and developmental research. And that *is*, in fact, the case; these are wonderful areas to study comparatively. But comparisons and comparative politics consist of studying differences as well as similarities. And in this regard one cannot but be impressed by the important *differences* between these two areas as well. Indeed, the differences are so great that they raise again the question with which we began this book as to whether a single common model, the transition-to-democracy approach, is sufficient to capture the immense variation in the Southern European and East European experiences.

DIFFERENCES

The image that one might keep in mind is a funnel, like the funnel through which you put oil or antifreeze into your car. The funnel is wide at the top, then tapers off and becomes narrow at the bottom. Except that this funnel is one of causality. At the top are the broadest, most general explanations. Then the explanations narrow and become more specific. Finally, at the bottom they become very specific, narrow, and focused on individual countries.

That is how I see the similarities and differences between Southern and Eastern Europe. At the top or widest part of the funnel are the broadest possible generalizations and explanations as to the similarities between Southern and Eastern Europe: both torn by long-term conflicts, instability, poverty, dependency, lack of institutionalization, and so on.

At a second, narrower level in my funnel of causality are the more recent transitions to democracy. At the most general level, all these countries, South and East, have held elections, established democracy, are freer now than before, have opened their markets, and have joined Europe. But as the funnel narrows even more, we cannot help noticing that the specifics of the individual cases differ more and more and that each individual country's experience is different. In other words, it is at the most general level that the broad comparisons and the models we use to explain general patterns are the most useful, but as we get down to specifics and individual cases, the usefulness of such models as the transition-to-democracy paradigm lessens.

At this stage, therefore, we need to emphasize the differences between the Southern and Eastern European experiences of transition. It is not that we want to deemphasize the similarities and commonalities of these two areas, only that a balanced view requires that we emphasize both the similarities *and* the differences:

1. By all the indicators we have, Eastern Europe, when it began its transitions in 1989, was quite a bit poorer than Southern Europe had been in the mid-1970s—less urban, less affluent, less middle class, and so forth. In other words, Southern Europe had a better socioeconomic base on which to start its democratization process than did Eastern Europe.
2. The political culture of Southern Europe—already oriented toward democracy and "Europeanness"—was better prepared for the transition than was Eastern Europe, for whom the abrupt transition beginning in 1989 represented a sharp break with the past and for which the area was not so well prepared.
3. Southern Europe in the mid-1970s already had a quasi-open press, almost no censorship, independent labor unions that the government tolerated, the beginning of a functioning political party system, and almost no secret-police controls anymore. Eastern Europe lagged way behind in all these respects.
4. With the Cold War still on and the fear of Communism's spread still strong, Southern Europe in the mid-1970s was the recipient of immense amounts of international investment, foreign aid, political advice and counseling by the United States and other countries; Eastern Europe, trying to democratize after the Cold War, has been the recipient of far less aid and assistance.
5. Once again we are impressed that in the mid-1970s, Southern Europe had banks, stock exchanges, financial institutions, regulatory agencies,

a dynamic entrepreneurial class, and all the economic preconditions and organizations that would enable it to make a rapid transition into the European and global economy. Eastern Europe had to start almost from zero on all these economic fronts.
6. We need to insist on the fundamental distinction between authoritarianism and totalitarianism. The facts are, it is *much* easier to transition from the looser, less rigid, less repressive authoritarianism to democracy than from totalitarianism ("total" control) to democracy. Once again, Southern Europe (authoritarian) had the advantage over Eastern Europe (which was still closer to totalitarianism).
7. Finally, we need to disaggregate our cases. That political-science term means we need to be careful about the use of a single, all-encompassing, but often too simple model and our applying it to all the cases in our two regions. The fact is, there is no one, single, "Southern European" model; instead, the democratic trajectories of Greece, Portugal, and Spain were very different. We need to look at the experiences of individual countries.

Similarly, in Eastern Europe, because they were all under Soviet control and "Communist," we have tended to assume that all the Eastern European countries were the same or very similar. But, in fact, each country of the area had a different history, political culture, different levels of socio-economic development, and even different experiences under Communism. It is, therefore, important that we consider them not just as a group but as separate, individual countries whose transitions to democracy will also be strongly affected by these differences.

WRAPPING UP

The modernization, democratization, and reintegration of the countries of Southern and Eastern Europe back to the mainstreams of modern European and Western life has to be one of the most exciting and important events of our times. Here we have a group of countries that were long isolated, poor, underdeveloped, and under repressive regimes that have now become free, open, democratic, and with a higher standard of living. It is hard not to stand up and applaud the Herculean efforts that went into making these transitions successful.

At the same time, we need to remember that many of these democratic transitions are still incomplete. Elections have occurred, new constitutions have been written, and institutions reformed, but have the underlying values and political culture also changed? Are the norms of civility, trust, egalitarianism, and participation fully incorporated? Changes in the political culture require a more difficult and time-consuming process and often require three or four *generations* to complete, not three or four years. In my view, the Southern European countries are much farther along the path to having a democratic political culture than are the Eastern European countries. Many of these remain still limited democracies, partial democracies, illiberal democracies. It will require far more time before they become complete democracies.

At some levels it is useful to employ broader theoretical models to understand these democratizing processes. We have called the Southern European countries "Mediterranean" and "authoritarian," and in political-culture and political-science studies we understand certain things by those terms. For example, we know that Southern, or Mediterranean, Europe was long dominated by clientelism and patronage, and that its authoritarianism, while certainly cruel and oppressive, was not as "total" as it would have been under totalitarianism. We employ these terms—*Mediterranean* and *authoritarian*—as shorthand ways of understanding the parallels and common features of these countries. But while such models are useful in understanding Southern Europe on a general level, we also understand that at some point you need to get down to individual cases and the unique experiences of individual countries.

Similarly, in Eastern Europe, the main models used were Marxist-Leninist or Communist and totalitarian. While all the countries conformed to some degree to these models, we also know already that each individual country had its own experience with Communism and that there were degrees of totalitarianism. Once again, our models are useful at a certain level of abstraction and generality, but they also need to be understood as providing only partial explanations. We need to know the situations of the individual countries.

Now we come to the recent transitions of these two areas to democracy. Two questions are involved: (1) Does this model, which emerged out of the Southern European experience, apply equally to all the countries of the area? The answer is yes and no: all the countries have transitioned to democracy, but Spain is probably the paradigm case, while Greece and Portugal lag somewhat behind. (2) Is this model from Southern Europe equally applicable in Eastern Europe? Once again the answer is yes and no. Obviously, much of Eastern Europe has transitioned to democracy but (a) at a fundamental level each country's experience was different, and (b) there was a fundamental set of differences, as outlined, between the Southern European and the Eastern European experiences.

The moral is this: Let us use such general models and interpretations as the transitions-to-democracy paradigm, but carefully, recognizing that they help us understand some of the processes involved at a general level.

But at some point we also need to understand the differences involved and get down to individual cases.

The author's view, to return to the practical level, is that the transitions to democracy of both Southern Europe and Eastern Europe are among the most encouraging and exciting events of the late twentieth, early twenty-first centuries. At the same time, let us remember those other countries, generally farther east and south, in the Balkans, in Caucasia, in Central Asia, along the border of the new Europe (Belarus, Ukraine, Moldova, Georgia), and Russia itself that have not yet made the transition to democracy and prosperity, or have made it only partially and incompletely. So while we warmly applaud the successful and enormously impressive transitions in Southern and Eastern Europe, let us also remember that there are still many very poor and not-very-democratic countries out there that, if we do not pay attention, assist, and bring them also into the democratic fold, are likely as potential failed states to cause many more problems for the world in the future.

DISCUSSION TOPICS

1. Summarize the differences and similarities of Eastern and Southern Europe.
2. Why is European enlargement important; why should the United States care?
3. What is the usefulness of the transitions-to-democracy literature as it applies to Africa, the Middle East, and other areas. How and why does it need to be modified and rethought to fit these other areas?

Suggested Readings

Anderson, Charles W. *The Political Economy of Spain* (Madison: University of Wisconsin Press, 1970).
Arango, Ramón. *Spain: Democracy Regained* (Boulder, Colo.: Westview, 1995).
Arendt, Hannah. *The Origins of Totalitarianism* (New York: Harcourt, Brace, Jovanovich, 1951).
Arrighi, Giovahni, ed. *Semiperipheral Development: The Politics of Southern Europe in the Twentieth Century* (Beverly Hills: Sage, 1985).
Baklanoff, Eric N., ed. *Economic and Business Perspectives on the Centennial of the Spanish-American War* (Tuscaloosa: University of Alabama, Bureau of Business and Economic Research, 1999).
Baklanoff, Eric. *The Economic Transformation of Spain and Portugal* (New York: Praeger, 1978).
Barnes, Samuel P., Antonio López Pina, and Peter McDonough. *The Cultural Dynamics of Democratization in Spain* (Ithaca, N.Y.: Cornell University Press, 1998).
Beer, Samuel H., et al. *Patterns of Government: The Major Political Systems of Europe*, 3rd ed. (New York: Random House, 1972).
Bell, Daniel. *The Coming of Post-Industrial Society* (New York: Basic Books, 1973).
Binedijk, Hans, ed. *Authoritarian Regimes in Transition* (Washington, D.C.: Foreign Service Institute, Department of State, 1987).
Bloch, Marc. *Feudal Society* (Chicago: University of Chicago Press, 1961).
Boilard, Steve D. *Russia at the Twenty-first Century* (Fort Worth, Tex.: Harcourt Brace, 1998).
Bonine-Blanc, Andrea. *Spain's Transition to Democracy* (Boulder, Colo.: Westview, 1987).
Braudel, Fernand. *The Mediterranean and the Mediterranean World in the Time of Phillip II* (New York: Harper and Row, 1972).
Brennan, Gerald. *The Spanish Labyrinth* (Cambridge: Cambridge University Press, 1971).

Bunce, Valerie. "Comparing East and South," *Journal of Democracy* 6 (July 1995): 87–100.
———. "Paper Curtains and Paper Tigers," *Slavic Review* 54 (Winter 1995): 979–87.
———. "Regional Issues in Democratization: The East versus the South." *Post-Soviet Affairs* 14 (1998): 187–211.
———. "Should Transitologists Be Grounded?" *Slavic Review* 54 (Spring 1995): 111–27.
Bruneau, Thomas, ed. *Political Parties and Democracy in Portugal* (Boulder, Colo.: Westview, 1997).
Bruneau, Thomas, and Alex MacLeod. *Politics in Contemporary Portugal* (Boulder, Colo.: Lynne Rienner, 1986).
Carr, Raymond. *Spain* (Oxford: Clarendon Press, 1966).
Clark, Robert P. *The Basques* (Reno: University of Nevada Press, 1979).
Clark, Victoria. *Why Angels Fall: A Journey through Orthodox Europe from Byzantium to Kosovo* (London: Macmillan, 2000).
Crisen, Sabina A.M., ed. *NATO and the Future of European Security* (Lanham, Md.: Rowman and Littlefield, 1998).
Crow, John. *Spain: The Root and Flowers* (Berkeley: University of California Press, 1985).
Deutsch, Karl, et al. *Comparative Government: Politics of Industrialized and Developing Nations*. (Boston: Houghton Mifflin, 1981).
Eaton, Samuel P. *The Forces of Freedom in Spain 1974–1979* (Stanford, Calif.: Hoover Institution Press, Stanford University, 1981).
Eberstadt, Nicholas. "Health, Nutrition and Literacy under Communism." *Journal of Economic Growth* 2 (Second Quarter 1987): 11–22.
Eckstein, Harry. "A Culturalist Theory of Political Change." *American Political Science Review* 82 (September 1988).
Einhorn, Eric S., and John Logue. *Modern Welfare States* (New York: Praeger, 1989).
Fish, Stephen M. *Democracy from Scratch: Opposition and Regime in the New Russian Revolution* (Princeton, N.J.: Princeton University Press, 1994).
Friedrich, Carl J., and Zbigniew Brzezinski. *Totalitarian Dictatorship and Autocracy* (New York: Praeger, 1962).
Fukuyama, Francis. *The End of History and the Last Man* (New York: Free Press, 1992).
———. *Trust: Social Virtues and the Creation of Prosperity* (New York: Free Press,1995).
Gellner, Ernest, and John Waterbury, eds. *Patrons and Clients in Mediterranean Societies* (London: Duckworth, 1977).
Graham, Lawrence S. *Romania: A Developing Socialist State* (Boulder, Colo.: Westview Press, 1982).
Graham, Lawrence S., and Douglas L. Wheeler, eds. *In Search of Modern Portugal: The Revolution and Its Consequences* (Madison: University of Wisconsin Press, 1982).
Grayson, George. *Strange Bedfellows: NATO Marches East* (Lanham, Md.: University Press of America, 1999).
Grew, Raymond, ed. *Crises of Political Development in Europe and the United States* (Princeton, N.J.: Princeton University Press, 1978).

Gunther, Richard, et al., eds. *The Politics of Democratic Consolidation: Southern Europe in Comparative Perspective* (Baltimore: Johns Hopkins University Press, 1995).

Gunther, Richard, Giacomo Sani, and Goldie Shabad, eds. *Spain after Franco* (Berkeley: University of California Press, 1986).

Hilton, Rodney, ed. *The Transition from Feudalism to Capitalism* (London: New Left Books, 1976).

Hooper, John. *The New Spaniards* (New York: Penguin, 1995).

Horowitz, Irving Louis. *Three Worlds of Development* (New York: Oxford University Press, 1972).

Howard, Marc Morje. "Institutional Design, Civilization or Prior Regime Type? Explaining Cross National Variation in Civil Society." Paper presented at the annual meeting of the American Political Science Association, Atlanta, Ga., 1999.

Huntington, Samuel P. "The Clash of Civilizations," *Foreign Affairs* (Summer 1993).

———. *Political Order in Changing Societies* (New Haven, Conn.: Yale University Press, 1968).

———. *The Third Wave: Democratization in the Late Twentieth Century* (Norman: University of Oklahoma Press, 1991).

Hyde-Price, Adrian. "Patterns of International Politics." In *Developments in Central and East European Politics*. Vol. 2, edited by Stephen White et al. (Durham, N.C.: Duke University Press, 1998), 255–75.

Inglehart, Ronald. "The Renaissance of Political Culture," *American Political Science Review* 82, no. 4 (December 1988).

Johnson, Lonnie R. *Central Europe: Enemies, Neighbors, Friends* (New York: Oxford University Press, 1996).

Karl, Terry Lynn, and Philippe C. Schmitter. "From an Iron Curtain to a Paper Curtain: Grounding Transitologists or Students of Postcommunism?" *Slavic Review* 54 (Winter 1995): 965–78.

Kenny, Michael. *A Spanish Tapestry* (Bloomington: Indiana University Press, 1962).

Kochanowitz, Jacek. "Leviathan Exhausted: Ideas on the State of the Post-Communist Transformation," *East Central Europe* 27, Pt. 1 (2000).

Kohler, Beate. *Political Forces in Spain, Greece, and Portugal* (London: Butterworth, 1982).

Kopstein, Jeffrey S. and David A. Reilly. "Geographic Diffusion and the Transformation of the Postcommunist World." *World Politics* 53 (October 2000): 1–37.

Linz, Juan. "Totalitarian and Authoritarian Regimes" in *Handbook of Political Science*, vol. 3, edited by Fred I. Greenstein and Nelson W. Polsky (Reading, Mass.: Addison Wesley, 1975).

Lipset, S. M. "Some Social Requisites of Democracy: Economic Development and Political Legitimacy." *American Political Science Review* 53 (March 1959): 69–105.

Magone, José. *European Portugal* (New York: St. Martin's, 1997).

Mangott, Gerhard, Harald Waldruch, and Stephen Day, eds. *Democratic Consolidation: The International Dimension* (Baden Baden, Germany: Nomos Austrian Institute for International Affairs, 2000).

Marias, Julián. *Understanding Spain* (Ann Arbor: University of Michigan Press, 1990).

Maxwell, Kenneth. *The Making of Portuguese Democracy* (New York: Cambridge University Press, 1995).

Michener, James. *Iberia* (New York: Random House, 1968).

Moreno, Alejandro. "The Democratic-Authoritarian Cleavage in New Democracies: Eastern Europe and Latin America in the 1990s." Paper presented at the annual meeting of the American Political Science Association, Atlanta, Ga., 1999.

O'Donnell, Guillermo, Philippe C. Schmitter, and Laurence Whitehead, eds. *Transitions from Authoritarian Rule* (Baltimore: Johns Hopkins University Press, 1986).

Opello, Walter. *Portugal's Political Development* (Boulder, Colo.: Westview, 1985).

Ortega y Gassett, José. *Invertebrate Spain* (New York: Norton, 1937).

Payne, Stanley. *A History of Spain and Portugal* (Madison: University of Wisconsin Press, 1973).

Prizel, Ilya. "The First Decade after the Collapse of Communism: Why Did Some Nations Succeed in Their Political and Economic Transformations while Others Failed?" *SAIS Review* 19 (Summer/Fall 1999): 1–15.

Przeworski, Adam, *Democracy and the Market* (Cambridge: Cambridge University Press, 1991).

———. *The Sustainability of Democracy*. Vol. 1 (Cambridge: Cambridge University Press, 1991).

———. *The Sustainability of Democracy*. Vol. 2 (Cambridge: Cambridge University Press, 1995).

Reiter, Erich. *The Effects of NATO and EU Enlargement* (Vienna: Landesverteidigungsakademie/Militärwissenschaftliches Büro, 1999).

Rice, Condoleezza, and Philip Zelikow. *Europe Unified and Transformed: A Study in Statecraft* (Cambridge, Mass.: Harvard University Press, 1995).

Rodó, José Enrique. *Ariel* (Austin: University of Texas Press, 1988).

Rose, Richard, and Christian Haerpfer. *Trends in Democracies and Markets: New Democracies Barometer, 1991–1998* (Glasgow: University of Strathclyde, Center for the Study of Public Policy, 1998).

Rostow, W. W. *The Stages of Economic Growth* (Cambridge: Cambridge University Press, 1960).

Rupnik, Jacques. "The Postcommunist Divide." *Journal of Democracy* (January 1999), 159–61.

Schmitter, Philippe C., and Terry Lynn Karl. "The Conceptual Travels of Transitologists and Consolidologists: How Far to the East Should They Attempt to Go?" *Slavic Review* 53 (Spring 1994): 173–85.

Schoepflin, George. "Culture and Identity in Post-Communist Europe," in *Developments in East European Politics*, edited by Stephen White, Judy Batt, and Paul G. Lewis (Durham, N.C.: Duke University Press, 1993): 16–34.

Skillings, Gordon H. *Interest Groups in Soviet Politics* (Princeton, N.J.: Princeton University Press, 1971).

Solsten, Eric, ed. *Portugal: A Country Study* (Washington, D.C.: Government Printing Office, 1994).

Solsten, Eric, and Sandra W. Meditz, eds. *Spain: A Country Study* (Washington, D.C.: Government Printing Office, 1990).

Spanakos, Anthony P., and Howard J. Wiarda. "Comparative Perspectives on Southern European Democratization." *Portuguese Studies Review* 5 (Fall/Winter 1996–1997): 93–96.
Sztompka, Piotr. "Dilemmas of the Great Transition." *Skisyphus* 2 (1992): 9–27.
Terry, Sarah M. "Thinking about Post-Communist Transitions: How Different Are They?" *Slavic Review* 52 (Summer 1993): 333–37.
Tiersky, Ronald, ed. *Europe Today* (Lanham, Md.: Rowman and Littlefield, 1999).
Tismaneanu, Vladimir. *The Poverty of Utopia: The Crisis of Marxist Ideology in Eastern Europe* (New Brunswick, N.J.: Transaction Press, 1988).
Walker, Martin. "Europe's Existential Crisis," *Wilson Quarterly* (Winter 2001), 30–53.
Wiarda, Howard J. *American Foreign Policy toward Latin America in the '80s and '90s* (New York: New York University Press, 1992).
———. *Corporatism and Comparative Politics: The Other Great "Ism"* (New York: M. E. Sharpe, 1997).
———. *Corporatism and Development: The Portuguese Experience* (Amherst: University of Massachusetts Press, 1977).
———. *Iberia and Latin America* (Lanham, Md.: Rowman and Littlefield, 1996).
———. *Introduction to Comparative Politics* (Belmont, Calif.: Wadsworth, 1993).
———. "Toward a Framework for the Study of Political Change in the Iberian-Latin World: The Corporative Model," *World Politics* 25 (1973): 205–35.
———. *U.S. Foreign and Strategic Policy in the Post–Cold War Era* (Westport, Conn.: Greenwood Press, 1996): 85–105.
———. *Where Does Europe End? The Politics of EU and NATO Enlargement* (Vienna: Austrian Institute of International Affairs, 2002); also published in *World Affairs* (Spring, 2002).
Wiarda, Howard J., and Margaret MacLeish Mott. *Catholic Roots and Democratic Flowers: Political Systems in Spain and Portugal* (Westport, Conn.: Greenwood Press, 2001).
Williams, Allan., ed. *Southern Europe Transformed: Political and Economic Change in Greece, Italy, Portugal, and Spain* (London: Harper and Row, 1984).
Zoellick, Robert B. *At the Frontiers: A New Agenda for US-EC Relations* (Washington, D.C.: Carnegie Endowment, 1993).

Index

abortion, 114
absolutism, 45, 70
Acquis Communautaire, 177, 197, 212, 231
Adolphus, Gustavus, 184
Adriatic, 177
advanced industrial nations, 17
Afghanistan, 163
Africa, 120
Albania, viii, 3, 66, 74, 75, 77, 160, 166, 189, 193, 198, 204, 240; people of, 190, 194
Albanian language, 63
alcoholism, 162, 169
Americas, the, 120
Anarchist, 41
Anarcho-Syndicalist, 41, 26
Andalusia, 110
Andean Pact, 139
Angola, 122, 128, 129, 143, 151, 163, 166
antisocial behavior, 169
Apodeti, 144
area specialists, 79
Argentina, 163
Arias, Carlos, 113, 136

Armenia, 221
army, 30, 37, 42, 46, 175
Arctic Circle, 177
Arctic Ocean, 179
Asia, 120
associational life, 49
Astúrias, 83
Australia, 145, 151
Austria, 178, 180, 188, 189, 191, 192, 194, 198, 222, 224, 238; investment of, 196, 222; people of, 192
Austrian, 196, 222
Austrians, 192
Austro-Hungarian Empire, 74, 178, 181, 208
autarky, 96, 101
authoritarian, 1, 155; corporatism, 103; regime, 6
authoritarianism, 5, 11, 22, 87, 96, 156, 157, 204, 247, 250, 251
autonomías, 105
autonomous groups, 71
autonomy, 110, 111; issues of, 112
Azerbaijan, 207
Aznar, José M., 105, 114, 139
Azores Islands, 127, 129

Baker, James, 183
Balkans, 166, 178, 179, 185, 186, 189, 191, 192, 207, 208, 252
Baltics, 171, 175, 177, 189, 190, 193, 202, 203, 208, 215, 219, 221, 223, 229, 230, 239, 240
Banco Bilbao, 138
Banco Central Hispano, 138
Banco Santander, 138
banks, 10, 249
Basque, 98, 110; country, 24, 111
Basque Nationalist Party, 111
Batista, 135
Belarus, viii, 3, 166, 175, 180, 188–90, 193, 197, 200, 202, 204, 206, 208, 218, 219, 221, 223, 227, 252, 193; people of, 178, 179, 193, 194
Belgium, 4, 22, 23, 223
Berlin Wall, 182, 207, 212
big bang, 237
Black Sea, 179, 225
Black Sea Cooperative Council (BSCC), 218
Black Sea Economic Cooperation (BSEC), 207
Bohemia, 185, 190, 191
Bonapartism, 156
Bosnia, 68, 75, 77, 175, 189, 193, 195, 205, 225, 227, 240
Bosnia-Herzegovina, 3, 191
Bosnians, 179, 194
Bratislava, 198, 222
Brazil, 139, 151, 163
Brenan, Gerald, 102
Brussels, 107, 220, 224, 228
Brzezinksi, Zbigniew, 184
Bucharest, 198
Budapest, 198
buffer states, 226, 227
Bulgaria, 3, 65–67, 74, 75, 77, 166, 171, 175, 180, 185, 188–90, 192, 193, 200–202, 204, 205, 216, 223, 230, 231, 234, 235, 237, 240; people of, 64, 190, 193, 194
bureaucracy, 50
bureaucratic state, 71
bureaucratization, 105

Bush, George H. W., 182, 225
Bush, George W., 236
business-entrepreneurial class, 37
business sector, 48, 50
Byzantium, 180

Caetano, Marcelo, 29, 32, 121
Calvo Sotelo, Leopoldo, 113
Camões Institute, 143
Cannes, 230
capitalism, 169, 171, 176n7
CARICOM, 139
Carlists, 41; wars of, 99
Carlos, Juan, 113
Carter, Jimmy, 163
Caspian Sea, 179
Catalan nationalism, 98
Catalonia, 24, 110
Catherine the Great, 182
Catholic Church. See Roman Catholic Church
Catholicism. See Roman Catholic Church
Caucasia, 252
caudilloism, 156
Cavaco e Silva, Aníbal, 122, 127
censorship, 104, 249
Center for Strategic and International Studies (CSIS), 243n14
center-periphery relations, 184
Central Asia, 166, 206–8, 218, 221, 225, 227, 241, 252
Central Intelligence Agency (CIA), 88, 159
centralism, 26
Charlemagne, 21, 97, 179, 180
Charter 77, 10
Chechnya, 175
China, 166, 169
Chisinau, 198
Christian, 193, 201
Christian Empire, 186
Christian Europe, 208
Christianity, 187
church and state, 69
church attendance, 169
church. See Roman Catholic Church

church-state relations, 26, 70, 72
CIA. *See* Central Intelligence Agency
CIS. *See* Commonwealth of
    Independent States
cities, 24
city-states, 26
civic culture, 173
Civic Forum, 206
civil society, 39, 47, 49, 89, 116, 165,
    202, 206, 207, 248
civil war, 25, 30, 38
civilization, 179
civilizational issues, 216, 241
"civilized," 178
civil-service, 49
clan, 4
class conflict, 26
classes, 35
clientelism, 251
Clinton, Bill, 228
Cold War, 3, 212, 219
collective security: agreement, 215;
    arrangement, 240; organization, 234
colonization, 120
common agricultural policy, 237
Common Market, 114
Commonwealth of Independent States
    (CIS), 3, 166, 170, 173–75, 182, 196,
    201, 207, 208, 214, 217, 221, 222, 233,
    240, 241
Communism, 72, 174, 248; as model,
    251; regimes of, 155, 167; in Russia,
    157; systems of, 174
Communist party, 41; countries, 10
comparative politics, 155, 156, 159, 175
Confederation of Portuguese
    Workers–National Intersindical
    (CGIP-IN), 124
Conference on Security and
    Cooperation for Europe (CSCE),
    232, 233
conflict, 31
Congress, 229, 238
conservatives, 24
conservativism, 112
consolidations of democracy, 79
consolidologists, 79; model of, 80

Constantinople, 21, 180
constitution, 110, 148
constitutional monarchy, 41
Convergence and Union, 111
co-optive political strategy, 39
Copenhagen, 230
core of Europe, 4
core-periphery relations, 23
corporate: bodies, 98; societal groups,
    45
corporatism, 3, 27, 39, 42, 48, 53, 58,
    108, 121, 135
corporatists, 18, 31; arena of, 43;
    regimes of, 28; system of, 83
corporativist unions, 38
corruption, 115
Cortes (Spanish parliament), 110
Council for Mutual Economic
    Association, 61
Council of Europe, 183
Counter-Reformation, 95, 181
crime, 169, 197, 223
Croatia, 3, 65, 68, 75, 77, 177, 180, 181,
    185, 188–90, 193, 200–202, 204, 205,
    207, 223, 240; people of, 68, 179,
    190–94
Cuba, 133, 138, 139, 163, 166
cultural changes, 82
culture, 2; crisis of, 161
Cunhal, Alvaro, 125
Curaçao, 152n5
customs unions, 237
Cyprus, 20, 216, 230, 232, 237, 240
Cyrillic alphabet, 63, 188
Czech lands, 180, 185, 188; people of,
    179, 193
Czech Republic, 3, 66, 67, 73, 74, 165,
    166, 171, 173, 175, 181, 189, 193, 197,
    200–205, 207, 214, 215, 222, 223, 228,
    231, 233, 239, 240
Czechoslovakia, 8, 10, 82, 85, 163, 172,
    173, 206, 230

Danes, 181
Danube, 180
Dark Ages, 21
Dayton Peace Accord, 195, 204

decision making, 43
Defense Department, 88
democracy, 28, 32, 33, 37, 46, 58, 86, 104, 115, 155, 170, 173, 174, 195, 196, 201, 215, 231, 247
democratization, 89, 200, 225, 250
Department of Defense, 228, 229
depression of the 1930s, 247
developing nations, 170
dictatorship, 28
Dili, 142, 143, 145, 146, 148
disaggregate, 250
disease, 20, 197
divorce, 114
Dole, Bob, 228
Dominican Republic. *See* Trujillo
drugs, 20, 223
d'Tocqueville, Alexis, 8, 44
Dutch, the, 142, 143
Dutch Caribbean, 152n5

Eanes, Ramalho, 126
East Asia, 2, 164
East Timor, 128, 129, 140, 149; as ungovernable, 149
Eastern Europe, vii, 3, 8, 19, 23, 61, 81, 89, 136, 158–61, 164, 167, 170, 174, 175, 245; invasions of, 246; participation in, 71; as religious, 4; tradition in, 4; as underdeveloped, 247
Eastern Orthodox Church. *See* Orthodox Church
Easterners, 178, 195
EC. *See* European Community
economic crisis, 161
economic development, 248
economic policy, 169
education, 70, 71
EEC. *See* European Economic Community
elections, 249
elite(s), 33, 37, 42
empires, 192
Endesa (Spanish utility), 138
England, 4, 22, 23
enlargement, 196

Enlightenment, 22, 184
entrepreneurial class, 250
Essen, 230
Estonia, 166, 175, 193, 200, 201, 204, 205, 207, 214, 219, 231, 239; people of, 179, 228
Ethiopia, 163, 166
ethnic groups, 4; cleansing of, 219; discontent of, 160; as minorities, 66; strife of, 246
ethnicity, 190
EU. *See* European Union (EU)
Euro Zone, 96
Europe, 129, 178–80, 182, 215, 221
European Association Agreements (EAA), 230
European Common Market, 128
European Community (EC), 3, 29, 107, 122
European Council, 230
European Economic Community (EEC), 19, 55, 180
European Monetary Union, 56, 128
European Union (EU), viii, 56, 96, 139, 177, 182, 193, 196, 206, 212, 214, 215, 219, 224, 225, 248; criteria for enlargement of, 231
Europeanness, 249
Euskadike Ezkerra, 111
"evil empire," 163

factions, 40
failed state, 149
family, 4; planning, 114; structure, 82
Fascism, 32, 95
Fascist, 27
federalism versus unitarism, 172
Ferdinand, 99, 109
feudal, 32
feudalism, 246
financial institutions, 5, 10, 249
Finland, 177
First Republic, 27
Folda Pass, 184
food, 168
foreign aid, 249
foreign assistance, 6

foreign policy, 132
framework agreements, 235
France, 4, 22, 23, 224, 247; people of, 181
Franco, Francisco, 6, 27–29, 31, 38, 39, 42, 44, 46, 54, 82, 84, 97, 99, 101, 113, 132, 133, 135; regime of, 103, 157
Freedom House, 203
Freedom Party, 194
free markets, 174
free-market system, 11
Free Masons, 99
French Revolution, 24, 30, 99
FRETILIN. *See* Revolutionary Front for the Independence of East Timor
Fukuyama, Francis, 2, 8
funnel of causality, 248

Galicia, 110
General Union of Workers (UGT), 124
geography, 81, 183, 185, 209
Georgia, viii, 3, 166, 179, 180, 190, 193, 202, 204–8, 218, 221, 223, 227, 252; people of, 178, 179
Germany, 4, 22, 23, 180, 181, 192, 194, 198, 223, 224, 233; investment of 196, 222; people of, 181, 190, 192
Garibaldi, Giuseppe, 26
globalization, 169
Goa, 142
Golden curtain, 177, 207, 209
González, Felipe, 113, 136
Gorbachev, Mikhail, 162, 163
Great Britain, 224
Greater Russia, 219
Greece, vii, 3, 4, 6, 7, 9, 11, 17–19, 21, 22, 24, 26, 28–30, 38, 54–56, 85–87, 164, 174, 179, 185, 215, 223, 245, 250, 251; people of, 190
Greece-Turkey conflict, 20
Greek Orthodox Church. *See* Orthodox Church
gross national product (GNP), 35
Gunea-Bissau, 122
Gusmão, Xanana, 146, 148
Guteres, Antonio, 125, 127

GUUAM, 207
Gypsies, 190

Haider, Jorg, 194, 223
Hapsburg(s), 98, 99, 109, 178, 188
Havel, Vaclav, 91, 192, 226
Helms-Burton restrictions, 138
Henri Batasuna, 111
hierarchical society, 18 27
high-income countries, 34
hispanidad, 134
Hispaniola, 134
hispanismo, 107, 134–36
historical memory, 102
history, 68, 105, 209
Hitler, 184
Hitlerism, 219
Hitler's Germany, 156, 157
Holland, 23
Holocaust, 219
Holy Roman Empire, 180
Hong Kong, 163
Horowitz, Irving Louis, 1
Hough, Jerry, 176n7
housing, 168
human rights, 163, 201, 202, 231
Hungarian language, 63, 64
Hungary, 3, 8, 65–67, 73, 74, 85, 163, 165, 166, 171, 173, 175, 180, 181, 188–93, 197, 200–207, 214, 215, 222, 223, 228, 230, 231, 233, 239, 240; people of, 68, 74, 179, 193
Huns, 181, 184
Huntington, Samuel, 2
Hyde-Price, Adrian, 184

Iberian Peninsula, 112
Iberoamerican summit, 138
ideology, crisis of, 160
immigrants, 20, 197, 220, 237
Individual Partnership Program (IPP), 235
individualism, 25
Indonesia, 140, 142–44, 171
Industrial Revolution, 22, 184
industrialization, 22, 26, 31, 96
Inquisition, the, 95, 101

Institute for Advanced Study, 243n13
institutionalization, 205
intellectuals, 99
interest groups, 44, 47–48; pluralism of, 44
international influences, 88
international investment, 249
Iran, 101; of the Shah, 157
Iraq, 101
Ireland, 224
Iron Curtain, 3, 177–79, 182, 207, 212
iron ore, 22
Isabella, 99, 109
Islam, 74, 178, 181, 189, 194; in Europe, 186, 208; fundamentalism of, 20
Israel, 101, 240
Italian city-states, 23
Italy, 3, 4, 17–19, 24, 26, 28–30, 38, 50, 55, 180, 198, 223; investment of, 222; of Mussolini, 157; people of, 181, 190

Japan, 112, 163
Juan Carlos, 136
Jews, 188, 190
jobs, 222
Johnson, Lonnie R., 190, 205
Joint Council, 235

Kaliningrad, 218
Kenny, Michael, 102
Kiev, 181, 198
King Juan Carlos. *See* Juan Carlos
Kissinger, Henry, 183
Kosovars, 179, 190, 194
Kosovo, 3, 68, 189, 191, 193, 195, 196, 225, 227, 240

labor, 53; problem, 26; shortage, 105; unions, 249
landholding class, 30
language, 63, 188
Latin America, 2, 107, 132, 133, 164, 170
Latvia, 3, 166, 175, 193, 200, 201, 204, 205, 207, 214, 219, 232, 239; people of, 179, 228

liberal democratic route, 1
liberalism, 30, 39, 121
liberals, 24, 25, 41
Libya, 101
life expectancy, 169
Lijphart, Arend, 114
limited pluralism, 114, 125, 157
limited representative government, 22
Linz, Juan, 82, 157
Lisbon, 127, 130
literacy, 168
Lithuania, 3, 166, 175, 180, 193, 194, 200, 201, 204, 205, 207, 214, 219, 232; people of, 179, 228
local autonomy, 26
Low Countries, 4, 22
Lufthansa Airlines, 221
Luso-phonic, 129
Luxembourg, 4

Maastricht Agreement, 128
Macao, 128, 129, 142
Macedonia, 3, 64, 68, 74, 77, 189, 200, 204; people of, 190
Mackinder, Harold, 184
Madeira, 129
"Madeleine's Map," 182
mafias, 197
Magyars, 181, 184, 190, 192; empire of, 181
Malacca, 142
Malta, 230, 232, 240
Mapfre, 138
market economy, 231
market reforms, 225
markets, 10, 165, 206; global, 56
Marshall Plan, 88
Marxism, 158
Marxism-Leninism, 160, 174; regimes of, 155; route of, 1
Marxist-Leninist model, 251
mass-based political parties, 41
masses, 33
Medical care, 168
Medieval model, 22
Mediterranean Europe, 17, 20, 57, 245
Mediterranean Sea, 179

MERCOSUR, 139
Metaxas, Ionnis, 28, 31, 38, 39, 42, 46
Mexico, 163, 198
Mezzogiorno, 19
Middle Ages, 190
middle class, 33, 37, 41, 128, 161, 249
Middle East, 20
Middle Eastern politics, 129
Middle Europe, 181, 226
military: dictatorship of, 31; interventions of, 33; juntas of, 156; orders of, 45, 98
Milosevic, Slobodan, 204
minorities, 231
Minsk, 198
modernization, 250
Moldova, viii, 3, 179, 180, 193, 198, 202, 204–8, 221, 223, 227, 252
Moldovans, 193, 194
Moluccas, 142
monarchies, 45
monarchists, 41
monarchy, 25, 26, 31, 98
Mongolians, 181
Montenegro, 3, 77, 189, 198, 204; people of, 179, 190
Moors, 109
Moran, Fernando, 137
Moravia, 185
morbific politics, 149
Morocco, 240
Moscow, 61, 198
Mozambique, 122, 128, 129, 143, 151, 163, 166
Museum of Europe, 179
Muslim. *See* Islam
Mussolini, Benito, 27, 28, 31, 38, 39, 42, 44, 46, 54; Italy of, 157
My Fair Lady, 185

Napoleon, 182, 184
nation building, 146
National Endowment for Democracy, 89
National Security Council, 233
NATO. *See* North Atlantic Treaty Organization

natural border, 236
natural resources, 22
Nazi Germany, 157
neocorporatism, 108
Netherlands, the, 4, 22, 151, 223
New Yalta, 177
Newly Industrialized Countries (NICs), 163
Nicaragua, 166
Nizhny Novgorod, 84
Nobel Prize, 234
nobility, 30, 37
nongovernmental institutions, 89
North, the, 23
North Africa, 20
North African politics, 129
North Atlantic Cooperative Council (NACC), 233
North Atlantic Treaty Organization (NATO), viii, 20, 29, 55, 76, 114, 177, 182, 196, 206, 212–14, 218, 224, 225, 227, 232, 238, 240, 248; expansion of, 219; political criteria of, 234
North Korea, 160, 166
Northern Europe, 22, 55

official party, 43
oligarchies, 58
oligarchy, 46
one-party states, 40
open-market systems, 171
organic society, 18
Organization for Economic Cooperation and Development, 100
Organization for Security and Cooperation in Europe (OSCE), 183, 218, 233
Organization of American States, 138
Organization of Petroleum Exporting Countries (OPEC), 101
Oriente Foundation, 149
Ortega y Gassett, José, 102, 103
Orthodox Church, 18, 21, 28, 65, 72, 74, 180, 186–88, 247
Orthodox countries, 188
Ottoman Turks, 178, 181, 189, 191

Pact of Moncloa, 108
parliamentary systems, 51, 126, 172
Partnership for Peace (PfP), 183, 218, 220, 232, 233
Partnership Work Program (PWP), 235
patrias chica(s), 22, 98
patrimonialist politics, 4, 33
patronage, 4, 41, 49, 172, 173, 251; agencies of, 42
patron-client, 33
peace and security, 220
peasant groups, 30, 38, 124
periphery, 32, 184; of Europe, 246
Permanent Joint Council (PJC), 218
Perón, 135
Perpignan, 83
Peter the Great, 182
Petroleum, 22
PHARE (Poland and Hungary: Assistance for the Reconstruction of the Economy), 230
Planning and Review Process (PRP), 235
pluralism, 39, 46, 69, 124, 173
Poland, 3, 8, 10, 66, 73, 74, 77, 85, 158, 163, 165, 166, 171, 175, 180, 185, 188–90, 192, 193, 197, 200, 201–7, 214, 215, 222, 223, 228, 230, 231, 233, 239, 240; people of, 63, 65, 66, 67, 69, 181, 193
policy reforms, 167
Polish-Lithuanian Empire, 181
political change, 172
political criteria, 234, 241
political-cultural heritage, 18
political culture, 6, 7, 9, 29, 62, 80, 81, 102, 115, 123, 162, 164, 173, 178, 197, 209, 216, 249, 251; as parochial, 29; and eighteenth-century split, 40
political development, 39
political economy, 206
political parties, 40, 104, 173
political party system (s), 125, 248, 249
polls, 224
poor, 246, 249
Popular Party (PP), 126, 114

Portugal, vii, 3, 4, 6, 7, 9, 11, 17–19, 22–24, 27, 28, 30, 38, 55, 84–89, 112, 120, 132, 140, 145, 164, 174, 185, 200, 215, 223, 245, 250, 251; discoveries of, 120
Portuguese Communist Party (PCP), 125
Portuguese Socialist Party (PSP), 125
poverty, 20, 33
Prague, 198
president, 52
presidential systems, 172
press, 249
Primo de Rivera, 38
privatization, 171
progressive, 24
prostitution, 197, 223
Protestant groups, 187
Protestant Reformation, 22, 181, 187
public opinion polls, 216
Public-Opinion Surveys, 195
public policy, 52
Puerto Rico, 133
Putin, Vladimir, 218, 220, 235
pyramid of power, 112
Pyrenees Mountains, 97

racism, 223
Reagan Doctrine, 163
Reagan, Ronald, 163
regional development funds, 237
regionalism, 105, 108
regions, 111
reintegration, 250
religion, 65, 82, 180, 186
religion: beliefs of, 18, 22; orders of, 45
Renaissance Europe, 181
republicanism, 26, 121
republicans, 41
republics, 41
resorgimento, 25
Respol SA, 139
Revolutionary Front for the Independence of East Timor (FRETILIN), 144, 145
Rhine River, 180

river systems, 22
robber-baron capitalism, 171
Roma, 188, 202, 211n19
Roman Catholic Church, 18, 28, 30, 37, 42, 46, 72, 74, 100, 124, 147, 158, 180, 181, 186, 187, 188, 247
Romania, 3, 64–66, 67, 74, 75, 77, 166, 171, 173, 175, 181, 185, 188, 189, 190, 192, 193, 200–202, 204, 205, 216, 223, 230, 232, 234, 235, 237, 240; people of, 190, 193, 194
Romanian language, 63
Rome, 21
rotativismo, 26
royal absolutism, 22
rule of law, 72
rules of the political "game," 38
Russia, viii, 10, 19, 84, 89, 136, 165, 170, 171, 173–75, 178, 179–82, 188, 189, 190, 193, 196, 200–202, 204–8, 214, 215, 217, 219–25, 229, 233, 236, 239, 240, 241, 252; people of, 178, 179, 181, 193, 194
Russian Revolution, 27, 31
Russian system, 70
Ruthanes, 190

Salazar, Antonio, 27–29, 31, 38, 39, 42, 44, 46, 54, 82, 121, 128, 132, 247; regime of, 103
Salazar-Caetano regime, 6
Sampaio, Jorge, 126
Saracens, 97
Scandinavia, 18, 22, 198, 223, 196; investment of, 221
Schengen, 238
Schengen (border control) Accord, 183; immigration rules of, 177; rules, 207, 222
science, 22
Scowcroft, Brent, 220
second-generation reforms, 215
secret police, 175
semifeudal, 32
September 11, 2001, 236
Serbia, 3, 68, 75, 77, 175, 178, 180, 181, 188, 189, 192, 193, 196, 202, 204, 205, 240, 247; people of, 64, 68, 179, 187, 190, 191, 193, 194
Sharansky, Natan, 162
sheepherders' guild (Mesta), 98
Singapore, 163, 176n7
Slovak language, 64
Slovak Republic, 232
Slovakia, 3, 66, 67, 74, 75, 166, 171, 173, 175, 181, 185, 188–93, 200–205, 207, 215, 216, 222, 223, 230, 238, 240; people of, 69, 179, 190, 192, 193, 228
Slovenia, 3, 65, 66, 68, 73, 74, 166, 171, 175, 177, 180, 181, 185, 188, 189, 190, 192, 193, 197, 200–207, 215, 222, 223, 230, 231, 240; people of, 179, 190–93, 228
Slovenian language, 64
Soares, Mario, 125, 126
social change(s), 6, 82, 102, 160
social contract, 70
Social Democratic Center (CDC), 126
Social Democratic Party (PSD), 122, 126
social indices, 200
social pact, 86, 165
social peace, 28
social policy, 167
social programs, 54, 128
social question, 52, 53
social structure, 34, 35, 247
Socialism, 41
Socialist International, 88
Socialist Party, 104
societal corporatism, 108
socioeconomic background, 34
socioeconomic base, 249
socioeconomic development, 197
Solidarity movement, 10, 89, 158, 206
Somoza, 135
Sophia, 198
Sotelo, Leopoldo, 136
South Korea, 163, 171
Southeast Europe, 189
Southern Europe, 3, 17, 18, 20, 29, 54, 80, 164, 174, 245; invasions of, 246; as "Mediteranean," 251; model of, 21; as patronage dominated, 18; as

religious, 4; tradition in, 4, 22, 24, 42; as underdeveloped, 247
Soviet Union, 9, 87, 89, 158–61, 163, 167, 169, 172, 173, 207, 212. *See also* Stalin
Spain, vii, 3, 4, 6, 7, 9, 11, 17–19, 22–24, 28–30, 38, 55, 82, 83, 85–89, 95, 112, 164, 174, 181, 185, 215, 223, 245, 250, 251; indigenous power structure of, 112; workforce in, 105
"Spanish miracle," 101
Spanish Socialist Workers Party (PSOE), 113
special favors, 173
Spice Islands, 142
Stalin, 158; Soviet Union of, 156
Stalinism, 219
state, 43, 44, 46, 47, 71, 112
state corporatism, 108
State Department, 233
state sectors, 49
state-society relations, 44, 47
statism, 72
stock exchanges, 249
structural reforms, 174
study groups, 83
Suárez, Adolfo, 113, 136
sub-Saharan Africa, 2, 20
Suharto, General, 144
sultanism, 156
Surinam, 152n5
Swedes, 181
Switzerland, 238
systems debate, 97, 178

Taiwan, 163, 171
Tatars, 181, 184
taxes, 197
technical criteria, 230
Telefónica, 139
terrorism, 20
theory, 90
Third Wave, the, 2
Third-World, 20
Timor Sea, 141
Timorese Democratic Union (UDT), 144

Timorese Social Democratic Association (ASDT), 144
Tirana, 198
Tlbisi, 198
tolerance, 173
Topasses, 142
totalitarian Communism, 5
totalitarian model, 158, 251
totalitarianism, 11, 86, 156, 159, 250, 251
tourism, 83
trade unionism, 26
trade-union movement, 38, 124
trade unions, 31
Transcaucasia, 166, 179, 227, 241
transformismo, 26
transitions to democracy, 2, 79, 155, 248, 249, 252; paradigm of, 251; approach to, 248; model of, 9
transitologists, 79; model of, 80; approach of, 90
Transylvania, 187, 193, 208
Trujillo, 135; Dominican Republic of, 157
Tuchman, Barbara, 27
Turkey, 21, 28, 178, 179, 181, 189–91, 193–95, 200, 204, 205, 208, 223, 230, 232, 239, 241
two-class system, 22, 37, 246

U.S. interests, 225
Ukraine, viii, 3, 166, 173, 175, 180, 181, 187–90, 193, 194, 197, 198, 202, 204–8, 218, 221, 223, 227, 241, 252; people of, 178, 179, 193, 194
Ulyssses, 179
UN. *See* United Nations
Underdeveloped countries, 32
underdevelopment, 33, 141, 186, 215; geographical, 22
Uniate, 193
unions, 104
United Nations (UN), 141, 145, 151
United States, 89, 129, 133, 145, 151, 221, 225, 239, 249
Ural Mountains, 179, 184
urbanization, 105
Uzbekistan, 207

Venezuela, 163
Venizelos, Eleuthérios, 28
Vienna, 189
Vietnam, 163, 166, 169
Visegrad Four, 238
Vojvodina, 187, 189, 191, 193, 208

Walesa, Lech, 163
Walker, Martin, 208
war on terrorism, 235, 237
war, 181, 246
Warsaw Pact, 61, 89, 182, 206, 212
Warsaw, 198

West, the, 180, 196
Western civilization, 216, 224, 236
Westernness, 201
women, 82
worker movements, 31
World War II, 247

Ximenes Belo, José Ramos-Horta, 145

Yugoslavia, viii, 3, 64, 68, 166, 172, 173, 185, 190, 192, 201, 214, 241

Zagreb, 198

About the Author

Howard J. Wiarda is the Dean Rusk Professor of International Relations and head of the Department of International Affairs at the University of Georgia. Much of his career was spent as professor of political science and comparative labor relations and the Leonard J. Horwitz Professor of Iberian and Latin American Studies at the University of Massachusetts, Amherst. He retains his positions as public-policy scholar of the Woodrow Wilson International Center for Scholars, and senior associate at the Center for Strategic and International Studies (CSIS) in Washington, D.C. Professor Wiarda began his career as a scholar of Latin American politics, and his writings on Latin America, Spain, Portugal, and the developing nations are well known in the field. While continuing these research and writing interests, over the last twenty years his scholarly interests have broadened to include Russia, Asia, Europe, sub-Saharan Africa, comparative democratization, civil society, and general comparative politics and American foreign policy.